BETH PIPE & SIAN LEWIS

Contents

PLAN YOUR TRIP
Welcome to England 4
My Perfect Day Walk 6
Our Picks 8
When to Go 14
Get Prepared for England 16

BY REGION

CUMBRIA & THE LAKES 21
Langdale Pikes 24
Hallin Fell 26
Catbells 28
Old Man of Coniston 30
Haystacks 32
Castle Crag 34
Helvellyn & Striding Edge 36
Scafell Pike 40
Millom to Silecroft 44
Shap & Swindale 48
Whitbarrow Scar 52
Also Try 56

DEVON & CORNWALL 59
Teign Gorge 62
Wistman's Wood 64
River Dart Walk 66
Kynance Cove & Lizard Point 68
St Agnes & Chapel Porth 70
Brown Willy & Rough Tor 72
Porthcurno to Land's End 74
Tintagel to Boscastle 78
Isles of Scilly 82
Combe Martin 86
Also Try 90

SOUTHWEST ENGLAND 93
Bath Skyline 96
Glastonbury Tor 98
Avebury & Silbury Hill 100
Tarr Steps 104
The New Forest 106
The Ridgeway 108
Corfe Castle to Langton Matravers 112
Lulworth Cove to Durdle Door 116
Also Try 120

NORTHERN ENGLAND 123
Ingleborough 126
Pendle Hill 130
Dunstanburgh Castle 132
Hadrian's Wall 134
Malham Landscape Trail 138
Robin Hood's Bay 140
Rievaulx 142
Berwick-upon-Tweed 144
Blyth to Tynemouth 148
York 152
Also Try 156

CENTRAL ENGLAND 159
Kinder Scout 162
Mam Tor 166
Stanage Edge 168
The Malvern Hills 170
Caer Caradoc 172
The Cotswold Way 174
Birmingham City & Canals 176
Kinver Edge 180
Also Try 184

SOUTHEAST & EAST ENGLAND 187
The Seven Sisters 190
Blakeney Point 194
The Backs 196
Leith Hill 198
Rye to Winchelsea 200
St Albans 204
The Viking Trail 206
Devil's Dyke 210
Mersea Island 214
Also Try 218

LONDON 221
Regent's Canal 224
Thames Path 228
New River 230
Hampstead Heath 232
Richmond Park 233
Tottenham Marshes 234
Roman London 238
Also Try 242

BACK MATTER
Arriving 244
Getting Around 245
Health & Safe Travel 246
Responsible Travel 247
Accommodation 248
Nuts & Bolts 249

Welcome to England

If one word could sum up all that England has to offer walkers it would be 'variety'. From the wildness of the white cliffs of Dover and the ancient histories of Rievaulx and Glastonbury Tor to the modern industrial landscape of Birmingham's canal network and the historical hidden depths of London, Bath and York, England has them all within just a few hours' travel of each other.

A good walk exercises the mind as well as the legs, so each walk is written by a knowledgeable companion, filling you in on the local landmarks and helping you to navigate the past that created the present landscape. You will also be pointed in the right direction for local food, drink and accommodation, as well as finding top tips on the best time of year to visit and how to find your way around local transport systems. So, welcome to England, and have a great walk!

Durdle Door (p117), Dorset
ALEX HIBBERT/GETTY IMAGES ©

My Perfect Day Walk

Beth Pipe

BERWICK-UPON-TWEED

P.144

I absolutely love this walk and I'm always excited to find an excuse to visit the town. For a small place, it really does punch well above its weight when it comes to history and breathtaking scenery. From the magnificent town walls to the elegant sweeping arches of the railway bridge, history lies in wait for you around every corner. And when you add spectacular sea views on top of all that, you really do have the perfect walk.

Berwick Old Bridge (p145), Berwick-upon-Tweed

Best Scenic Walks

1. Castle Crag
For the biggest view from the smallest climb, this is the route to take.

2. Dunstanburgh Castle
Sweeping sea views, ancient castles and breathtaking beaches; a walk crammed with delights.

3. Kynance Cove & Lizard Point
Add a few steps to this impressive walk to reach the top of the Lizard Lighthouse.

4. Kinder Scout
Views so stunning that they inspired civil disobedience and the birth of modern rambling.

5. The Seven Sisters
Wave 'bonjour' to France on a clear day as you breathe in the salty sea air.

Best Urban Walks

1 Birmingham Canals
From smoggy industrial heritage to modern vibrant city, track the region's transformation as you go.

2 New River
A side of London most people miss. It includes a revolutionary water supply and several parks.

3 Bath Skyline
A bird's-eye view of an ancient city. Admire the architecture from near and far.

4 York City Walls
A lap of the city and a very short street with an impressively long name.

5 St Albans
Follow the footsteps of England's ancestors around the city and cathedral and up to the Roman Theatre.

Sian Lewis
PORTHCURNO TO LAND'S END
P.74

On a summer's day you can't beat the South West Coast Path. This long-distance trail stretches for 630 miles through Somerset, Devon, Cornwall and Dorset, but I think the most magical day hike along it is at Britain's tip, walking from Porthcurno to Land's End in Cornwall, passing the atmospheric Minack theatre and seeking out secluded Treen Cove, where I always feel like a real castaway.

Treen Cove (p75), Cornwall

Best Family Walks

1 Hampstead Heath
Pack a picnic and a swimsuit to make the most of the finest park in London.

2 The New Forest
Plenty of variety and crammed with diverse wildlife, including the ponies and, occasionally, even pigs.

3 River Dart Walk
A gentle amble along the estuary path, plus ferry rides at the start and finish.

4 Berwick-upon-Tweed
Criss-cross the ancient town and enjoy a stroll on the beach on your way back.

5 Millom to Silecroft
A longer walk that traverses huge sea walls and giant dunes on the final stretch.

Our Picks

BEST HISTORY WALKS

Whoever said history was boring was just plain wrong! History surrounds us on every walk but, most of the time, we just don't know what to look for. These walks lift the lid on the telltale signs of the past and allow us to follow in the footsteps of England's ancestors, discovering the stories behind some of the country's most famous sites and revealing how the past has changed the landscape of today.

QUICK FACT

Many modern English roads follow routes originally laid down by the Romans over two thousand years ago.

Roman London
Unearth the Roman roots of Londinium hidden deep within the heart of the city.
P.238

The Viking Trail
Discover your inner Viking along the windswept coast where the invaders first reached Britain.
P.206

York
Walk the walls that encircle a city where history is present with every footstep you take.
P.152

Tintagel to Boscastle
Immerse yourself in myths and legends as you explore Merlin's Cave and the tales of King Arthur.
P.78

Avebury & Silbury Hill
A stone circle so large that they built an entire village inside it – but nobody knows why.
P.100

Tintagel Castle ruins (p78), Cornwall

Right: Avebury (p100)

Our Picks

BEST WILDLIFE WALKS

England may not boast the highest peaks or the longest rivers in the world, but it is home to an outstanding array of native wildlife, and you don't always need to venture far from the cities to see it. The famous parks of London are home to many indigenous species, while England's wilder habitats are important stopping-off points for migrating birds, as well as hosting spectacular resident populations.

QUICK FACT

The New Forest pony is a distinct breed, and each pony is owned by a member of the commoning community.

The New Forest
A portal to a wild world brimming with deer, otters, ponies and a rich and varied landscape.
P.106

Richmond Park
Take a short jaunt from the city to the park where deer have roamed since 1637.
P.233

Wistman's Wood
Roam the mossy ancient woodland that was once part of a mighty English forest.
P.64

Millom to Silecroft
An unexpected gem on the Cumbrian coast where a reclaimed industrial site is now a wildlife haven.
P.44

Blakeney Point
Bring your binoculars for seal-spotting along the coast and bird-spotting in the marsh.
P.194

Ponies, New Forest (p106)

Our Picks

BEST WALKS BY WATER

Living on an island surrounded by water and crossed by dozens of beautiful rivers, is it any wonder that the English love a watery walk? Then there are the stunning lakes of the Lake District plus an impressive network of canals, built for transportation in an industrial age, but today offering perfect paths that connect cities across endless countryside, often with plenty of traditional pubs along the route.

Sunrise from Hallin Fell (p26)

Berwick-upon-Tweed
Far-reaching views out across the North Sea and sweeping bridges over the River Tweed.
P.144

River Dart Walk
Uncover the mysteries of one of England's finest river estuaries and reveal a crime writer's hideaway.
P.66

Hallin Fell
A short, sharp walk to enjoy a bird's-eye view of one of the prettiest lakes in England.
P.26

Thames Path
A walk that connects London's most famous ancient landmark to a modern engineering marvel.
P.228

Birmingham City & Canals
Take a trip into England's industrial past with a walk through the very heart of the country.
P.176

Our Picks

BEST GEOLOGICAL WALKS

Rocks underpin everything else – literally and figuratively. They are the reason the rivers flow where they do, they dictate the vegetation that grows on them and, for millennia, they have influenced where settlements have evolved and flourished. Local rocks also create the feel of the local towns, from the honey-coloured sandstones of the Cotswolds to the distinctive grey cottages of Cumbria.

Langdale Pikes
Perfect pinnacles that were once home to a neolithic axe factory using local rocks.
P.24

Porthcurno to Lands End
Rugged coastline at its finest, with a rock theatre thrown in for good measure.
P.74

The Seven Sisters
Walk the length of the giant chalk cliffs – arguably England's most famous natural feature.
P.190

Lulworth Cove to Durdle Door
A perfect opportunity to view one of England's finest geological landmarks.
P.116

Malham Landscape Trail
The largest area of limestone pavement in the country and a filming location for *Harry Potter*.
P.138

Walking the Seven Sisters (p190)

Our Picks

BEST MINDFUL WALKS

Finding headspace in a chaotic world is never easy; sometimes we just need a little time out. Any walk can be a mindful walk if we employ all of our senses. Pause along the way to see, hear, smell and touch the things around you. Stop for a drink and a bite to eat to allow yourself time to rest, relax and truly take in England's glorious landscapes...

TOP TIP
You can find peace and quiet on popular routes by visiting outside busy times or during low season.

Mersea Island
Unearth the 'best kept secret in Essex' to explore quiet sandy beaches and tranquil nature reserves.

P.214

The Malvern Hills
Immerse yourself in the sumptuous landscape that inspired JRR Tolkien, CS Lewis and Edward Elgar.

P.170

Malvern Hills (p170)

Isles of Scilly
Take a walk around England's archipelago, picnic on deserted beaches and swim in the turquoise sea.

P.82

Shap & Swindale
Escape the Lake District crowds and explore the gentle hills around Shap, with only sheep for company.

P.48

Blyth to Tynemouth
Hop from hidden cove to hidden cove and explore the coastline that most visitors never find.

P.148

BEST DAY WALKS: ENGLAND

When to Go

Picture perfect all year round, but it's best to pack a waterproof, just in case.

Four seasons in one day is a common experience, particularly in the west of the country. Late spring and early autumn are perfect for walking in England. The bright colours of daffodils and tulips will light up your springtime routes while in autumn the reds and golds of the trees will brighten up any drizzly afternoon.

The maritime influence on the weather means that summers can be variable and often wet, but rarely as extreme as the rest of Europe. Expect regular highs in the south of 25°C+ and a few degrees less in the north. Winter extremes are also rare. Most areas experience some snow and high routes will be especially vulnerable.

Accommodation

Consider public transport options to find cheaper accommodation away from overly popular spots. School holiday periods are notoriously expensive so avoid these if you can and plan ahead – chains such as Travelodge offer significant discounts for advance bookings.

> **I LIVE HERE**
>
> **CRISP WALKS ALONG KINVER EDGE**
>
> **Ruth Lewis is an outdoor enthusiast, dog walker and two-time cancer survivor**
>
> 'I love walking Kinver Edge in summer – it is a truly beautiful place in all seasons. The wooded sections are lovely in autumn – I really enjoy crunching through the fallen leaves on a windy day, but best of all is a bright, crisp, winter's day. The absence of leaves reveals gorgeous views on both sides and as you leave the wooded sections and climb past the Roman fort towards the viewpoint they become even more stunning. The air is clean and fresh and you feel like you are on top of the world!'

BRING A BROLLY!

'It always rains in England', right? We have the sea to thank for our temperate climate, but it does bring rain with it. The west generally experiences higher levels of rainfall than the east. For example, Cornwall averages 1200mm per year whereas Northumberland averages 650mm per year.

Weather Watch (Birmingham)

JANUARY	FEBRUARY	MARCH	APRIL	MAY	JUNE
Average daytime max: **7°C**	Average daytime max: **8°C**	Average daytime max: **10°C**	Average daytime max: **13°C**	Average daytime max: **16°C**	Average daytime max: **20°C**
Days of rainfall: **13**	Days of rainfall: **9**	Days of rainfall: **9**	Days of rainfall: **10**	Days of rainfall: **9**	Days of rainfall: **9**

Falmouth International Sea Shanty Festival

MUSIC FESTIVALS & OTHER HIGHLIGHTS

Based in Suffolk, **Latitude** is a top music and arts festival for the whole family. **July**

Set in the superb scenery of the Lake District, **Kendal Calling** attracts big names and indie faves. **August**

An endlessly classy affair in the heart of East Sussex, **Glyndebourne Festival** is an absolute must for opera lovers. **May–August**

Brighten up a winter visit with a spectacular display of lights and lanterns at Wiltshire's **Longleat Festival of Light**. **November–January**

EAT, SING & DANCE

Another Fine Fest in Ulverston includes street theatre and circus performances. **June**

Enjoy exclusive menus and diverse dining experiences during the **Birmingham Restaurant Festival**. **August**

Fully immerse yourself in Cornish life and traditions at the **Falmouth International Sea Shanty Festival**. **June**

Lindisfarne Festival offers a perfect smorgasbord of music to suit all tastes. **August/September**

SUNSEEKING

The daylight hours across the UK vary dramatically with the seasons. In the heart of winter, the sun will set in Cumbria at 4pm but, in summer, it enjoys longer daylight hours than London with the sun rising at 4.30am and not setting until nearly 10pm.

I LIVE HERE

COAST & COUNTRYSIDE IN CORNWALL

Helen Venus is a walking guide and founder of Wild Rambling (wildrambling.com)

'Walking in Cornwall is special in any season, but my favourite time has to be late spring. Each step brings such an assault on the senses: seas of aromatic bluebells, the sound of bees, wild garlic in abundance, and the frothy blossom on the trees. It's always a thrill to stroll along the coastal path, accompanied by the soundtrack of the surging sea, but head inland to discover this land's diverse history: from ancient pagan burial sites and primitive villages to the fascinating industrial archaeology of the recent past.'

JULY	AUGUST	SEPTEMBER	OCTOBER	NOVEMBER	DECEMBER
Average daytime max: **22°C**	Average daytime max: **21°C**	Average daytime max: **19°C**	Average daytime max: **14°C**	Average daytime max: **10°C**	Average daytime max: **8°C**
Days of rainfall: **8**	Days of rainfall: **10**	Days of rainfall: **10**	Days of rainfall: **12**	Days of rainfall: **13**	Days of rainfall: **13**

Get Prepared for England

Useful things to load in your bag, your ears and your brain

Clothing

The secret to dealing with the English weather is layers that can be added or subtracted with ease and, as Alfred Wainwright said, 'There's no such thing as bad weather, only unsuitable clothing'.

Lightweight waterproof: Should always be tucked in the bottom of your backpack, just in case.

Base layer: Get a good quality one that will wick moisture and keep you warm in winter and cool in summer.

Long hiking trousers: Avoid the temptation to bare your legs on hilly hikes as you may pick up a tick. Long trousers will protect you from ticks and help you avoid sunburn.

Walking socks: Get good ones; merino wool if you can. These will cushion your feet and regulate their temperature.

Decent walking boots: You get what you pay for so if you're planning on long walks then you'll need good boots. What you invest in boots you'll save in blister plasters.

Waterproofs: A Gore-Tex jacket and trousers will keep you warm and dry, but still allow the air to flow.

Hat: One to keep the sun off in the summer, and one to keep your head warm in winter.

Walking poles: Not technically clothing, but hugely helpful on high, hilly hikes.

WATCH

Cumbria: The Lakes and Coast
(Channel 5; 2024) Exploring the whole county and the people who make it tick.

Vera
(ITV; 2011–25) A popular crime drama filmed around Newcastle and northeast England.

The Unlikely Pilgrimage of Harold Fry
(Hettie Macdonald; 2023) The fictional story of a man who walks the length of England.

Cornwall with Simon Reeve
(BBC; 2021) Documentary about the people, businesses and culture of Cornwall.

Descent from Scafell Pike (p40)

Words

Ordinance Survey (OS) maps: The go-to maps for route planning and hiking. Available in paper form or via an app

Public footpath: In England there are clear and specific public rights of way that are protected by law; these will be clearly indicated on your OS map

Bridleway: Larger rights of way that also allow bikes and horses

Pub: Not just a place to drink, they also usually offer food and plenty of handy local pointers

Cheers: A common friendly greeting that can mean hello or goodbye

Quid: Informal word for pound, as in 'that'll be five quid for the ticket'

Loo: An informal word for toilet

Hooley: Strong wind. 'It's blowing a hooley out there'

Raining cats and dogs: Heavy rain

Buttie: Sandwich. Also, bacon buttie (bacon sandwich), a popular breakfast

Crisps: Brits love their crisps! Known as 'potato chips' in the US, but ours come in a mind-boggling array of flavours

Scotch egg: A boiled egg encased in sausage meat and deep fried; available in most delicatessens and a handy, self-contained, hiking snack

Chippy: Fish and chip shop. A staple of every English high street and the perfect treat at the end of a long hike

LISTEN

Countrystride Podcast
(Mark Richards; 2019–present) Celebrating the landscapes, culture, heritage and people of Cumbria and the Lake District.

National Trust podcasts
(Ongoing) A wide range of recordings exploring the history and wildlife of England.

Who's on the Bookshelf?
(Suffolk Libraries; 2023 to present) Talks to a range of local authors about their books.

The Cornish Bird
(Elizabeth Dale; 2020 to present) Digging in to Cornwall's hidden past and forgotten stories.

READ

The Salt Path
(Raynor Winn; 2018) An enthralling account of walking the South West Coast Path.

Brewers Loop
(Beth and Steve Pipe; 2023) Discovering the history of the Lake District via microbreweries.

H is for Hawk
(Helen Macdonald; 2014) A story about wildlife and recovery in Cambridgeshire.

Walking Home
(Simon Armitage; 2012) Following the Pennine Way and paying his way with words.

EXPLORE

Hadrian's Wall (p134)

Contents

CUMBRIA & THE LAKES 21

DEVON & CORNWALL 59

SOUTHWEST ENGLAND 93

NORTHERN ENGLAND 123

CENTRAL ENGLAND 159

SOUTHEAST & EAST ENGLAND 187

LONDON 221

Wastwater (p41) and Scafell Pike (p40)

Cumbria & the Lakes

01 Langdale Pikes
Classic Lakeland circuit. **p24**

02 Hallin Fell
A little fell with mighty views. **p26**

03 Catbells
A family-friendly fellwalk. **p28**

04 Old Man of Coniston
Hike high above Coniston Water. **p30**

05 Haystacks
Visit Wainwright's favourite mountain. **p32**

06 Castle Crag
Gaze over the fields of Borrowdale. **p34**

07 Helvellyn & Striding Edge
A lofty ridge walk par excellence. **p36**

08 Scafell Pike
Climb to the very top of England. **p40**

09 Millom to Silecroft
Discover Cumbria's lovely coastline. **p44**

10 Shap & Swindale
Take a gentle lowland ramble. **p48**

11 Whitbarrow Scar
Wind through ancient woodlands to admire views across Morecambe Bay. **p52**

BEST DAY WALKS: ENGLAND   21

Explore
Cumbria & the Lakes

The soaring landscape of Cumbria has inspired poets, artists and hikers, but what many today see as England's greatest adventure playground was built on heavy industry and the hard work of the farming community. The fells of the Lake District National Park are the undoubted stars of the show but, away from the wild mountains, you'll find pristine coastline, spacious glacial valleys, ancient woodlands and hidden villages that will transport you far away from the chaos of modern life. The Lake District National Park was recognised as a UNESCO World Heritage Site in 2017; you'll soon see why this is the UK's most popular national park.

Barrow-in-Furness

Many people will already be familiar with the hot spots of Windermere, Keswick, Grasmere and Ambleside, and they do have plenty to offer when it comes to shopping and entertainment, but it's worth exploring towns that see less of the spotlight if you want to get a real feel for the county.

Barrow-in-Furness might not be top of every travel itinerary, which is a shame as it's a great base for exploring the south of the county and is well served by public transport. It burgeoned from a sleepy fishing port to a major town in the space of a decade, thanks to mining, shipbuilding and the boom in railway travel. Today, it's a cost-effective place to stay, with many great attractions on its doorstep. There's always something going on at the Dock Museum (dockmuseum.org.uk), with large-scale replicas of many of the boats built here over the years, and Walney Island, just a short drive away, boasts a seal colony and miles of pristine sand dunes.

Kendal

Kendal once sat at the heart of the international wool trade (the town motto translates to 'wool is my bread') and it has not one, but two castles to explore. It is home to various festivals throughout the year including the Torchlight Carnival, Walking Festival and the Kendal Mountain Festival – one of the most popular outdoor festivals in the world. The town is crammed with ginnels (alleyways) – a relic of its woollen past – just waiting to be explored, and a riverside stroll is the perfect way to stretch your legs after a long day on the fells.

Cockermouth

Cockermouth is only a 15-minute drive from Keswick but is a world away from the chaos of the summer crowds. Visit the birthplace of William Wordsworth (nationaltrust.org.uk/visit/lake-district/wordsworth-house-and-garden) and explore the wide avenues of the town that also gave us Fletcher Christian. The town lies at the confluence of two rivers, the Derwent and the Cocker, which means that there are endless river walks to explore.

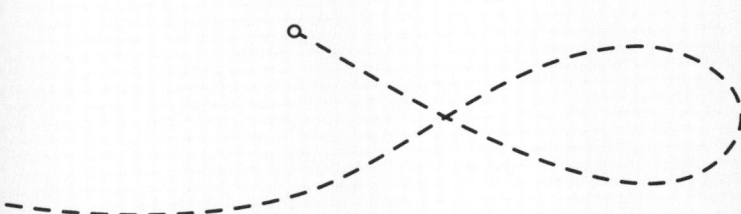

Whitehaven

Over on the west coast is Whitehaven, which, along with Cockermouth, is one of only 51 'Gem Towns' in the country – places that are deemed to be 'particularly splendid and precious'. The grid-like street layout is said to have inspired settlers arriving in America, who designed their towns in the same format. The historic harbour has much to offer, with cafes, pubs and the excellent Beacon Museum (thebeacon-whitehaven.co.uk).

 ## When to Go

Spring and autumn are the perfect times to visit. In spring the woodlands are filled with wild garlic and bluebells, with the famous Rannerdale bluebells attracting visitors from around the world. Autumn is perfect for blustery hikes and evenings in front of a roaring fire. Summer can be busy in the hot spots, but there are still places to escape the crowds.

 ## Transport

Aside from peak summer season, there is little in the way of heavy local traffic. Oxenholme (Kendal) is a three-hour train ride from Euston, and a change at Lancaster will give you access to the Cumbrian Coast train. The region is keen to promote car-free travel; more details can be found at visitlakedistrict.com/explore/travel/carfree.

 ## Where to Stay

Crumble Cottages (crumblecottages.co.uk) in Cartmel give you the chance to stay in a traditional Cumbrian stone cottage, plus there are pristine gardens to explore. It's also just a mile from L'Enclume – the first restaurant outside the southeast to earn three Michelin stars.

At award-winning Sunnyside Guest House (sunnysideguesthouse.com) in Keswick you are guaranteed parking, local food, a warm welcome and an unforgettable stay a stone's throw from the town centre.

If you're on a budget then there are plenty of hostels to choose from, including Kendal Hostel (kendalhostel.co.uk), an independent hostel run by a local family.

Resources

Visit Lake District (visitlakedistrict.com) For events, guides and inspiration.

Mayor's Parlour in Kendal (kendaltowncouncil.gov.uk/heritage/kendal-mayor) Make a free appointment to see the Mayor's Parlour – it's a different way to explore Cumbria's past.

AdventureSmart (adventuresmart.uk) Everything you need to stay safe in the fells.

Made in Cumbria (madeincumbria.co.uk) A guide to locally made goods and produce.

What's On

Dalemain World Marmalade Awards (dalemain.com; Apr) Sample the finest preserves from around the world.

Great North Swim (greatswim.org/great-north-swim; Jun) The largest open-water swimming event in the UK, in England's largest swimming pool.

Grasmere Rushbearing (english-lakes.com/grasmere_rushbearing.html; Jul) Upholding local historical traditions.

Westmorland County Show (westmorlandshow.co.uk; Sep) A showcase of local rural life.

Kendal Mountain Festival (kendalmountainfestival.com; Nov) Outdoors films, talks and events.

01
Langdale Pikes

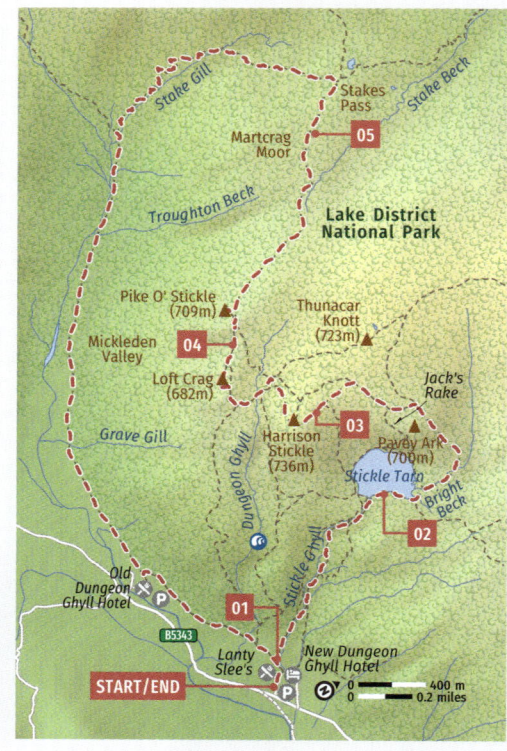

DURATION	DIFFICULTY	DISTANCE	START/END
5-6hr	Hard	7 miles/ 11.5km	New Dungeon Ghyll Hotel

TERRAIN	Rocky, high fells

The classic circuit of Great Langdale ticks off between three and five Wainwrights depending on your route. It covers some steep, hard-going miles, but the stirring views over the Langdale and Mickleden Valleys are worth the effort.

Getting Here
Parking spaces in Langdale can be scarce in summer. There are National Trust car parks at Stickle Ghyll and the Old Dungeon Ghyll hotel (free for NT members), plus an NPA car park opposite the New Dungeon Ghyll, but all are often full by 10am. Local farmers often open fields to act as an overflow. Bus 516 (six daily) from Ambleside stops at Skelwith Bridge, Elterwater and the Old Dungeon Ghyll.

Starting Point
Hikers gather in the car park beside the New Dungeon Ghyll Hotel; the nearby Lanty Slee's is a good place for a pre-hike snack.

01 **Langdale** (from the old Norse for 'long valley') is a classic u-shaped glacial valley, but it's unusual in that it doesn't have a lake at the bottom. The summits along its northern edge, known as the Pikes, are a favourite of fellwalkers. You'll be covering seven steep, hard-going miles, and several thousand feet of ascent, so it would be sensible not to make this your first fell walk. The trail starts behind the New Dungeon Ghyll Hotel, leading steeply up the ravine of Stickle Ghyll. The easiest path starts on the beck's left bank, then crosses over stepping stones halfway up, climbing sharply to **Stickle Tarn** (pictured).

02 Take a breather at the tarn and admire the craggy views of your next target, **Pavey Ark** (700m). There are several routes to the summit, including the treacherous scramble up the face of

Langdale Axe Factory

On the scree slopes beneath Pike O' Stickle and Harrison Stickle in Great Langdale is one of the largest Neolithic axe factories in Britain. The area has rich deposits of a form of greenstone, a hard form of volcanic stone that can be worked to a fine, sharp edge. Hundreds of 'reject' axe heads still litter the quarry site. Amazingly, around 27% of the Neolithic axes discovered in Britain originate from Langdale, with examples found as far afield as Ireland and Cornwall.

OLIVER BERRY/LONELY PLANET ©

Best for

WILD VIEWS

Pavey Ark known as 'Jack's Rake'. A popular ascent is the route dubbed by Wainwright as North Rake. The trail leads up Bright Beck, and climbs a scree gully to the summit; take care near the edge. Pavey Ark is actually an outlying peak of Thunacar Knott, so peak-bagging purists will want to head northwest for 500m to the summit. There's no path; just head across the grass for the highest point.

03 From here, pick up the well-worn trail along the cliff from Pavey Ark, and follow it to the top of **Harrison Stickle**, at 736m the highest of the Pikes.

04 The path drops down the fell's west side and climbs over the rubbly ridge of **Loft Crag** (682m), leading northwest to the distinctive hump of **Pike O' Stickle** (709m). There's some scrambling involved in getting to the top – the drops are daunting but the views are worth it, so take your time and be sure of your footholds.

05 Once you've conquered the Pikes, follow the faint path across the grassy slopes of Martcrag Moor to the junction at **Stakes Pass**; the trail isn't always distinct here. When you reach the pass, turn south and follow the zigzagging trail downhill for around 3 miles into the Mickleden Valley, ending at the Old Dungeon Ghyll Hotel. From here it's an easy amble back along the road to the car park at New Dungeon Ghyll.

Take a Break

The **Old Dungeon Ghyll** (015394-37272; odg.co.uk; Great Langdale;) – affectionately known as the ODG – is awash with Lakeland heritage: many famous walkers have stayed here, including King Charles and mountaineer Chris Bonington. The slate-floored, fire-warmed Hiker's Bar is a must for a posthike pint.

02
Hallin Fell

DURATION	DIFFICULTY	DISTANCE	START/END
3½-4hr	Moderate	7½ miles/ 12.2km	Howtown Pier/ Glenridding

TERRAIN	Grassy fell and lakeshore

Like Catbells (p28), Hallin Fell might be little compared to many Lakeland fells, but it offers one of the best bang-for-buck views in the national park – an Ullswater show-stopper.

Getting Here
By far the best way to get to the trailhead at Howtown is aboard the handsome Ullswater Steamers, either from Glenridding or Pooley Bridge.

Starting Point
From the steamer jetty in Pooley Bridge, you'll have a grand view south across Ullswater. Hallin Fell is on the lake's west side, dwarfed by much higher peaks behind.

01 Hop off the steamer at **Howtown Pier**. Cross over the bridge and follow wooden signs pointing to Sandwich. You'll go through a couple of swing gates, then start to climb up the fell following the line of an old drystone wall. The path tracks roughly along the roadside to begin with, so it's hard to get lost. Then it bears right and begins to climb gently up the fell's southern side.

02 Continue uphill. It's a fairly straightforward climb of about 20 minutes to the top at 388m. When you take a breather, remember to turn round and admire the views down into the neighbouring valleys of Boredale and Martindale, which is home to a beautiful 16th-century church.

03 There are several rocky humps dotted around the fell's top; the true summit is marked by a **stone trig point**. The view from here is really quite something: a bird's-eye perspective looking north across Ullswater all the way to Pooley Bridge (you might be able to spy one of the lake steamers beetling

 Ullswater Steamers

Ullswater's historic **steamers** (☎ 017684-82229; ullswater-steamers.co.uk; full-lake return adult/child £24/14.50) are a memorable way to explore the lake (although strictly speaking they haven't actually 'steamed' for decades). The various vessels include the stately *Lady of the Lake*, launched in 1877 and supposedly the world's oldest working passenger boat. The boats run east–west from Pooley Bridge to Glenridding via Howtown; there are nine daily sailings in summer, three in winter.

along far below). To the south, you should be able to see right across to the Helvellyn range. Take your time up here – it's a real corker of a lunch spot.

04 Backtrack down the fellside. When you reach the road, turn west past Hause Farm, crossing the fields as you follow the course of Sandwick Beck. The path skirts around the northern side of Sleet Fell through Scalehow Wood, then loops southwest along the wooded shores of Ullswater (pictured). You're now following the **Ullswater Way** (ullswater.com/the-ullswater-way), a newly established route that circumnavigates the whole lakeshore. Ullswater is famous for its displays of springtime daffodils – they inspired Wordsworth's best-known poem (you know the one – it begins 'I wandered lonely as a cloud...').

05 After a while you'll reach the distinctive headland of **Silver Point**, overlooked by the imposing face of Silver Crag, an outlying peak of nearby Place Fell. This was a favourite beauty spot of Alfred Wainwright's, with an amazing view up the lake and across towards the Helvellyn massif. There is a route up to the top of the crag, but it's scrambly.

06 Continue south past the rock formation known as the **Devil's Chimney** and the inlet of Blowick Bay, rounding the lake's southernmost point through Side Farm. The route then follows the main road back to Glenridding, where you can catch the return ferry back to Pooley Bridge.

 Take a Break

The endearingly old-fashioned **Howtown Hotel** (howtown-hotel.co.uk) is a cosy place for a pre-hike lunch, with a small cafe on the side serving hot soup, sandwiches and snacks. Otherwise, there are pubs and cafes in Patterdale and Glenridding.

BEST DAY WALKS: ENGLAND

03
Catbells

DURATION	DIFFICULTY	DISTANCE	START/END
2½hr	Easy	3.8 miles/ 6.2km	Hawse End jetty

TERRAIN	Grassy fell

Though it's only 451m in height, the mini-mountain of Catbells packs a photogenic punch despite its modest dimensions, with sweeping views over dreamy Derwentwater.

Lakeland's most famous hillwalker described the mini-mountain of **Catbells** as 'one of the great favourites, a family fell where grandmothers and infants can climb the heights together, a place beloved'. Alfred Wainwright's words in *Book Six: The Northwestern Fells* may certainly be true, but the family will still need to be fit. This is a brilliant first-timer fell, and for many a walker, it's served as the gateway to a lifetime of Lakeland walking.

The classic path starts near the **Hawse End jetty** on Derwentwater's west side; the best way to get there is aboard the Keswick Launch. From Hawse End, the path rises steeply for around 1.5 miles to the summit, which gives a really fine panorama over Skiddaw, the Newlands Valley and Derwentwater (pictured). The route then drops down the fell's southern flank to **Brackenburn** and **Manesty Park**.

From here, you can either choose to continue along the fellside path, or follow a lower path through the woods of **Brandlehow Park** back to the jetty. If you're lucky, you might spot a red squirrel darting through the treetops; Beatrix Potter is said to have had the idea for *The Tale of Squirrel Nutkin* while she was wandering in the woods around Derwentwater.

In case you're wondering about the fell's rather curious name, Catbells probably derives from 'cat's bield', a wild cat's shelter – a handy factoid with which to impress your fellow walkers.

04

Old Man of Coniston

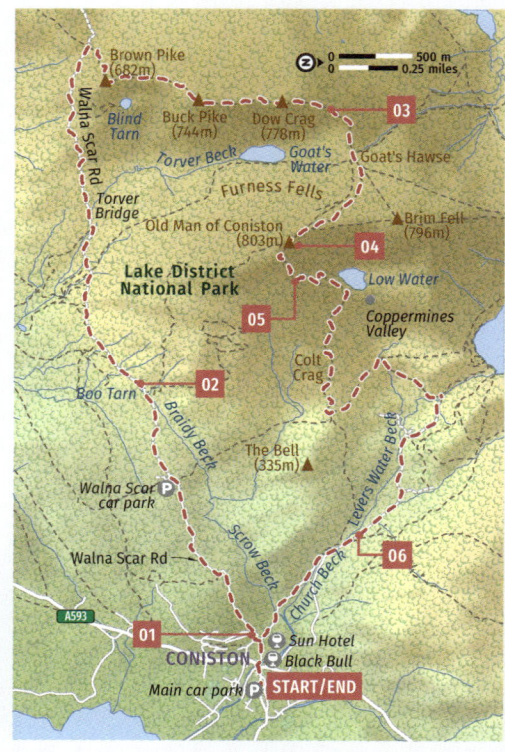

DURATION	DIFFICULTY	DISTANCE	START/END
4-5hr	Moderate	7.1 miles/ 11.4km	Coniston

TERRAIN	Rocky fells, old mine workings

Hunkering above Coniston like a benevolent giant, the Old Man (803m) presents an irresistible challenge. The most popular route shoots straight up from the village, but it's a leg-shredding slog – a much more rewarding route circles round behind the Old Man via Brown Pike and Dow Crag.

Getting Here

Coniston is 8 miles from Ambleside. Bus 505 runs hourly. The Coniston Bus-and-Boat ticket (golakes.co.uk/Windermere-Coniston-Bus-and-Boat) includes a return ticket on the 505, a trip on the Coniston Launch (conistonlaunch.co.uk) and entry to John Ruskin's house at Brantwood (brantwood.org.uk).

Starting Point

There is a large car park in the centre of Coniston. Alternatively, you can cut off a bit of the walk by parking at the end of Walna Scar Rd.

01 Follow the road past the Sun Hotel for half a mile to the start of Walna Scar Rd. Go through the gate and head west along the track, admiring the view across the barren expanse of **Torver High Common**.

02 The path leads west, passing the tiny pond of Boo Tarn after about a mile. Ignore the side-trail on your right that leads north towards the pool of Goat's Water. Instead, continue west, following the trail as it climbs the south flank of **Brown Pike** (682m) and traces the ridgeline across **Buck Pike** (744m) and **Dow Crag** (778m). The views east across Goat's Water to the Old Man are superb, but the drop is severe; take care near the edge, especially when it's windy.

Steam Yacht Gondola

Built in 1859 and restored in the 1980s by the National Trust, this wonderful Coniston Water **steam yacht** (📞015394-63850; nationaltrust.org.uk/steam-yacht-gondola; Coniston Jetty; adult/child/family half lake £17.50/8.75/43.75, full lake £23.50/11.75/58.75) looks like a cross between a Venetian *vaporetto* and an English houseboat, complete with cushioned saloons and polished wood seats. It's a stately way to see the lake, especially if you're visiting Brantwood, and it's ecofriendly – since 2008 it's been powered by waste wood.

03 From Dow Crag, the trail circles round **Goat's Water**, dropping into the saddle of Goat's Hause before ascending the calf-testing incline up the Old Man's west side. This is the toughest part of the day, a real stamina-sapper, but eventually you'll find yourself standing on the Old Man's head.

04 At 803m, the **summit** is the highest of the Furness Fells. The panorama extends east over Coniston Water, north towards Swirl How and Wetherlam, and west towards Dow Crag and the Seathwaite Fells beyond. If you're lucky, you may see Morecambe Bay glinting away.

05 From the cairn at the top, a zigzag trail tracks sharply down the mountain's northern side into **Coppermines Valley** (pictured). The side of the hill is littered with spoil heaps, and the rocks can be quite slippy, so watch your step. Follow the slip-slidy path down to Low Water, then east through the abandoned slate quarries beneath Colt Crag; a stone staircase has been cut out at points, but it's steep. Mining remains are scattered all around: ruined buildings, old tram lines, winding engines, winches and steel cables, a reminder that the Lake District was an industrial centre long before it became a beauty spot.

06 The path winds down the valley along the southern bank of Levers Water Beck and Church Beck, then descends back to the village.

 Take a Break

The **Sun Hotel** (📞015394-41248; thesunconiston.com; ⏰10am-11pm) has a fell-view beer garden and serves decent grub. A little further into the village, the **Black Bull** (📞015394-41335; blackbullconiston.co.uk/bar; Yewdale Rd; ⏰noon-11pm) brews its own ales, including Bluebird Bitter and Old Man Ale.

05
Haystacks

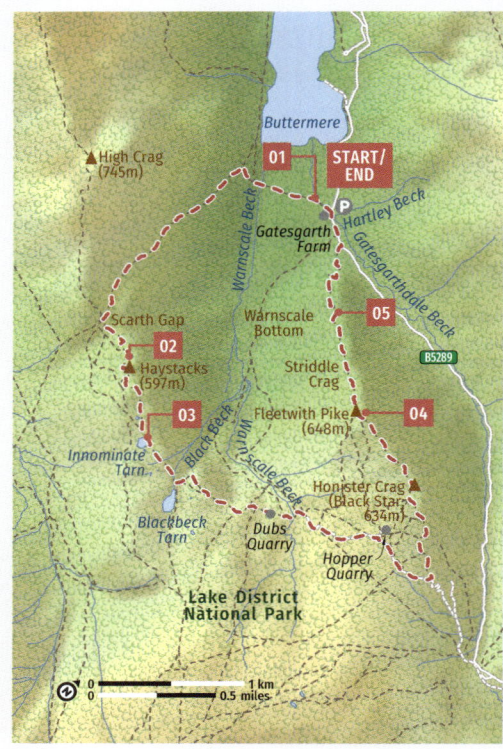

DURATION	DIFFICULTY	DISTANCE	START/END
4–5hr	Moderate	5.5 miles / 8.8km	Gatesgarth Farm

TERRAIN	Rocky fells, quarry paths

'For a man trying to get a persistent worry out of his mind, the top of Haystacks is a wonderful cure.' So said Alfred Wainwright in Book 7 of his *Pictorial Guides,* and if anywhere sums up what he loved about the Lakeland fells, it's Haystacks, his favourite mountain and final resting place.

Getting Here
Buttermere is 9 miles drive from Keswick via Whinlatter Pass. The valley has an excellent bus service: the 77/77A (seven daily Monday to Saturday, five Sunday) makes a circular route from Keswick via Portinscale, Borrowdale, Honister Pass, Lorton and Whinlatter.

Starting Point
The walk begins in the heart of Buttermere, surrounded by magnificent fells on every side; there is a small car park near Gatesgarth Farm.

01 This route follows Wainwright's preferred ascent from Gatesgarth, and descends via the arête of Fleetwith Pike. As always, a map is helpful as the paths can be confusing. Park at Gatesgarth Farm (or better still, catch the 77 bus from Buttermere). Head southeast across Peggy's Bridge, and follow the path as it winds up to the saddle of **Scarth Gap**, a good place for a breather before you tackle the rocky buttress of Haystacks itself.

02 The climb to the summit is steep but not too testing, although there are a few bits of clambering. After 20 minutes or so, you'll reach the top of **Haystacks**, with its twin cairns and cluster of little pools. The panorama from the top is grand, stretching northwest across Buttermere, west into Ennerdale and south towards Pillar and Great Gable. In *Fellwalking with Wainwright,* the hillwalker likened the fell to a 'shaggy and undisciplined terrier'.

Alfred Wainwright

The inveterate fellwalker, cartographer and author Alfred Wainwright (AW to his fans) penned seven volumes of *The Pictorial Guides to the Lakeland Fells*. Well over half a century after their original publication, Wainwright's guides are still the preferred choice for many fellwalkers, thanks to their hand-illustrated maps, painstaking route descriptions and quirky writing – but most of all, perhaps, for Wainwright's enduring love of the Lakeland landscape, which is plainly apparent on every page. They're more than guidebooks; they're works of art.

03 From here, the path meanders eastwards past two high tarns: the reedy pool of **Blackbeck Tarn**, and **Innominate Tarn**, where Wainwright's ashes were scattered in 1991, as requested in his will. In his autobiographical book *Memoirs of a Fellwanderer*, he noted (with typically pithy humour): 'if you, dear reader, should get a bit of grit in your boot as you are crossing Haystacks in the years to come, please treat it with respect. It might be me.' As you descend east, you'll pass a left-hand path into Warnscale Bottom, an easy escape route that avoids Fleetwith Pike.

04 To reach Fleetwith Pike, descend towards the slate piles of Dubs Quarry and follow the quarry roads before cutting west under Honister Crag (Hopper Quarry is still in use). The path leads northwest along the ridge to the summit cairn of **Fleetwith Pike**, with a mind-blowing vista (pictured) along the length of Buttermere and Crummock Water beyond.

05 From the top, a clear but rocky path leads sharply down the spine of the pike; it's not too difficult, but it is steep and rubbly in places. The impressive views offer ample opportunity to pause for a photographic rest stop. At the bottom, the path levels out down to Gatesgarth.

Take a Break

Buttermere has good options for a post-hike lunch, including **Syke Farm** (sykefarmcampsite.com), which serves sandwiches, cream teas and homemade ice cream. It's also worth heading over to nearby Loweswater for the **Kirkstile Inn** (kirkstileinn.com), which brews its own ales.

06
Castle Crag

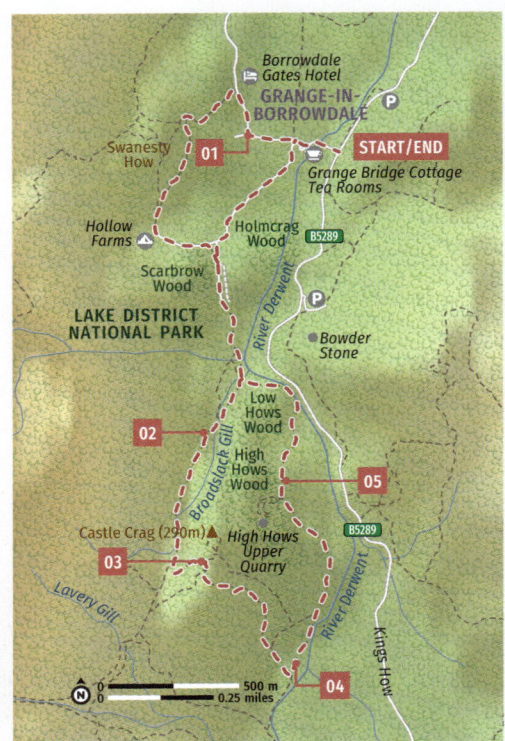

DURATION	DIFFICULTY	DISTANCE	START/END
2hr	Easy	4.5 miles/ 7.2km	Grange-in-Borrowdale

TERRAIN	Woodland and slate quarries

Borrowdale has many fells to conquer, but one of the most spectacular also happens to be one of the smallest. The former slate quarry of Castle Crag is less than a thousand feet in height, but offers a wraparound scene of the green farms and fields of Borrowdale.

Getting Here

Grange-in-Borrowdale is 5 miles south of Keswick. The easiest way to get here is on the 78 bus (at least hourly, half-hourly on weekends from July to August), which shuttles through Borrowdale as far as Seatoller, then heads back the same way to Keswick. Parking can be tricky: there is a small roadside car park a little north of Grange, and another larger one to the south near the Bowder Stone.

Starting Point

Grange-in-Borrowdale makes a lovely place to begin the walk, with its whitewashed cottages and pretty stone bridge.

01 Cross over the double-arched footbridge in Grange. This area was once the site of a monastic farm that belonged to the monks of Furness Abbey. Cross the bridge, walk through the village and follow the road towards the Borrowdale Gates Hotel. A gate leads left onto a path heading south past Swanesty How and Hollow Farms campsite. At the next junction, turn right along the edge of Holmcrag Wood.

02 At the next junction, follow the trail left past Dolts Quarry, with Low Hows Wood on your left. Near the southern edge of the wood, a path leads left (east). Take this, and then look out for another left-hand turn soon afterwards, which

Millican Dalton

Born in 1867, Millican Dalton pioneered a backwoods lifestyle long before Bear Grylls or Ray Mears. Having worked briefly in London as an insurance clerk, Dalton struck out for adventure in the 1920s, moving into an abandoned cave on the side of Castle Crag, where he spent most of the rest of his life, practising a self-sufficient lifestyle while leading people on hiking, climbing and camping adventures. A self-styled 'Professor of Adventure' and lifelong bachelor, he made most of his own clothes, and was never seen without his natty Tyrolean hat. He died in 1947, aged 79; his self-penned journal, *Philosophy of Life*, was sadly lost after his death.

crosses a couple of stiles before the climb up **Castle Crag**. It's a fairly short walk up, but it is very steep – and there is one section near the summit that zigzags up and over a mass of shattered slate. Take extra care here, as the stone is unstable underfoot and can be very slippy in wet weather. Walking poles may come in handy.

03 At the top you'll enter the **old quarry** (pictured), surrounded by upstanding stones and cairns arranged by previous hikers. For the best views, climb up a bit further to the grassy plateau just above: a dramatic vista opens up of a patchwork of green fields and farms, stretching away south and southwest to the summits of the Borrowdale and Buttermere Fells. This is a fantastic spot for a picnic.

04 Retrace your steps back down the crag, crossing the stiles until you reach the main path. Turn left (southeast) and follow the trail along the edge of the woods, before turning north along the banks of the River Derwent. You'll enter **High Hows Wood**; look out for a side trail on the left leading to an area of old quarry workings and caves. The legendary woodsman Millican Dalton lived here for nearly 30 years.

05 On the north side of Low Hows Wood, you'll rejoin the trail back to Grange. At the next junction, take the right-hand fork through **Holmcrag Wood**. Before long you'll be back in the village, enjoying a well-earned cuppa and slice of cake.

Take a Break

Many a walker stops off for tea and cake or a slice of leek-and-ham pie at the quaint **Grange Bridge Cottage Tea Rooms** (01768-777201), in an idyllic spot right next to the bridge in Grange. The prime tables are right by the river, but they fill up very fast on sunny days.

BEST DAY WALKS: ENGLAND

07

Helvellyn & Striding Edge

DURATION	DIFFICULTY	DISTANCE	START/END
6-7hr	Hard	8 miles/ 12.5km	Glenridding

TERRAIN	Exposed mountain ridge

Next to Scafell Pike, Helvellyn is the Lakeland fell that everyone has on their bucket list. The classic ridge route along Striding Edge and Swirral Edge is definitely not for the faint of heart, but few English hikes are quite as buttock-clenchingly thrilling.

Getting Here

Bus 508 travels from Penrith to Glenridding and Patterdale. Five buses continue over Kirkstone Pass to Windermere. The Ullswater Bus-and-Boat Combo ticket includes a day's travel on bus 508 with a return trip on an Ullswater Steamer; buy the ticket on the bus.

Starting Point

The trail begins at a very large public car park in Glenridding, next to the **Lake District National Park Ullswater Information Centre** (☎01539-724555; ullswater tic@lake-district.gov.uk; ⓘ9.30am-5.30pm Apr-Oct, to 3.30pm Sat & Sun Nov-Mar). There are several shops in the village where you can pick up supplies and gear for the trail.

01 Cumbria's third-highest mountain – at 950m – is a fairly formidable proposition even for experienced walkers, with dizzying drops and some all-fours scrambling. It's definitely best avoided if you're even slightly wary of heights, and don't even think about it in wintry conditions, when the arête is cloaked in treacherous ice and snow. Queues are also a problem in high summer, so this is another one to save for a clear, quiet day in late spring or early autumn. But don't let the challenges put you off: Helvellyn is well within the reach of most ordinary walkers. The key is not to rush, to watch your step on the trickier sections, and to try and take the easiest route wherever you can. You'll be on the top in no time. Well, alright – maybe not no time, but no more than 3½ hours for the averagely fit walker.

There are many possible routes to the top, but we've gone with the classic, starting in Glenridding. Follow the road up past the Travellers Rest pub, and take the bridleway signed to Glenridding Bridge. You'll pass Gillside Farm campsite, then take another steepening path along Mires Beck, climbing quite sharply up Birkhouse Moor. From here, the path continues to climb up to a drystone wall, crossing over at a well-known point known as **Hole-in-the-Wall**, before emerging onto the ridgeline of **Bleaberry Crag**.

02 Follow the ridgeline along to High Spying How. This is where the real ascent begins. Dead ahead of you looms the formidable ridge of **Striding Edge**. It looks imposing, even impossible, but it's actually very achievable, as long as you take things slow and steady, and watch your footing. Several possible trails wind their way along the edge, offering various degrees of difficulty; the hardest involves scrambling directly up the ridge, but a path along the right side avoids most of the hand-over-hand work. Whichever route you decide to take, the drops are pretty formidable, but you'll be fine if you take your time and watch your step.

03 At the end of the ridge, a final, semi-scrambly section heads up a rock buttress before levelling out onto Helvellyn's surprisingly flat summit plateau. After the airy ridge ascent, it seems rather strange that the mountain's top is so level. The views are truly fabulous: the glassy expanse of **Red Tarn** stretches out way beneath

Helvellyn's Hardiest Hikers

While you're tackling Helvellyn, spare a thought for the steel-legged Fell Top Assessors, who are employed by the national park to climb the mountain every day between December and Easter to assess the risk of possible avalanches, and to measure weather conditions such as wind chill, snow depth and temperature.

The information is recorded on the **Lake District Weatherline** (0870 055 0575; lake-district.gov.uk/weatherline), a vital weather service relied upon by hundreds of thousands of hill walkers.

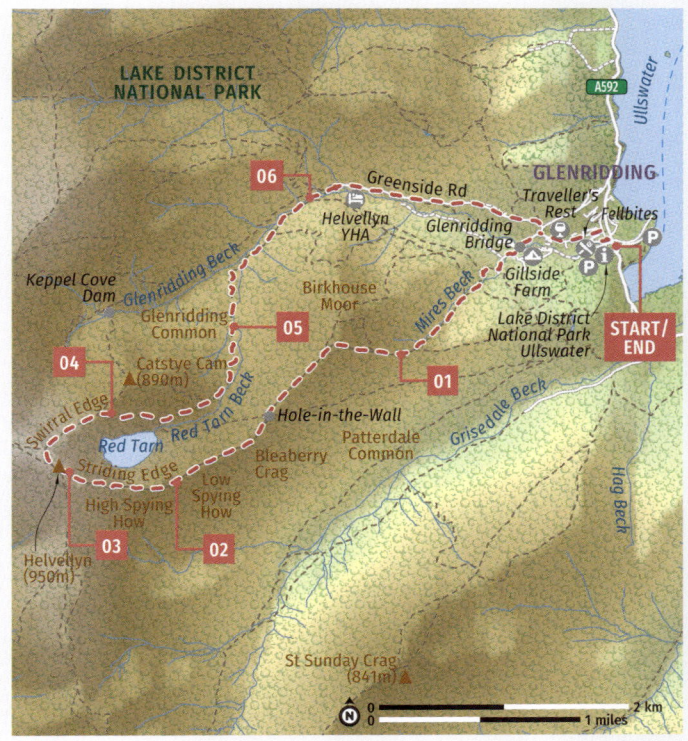

BEST DAY WALKS: ENGLAND 37

you, along with the needle-thin arêtes of Striding Edge and Swirral Edge, both cut out by the long-gone glacier that carved out the entire massif. Big views loom on all horizons: southeast to St Sunday Crag, northeast to the pointy peak of Catstye Cam, west to Thirlmere and east to Ullswater. Beyond, when the weather is really clear, you should be able to see all the way to the Solway Firth, Morecambe Bay and the Irish Sea.

Three **memorials** can be found around Helvellyn's summit. One commemorates the artist and climber Charles Gough who, in 1805, became the first recorded person to fall off the mountain. His body was found three months later; according to legend, his faithful dog Foxie was still waiting beside the skeleton (William Wordsworth wrote a poem about the dog's devotion called *Fidelity*, conveniently overlooking the rather inconvenient likelihood that Foxie more than likely survived by eating the remains of his owner). Another memorial concerns local man Robert Dixon, who slipped off the peak while following a foxhounds' trail in 1858. A third memorial champions two daring pilots, John Leeming and Bert Hinkler, who amazingly managed to land their planes on the top of Helvellyn in 1926.

The natural drama of Helvellyn made it a particular favourite of Wordsworth, who lived much of his life at nearby Grasmere. He is known to have ascended the mountain several times; one of the best-known portraits of the poet, painted by Benjamin Robert Haydon in 1842, depicts him deep in thought with Helvellyn as an über-romantic backdrop. Samuel Taylor Coleridge is also known to have climbed Helvellyn a number of times: an entry in Dorothy Wordsworth's diary records an occasion in 1800 when the poet came to visit them at around ten in the evening, having climbed the mountain the same day. The mountain's name is thought to derive from an ancient Celtic term for 'yellow moorland', although there is some debate about this, not least since the mountain isn't really very yellow at all.

DUNCAN ANDISON/SHUTTERSTOCK ©

04 The entire landscape around Helvellyn was carved out by massive glaciers that gouged out the surrounding rock during the last Ice Age (those boring geography lessons at school all about drumlins, moraines and cirques might finally come in handy). The descent from the summit is via **Swirral Edge** (pictured p36), another classic glacial arête that loops around the northern side of Red Tarn, a high lake formed by glacial meltwater. Water from the tarn was once used to power machinery at the nearby Greenside mines. The edge is steep and fairly exposed; in fact, some walkers find that they actually feel more exposed here than on Striding Edge – but it's the thrilling, tightrope-like walk that

38   BEST DAY WALKS: ENGLAND

 On the Edge

Striding Edge (pictured) is a classic arête, a sharp mountain ridge formed by the action of glacial erosion. When snow and ice accumulates in hollows, known as corries, on opposite sides of the mountain, and slowly slips down the mountainsides, the underlying rock is gradually worn away. Over millennia, the rock is reshaped into a narrow, knife-edge ridge; the ice then melts away, leaving behind glacial pools like Red Tarn.

makes it the perfect companion piece. The ridge is overlooked by the pyramid-shaped peak of **Catstye Cam** (890m), another popular target for peak-baggers. Soon the trail heads down off the ridge and leads to a junction at the lake's eastern edge.

05 Bear left (north), following the course of Red Tarn Beck northwards through the old mine workings on the north side of Birkhouse Moor. As you cross Glenridding Common, you'll see **Keppel Cove** to the west; this was the site of a major disaster in 1927, when a dam failed following a severe storm, flooding the Glenridding valley below. Miraculously, no-one lost their lives – but the local topography means that the area continues to be extremely flood-prone. The most recent floods were in 2015, when Storm Desmond swept through the village, causing Glenridding Beck to break its banks twice in a matter of days, resulting in major damage.

06 When you reach the old mine workings, the path crosses over Glenridding Beck and leads past **Helvellyn YHA** (0845 371 9742; yha.org.uk; Greenside; dm £16-30; Easter-Oct), where many walkers choose to spend a night in order to beat the crowds by getting an early start on the mountain. From the hostel, it's a straightforward trek back down the old Greenside Road into Glenridding village.

☕ Take a Break

Fellbites (017684-82781; lunch mains £8-10, dinner mains £15-24; 9am-8.30pm Thu-Tue, to 5.30pm Wed), beside the car park in Glenridding, has something to fill you up at any time of day: fry-ups for breakfast; soups, burgers and rarebits for lunch; lamb shanks and duck breast for dinner.

The luxurious **Another Place, The Lake** (017684-86442; another. place; Watermillock; r £295-397, f £520-600; P) has a couple of in-house restaurants, and also offers lake activities including SUP, kayaking and wild swimming.

BEST DAY WALKS: ENGLAND 39

08
Scafell Pike

Best for

A POST-HIKE PINT

DURATION	DIFFICULTY	DISTANCE	START/END
4-5hr	Hard	5.8 miles/ 9.4km	Wasdale Head

TERRAIN	Rocky, exposed mountain

In terms of bragging rights alone, this is the biggest day out in England: the nation's highest hiking challenge at 978m. It might be relatively small compared to say, the Alps, but make no mistake, this is a proper, full-blown mountain: stark, wild and packed with drama.

Getting Here
Wasdale Head lies in a deep valley, 5 miles' drive from the Cumbrian coast. There are no bus services, so the only option is to drive, cycle or take a cab: try **Gosforth Taxis** (019467-25308).

Starting Point
The car park at Wasdale Head fills up fast in summer. There is a second National Trust car park at the end of Wastwater.

01 Every year thousands of hikers set out to conquer England's highest mountain and, despite its elevation, it's achievable as long as you're fit and properly equipped – but it's a tough walk, no two ways about it. The exposed summit and altitude make this walk dangerous and difficult to navigate during bad weather. It's at its best on a clear day, or at the very least one without too much low cloud. It's important to stick to the path wherever possible, as trail erosion is becoming a big problem on Scafell Pike – the peak's popularity inevitably puts the mountain's delicate habitat under severe pressure, so you want to avoid adding to the problem if you can. A map and proper walking gear are essential for this walk; if you're attempting it in bad weather, which we don't advise, a compass is also mandatory.

As with most fells, there's a multitude of ways to conquer Scafell Pike, many starting from Wasdale Head. We've chosen one that also takes in the summit of nearby Lingmell, which offers a great view of the Scafell mountain massif, and is generally much quieter than the main motorway route through Hollow Stones. **Wasdale Head** is a dramatic place to begin a walk in its own right: hemmed in by brooding peaks on all sides, it's a view that's often voted one of the best in Britain, and that's before you've even got out of the car park. Take the trail leading southeast, crossing over **Lingmell Gill** via the footbridge. The path is faint to begin with, then becomes clearer as it ratchets up the west side of Lingmell. It's a taxing, tiring climb – on the plus side, it gets a good chunk of the ascent out of the way early, when your legs are still relatively fresh.

02 It's a steep push up the ridge, increasingly strewn with scree and rocks around **Goat Crags**. At around 550m, the path starts to level out and climb more gently eastwards towards the fell top. It veers around the Goat Crags, climbing up a gully towards the peak of **Lingmell**, which you'll reach at 807m. To the north, the moody summits of Kirkfell and Great Gable loom; to the east rises Great End; and to the south, the stark ridge line of Scafell Pike and the distinctive notched profile of Scafell occupy the sky. But the best part of the view from Lingmell is to the west – the long, glassy stretch of **Wastwater** (pictured), England's deepest lake, and the distant shimmer of the Irish Sea beyond. The summit cairn is a good place for a picnic and a rest before stage two: the push up to the Pike.

03 From Lingmell, the path drops south into the grassy dip of **Lingmell Col**, where you'll come to a junction with two alternative paths: the 'Corridor Route' from Seathwaite in Borrowdale, and the 'Hollow Stones' route from Wasdale Head. Make a mental note of

Scafell or Scawfell?

Scafell Pike's name derives from the Old Norse *skalli fjall*, meaning 'the fell with the bald summit'; pike comes from *pic*, or peak. To early tourists, the mountain formed part of a circuit known as the Scawfell Pikes, along with nearby Ill Crag and Broad Crag (scawfell roughly reflects how it sounds when pronounced in a thick Cumbrian accent, and was used on maps for decades). Initially, early cartographers thought that Scafell was actually higher than Scafell Pike; in fact it's 14m lower.

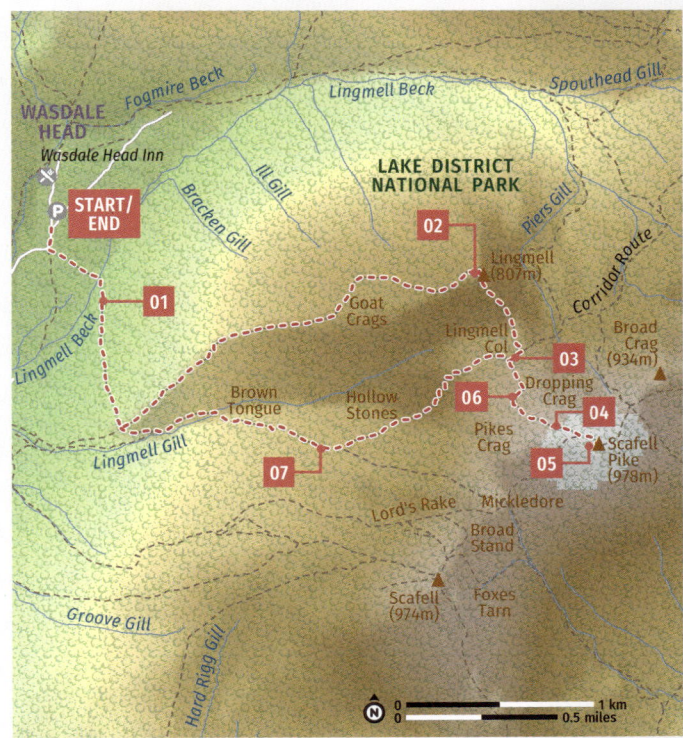

this junction, as you'll be coming back to it later. It can be incredibly windy up on the col, so keep a tight grip on anything that has the potential to fly off into the great blue yonder.

04 South of the Lingmell Col junction, you begin to share the path with the main 'tourist' route up Scafell Pike, so you are pretty much guaranteed to encounter more crowds after the glorious quiet of Lingmell. From the col, the path climbs between **Dropping Crag** and **Pikes Crag**, becoming ever more rocky as you ascend.

05 A great shattered expanse of broken rock and scree covers the summit plateau; it looks like something from an extraterrestrial planet, altogether harsher and more unforgiving than some Lakeland fells. There's no defined path as such, but when the weather's clear, it's fairly obvious where you need to go – cairns mark the way, and unless you're an extremely early bird, there are bound to be other walkers there before you. In bad weather, however, it's very easy to lose your way here, when the summit is likely to be blanketed in cloud. Without a compass, it's easy to get lost in the mist.

At 978m, **Scafell Pike** is known to every schoolchild as England's highest mountain, but it wasn't always this way: until the peak was properly surveyed in the early 19th century, most people believed that either Skiddaw, near Keswick, or Helvellyn, near Ullswater, was Lakeland's loftiest

RICHARD WHITCOMBE/SHUTTERSTOCK ©

peak. Among those early walkers was Samuel Taylor Coleridge, who wrote a letter from the summit in 1802, and Dorothy Wordsworth, William's sister, who commemorated climbing the mountain in her journal (a rather extraordinary achievement at a time when hillwalking – let alone by a solo woman – was still in its infancy). In 1919 the peak was donated to the National Trust by its owner, Lord Leconfield, in memory of all the many Lakeland servicemen who laid down their lives during the Great War. The views across the valley are astounding, especially the interlocking panorama of peaks to the north, including Lingmell, from which you've just climbed – but if it's cloudy there won't be very much to see at all. Be prepared for fierce winds up on the top: Scafell Pike's welcome can be a bit brutal.

Two paths lead away from the summit: one northeast over Broad Crag, the other southwest along the ridge of Mickledore. If you want to push on to the top of Scafell Pike's sister peak, Scafell, it's the Mickledore route you need to follow. When you reach the ridge, you'll find the way to the summit blocked by a massive, rather terrifying wall of rock. This is **Broad Stand**, a formidable challenge for the most seasoned rock-climbers (notoriously, this is the point at which Samuel Taylor Coleridge became 'cragfast' during his 1802 climb). Another equally treacherous route ascends westwards via the gully scramble known as **Lord's Rake**. Neither of these

Wastwater

In his 1810 *Guide to the Lakes*, William Wordsworth described Wastwater (pictured) as 'long, narrow, stern and desolate', and it's a description that still seems apt. The lake itself is owned by the National Trust and is the deepest body of water in the national park (around 79m at its deepest point). It's also the coldest, and one of the clearest; very little life can survive in its inhospitable waters, apart from the hardy Arctic char.

is remotely suitable for walkers. The only sane route for hikers to the summit of Scafell drops south then west via Foxes Tarn, before ascending sharply up to the summit at 974m. It's doable for experienced walkers, but still a tricky, scrabbly climb that should be avoided in bad weather; a ridge walk then heads west back to Wasdale Head.

06 However, if you don't feel up to tackling Scafell, simply retrace your steps back from the summit of Scafell Pike to Lingmell Col and the junction you passed on the way down from Lingmell. In good weather, it shouldn't be too hard to follow the stone cairns – but there's no clearly defined path as you're walking through a fairly featureless plain composed of rock and scree, so you need to pay close attention not to lose your way. This is where a compass really comes in handy if the weather has set in – you can just take bearings off the map to make sure you're on the right path. In practice, however, you're extremely unlikely to be alone on the summit – so if in doubt, there's no harm in asking another hiker if they're happy for you to follow them back down.

07 When you reach the junction at Lingmell Col, follow the path west down along the **river valley**. This is the well-trodden main path up and down from the Pike which most people follow, leading west through Hollow Stones, Brown Tongue and Wasdale Head. Once you're back at the bottom, give yourself a pat on the back – you've just conquered England's rooftop. Now you've just got Ben Nevis and Snowdon to tick off...

Take a Break

A slice of hill-walking heritage awaits at the **Wasdale Head Inn** (019467-26229; wasdale.com; per person per night from £100, minimum 3nt stay;). Hunkering beneath Scafell Pike, this 19th-century hostelry is gloriously old-fashioned and covered in vintage photos and climbing memorabilia. The wood-panelled dining room serves fine food, with pub grub and ales in Ritson's Bar, where many a Scafell Piker has congregated.

09
Millom to Silecroft

DURATION	DIFFICULTY	DISTANCE	START/END
4–4½hr	Moderate	10.2 miles / 16.4km	Millom / Silecroft

TERRAIN	Tarmac, hard track, dunes, farmland

Cumbria has much to offer aside from the soaring fells and shimmering lakes. The 182-mile coastal footpath wraps itself around the county and this stretch, in the far southwest corner, rarely attracts visitors but is perennially popular with those 'in the know'. The path is well signed throughout and takes in natural delights such as Duddon Estuary and Haverigg Dunes, as well as impressive artificial structures including immense sea barriers and numerous lighthouses.

Getting Here
The scenic coastal railway makes the entire footpath easy to explore by hopping on and off trains and walking between the stations.

Starting Point
This is a station-to-station walk, with the start at Millom train station. There is also ample parking available around the station.

01 Exit Millom train station onto the main road bridge crossing the line. Turn left and walk down Lancashire Rd, passing the Tesco supermarket. Follow this road to the end then continue over to the track beyond. When you reach the shoreline, turn right to follow the signed 'England Coast Path' route. Remain on this path, following the signs, until you emerge through woodland onto the Outer Barrier at **Hodbarrow Point**.

The River Duddon rises near Three Shires Stone, in the fells above Coniston at the point where the boundaries of the historic counties of Cumberland, Westmorland and Lancashire met and, with its vast tidal range, the estuary attracts many migrating

⚒ Industrial Millom

Millom was once the site of one of the richest iron ore deposits in the world. The ore here had an iron content of over 60%, so it's no surprise that an industry and infrastructure quickly sprung up around it. A steelworks was built nearby and, in its heyday, over 1000 people were employed here. The boom in the railways helped and as they grew and spread, so did demand for iron, and the mine remained prosperous for over 100 years. Flooding from the sea and easier access to imports from elsewhere lead to the final closure of the mine in 1968.

bird species each year. It has also attracted its fair share of admirers, including William Wordsworth who wrote 34 sonnets about it, and William Turner, whose painting *Duddon Sands* hangs in the Tate Gallery.

02 Walk along the barrier toward **Haverigg**. When you reach the far side, turn left through the car park, then right to follow the footpath towards the village. When you cross the bridge, turn left to return to the coast. The lighthouse (pictured) you pass along the way was built in 1905 and is one of only a very small number of lighthouses in the UK to be built from cast iron.

It was built to mark the completion of the Outer Barrier and was restored in 2003 after a fundraising effort by a local school.

03 Continue to follow the signs out onto the dunes. Please note that the path along this stretch can be overgrown and indistinct at times – tides permitting it is often easier to walk along the beach. The beautiful sculpture you pass just before you reach the shore is **Escape to Light**. It was created by renowned sculptor Josefina de Vasconcellos, who lived in Little Langdale and was, at one point, the oldest sculptor in the world. She completed this sculpture when she was 90. It originally stood at Rydall Hall but was moved here in 2003 to commemorate inshore rescue crews around the UK.

04 After rounding the headland look for the waymarked route back through Black Dub and towards the wind farm. Keep following the signs that will bring you through the dunes and back out onto the beach again. When you see three signs pointing inland, take the third one and follow a straight, broad farm track. Continue on this track towards Kirkstanton. After crossing a pretty little bridge turn left into Standing

Stones Farm and follow the tarmac lane to the houses. At the end of this track turn right to cross a stile. You can take a detour here to visit the **standing stones** 50m away in the field. As with many standing stones these are impressive, but the reason for their existence remains a mystery. They are thought to date back to the Bronze Age and one source suggests they were once part of an old burial mound, while others suggest they were ancient waymarkers pointing to a safe route between the hills.

05 When you're ready to proceed, return to the stile and follow the path along the field edge and along a beck. Cross the wooden footbridge and follow the waymarkers across the field to a gate on the far side. Go through the gate, following the enclosed track to a small road. Turn right here, then right again to follow the road to **Silecroft train station**.

The coastal railway line came into being one section at a time, rather than as one cohesive plan, and was driven into existence by the various heavy industries that dominated the coast during that period, from quarrying and smelting to shipbuilding. The route remains popular with visitors and provides an essential commuting route for the large employers in the area, such as Sellafield and BAE Systems.

Wildlife Haven

What was once a huge, noisy, industrial site is now a tranquil nature reserve managed by the RSPB. The carefully managed Hodbarrow Nature Reserve is now home to breeding terns, ringed plovers and redshanks, and the pinging call of oyster-catchers will provide the soundtrack for much of your walk. Between May and July the island in the lagoon is home to a colony of terns and there is access to a bird hide so you can observe them more easily. The carefully managed pools around the lagoon provide homes for endangered natterjack toads, as well as pillwort, the UKs only aquatic fern.

Take a Break

There are numerous stopping points if you have brought your own packed lunch. Between Hodbarrow Point and the start of Haverigg Dunes there are several well-placed benches, all with excellent views and, once you're in the dunes, you can take your pick of perfect picnic spots. There are ice-cream and snack vans in Haverigg, as well as a small shop. At Silecroft there's a new beach cafe in the car park serving a range of drinks and snacks.

10
Shap & Swindale

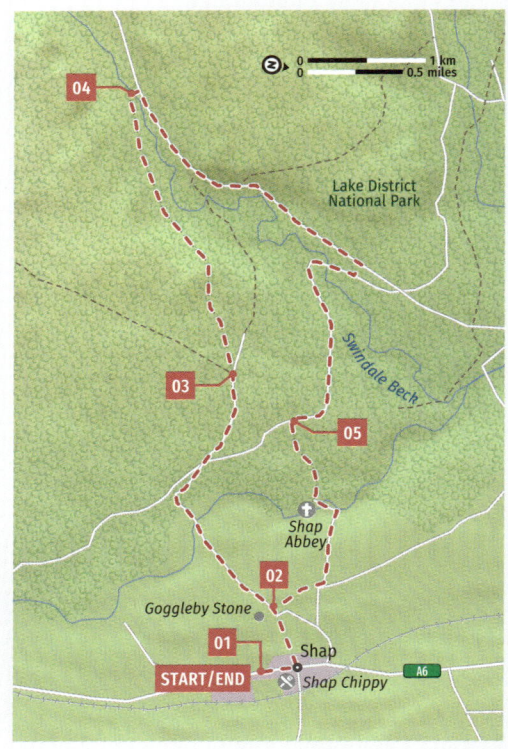

DURATION	DIFFICULTY	DISTANCE	START/END
3½-4hr	Moderate	8.7 miles/ 14km	Memorial Hall car park

TERRAIN	Mostly hard track/tarmac

Even on the sunniest days in the school holidays you'll find peace, and a free parking space, around Shap. The local fells are gentle, undulating and crammed with local history, from Bronze Age standing stones to robust concrete bridges, and from a modern-day rewilding project to an ancient abbey. Although this is a gentle and winding route there is little in the way of shelter, so whatever the weather has to offer you'll be fully immersed in the experience.

Getting Here
The Shap Memorial Hall car park is small and free. Directly outside the car park are the local bus stops. Bus 106 runs from Penrith and Kendal to Shap.

Starting Point
There are plenty of facilities near the start including well-kept toilets, and a local shop where you can stock up for the hike ahead.

01 Exit the **car park** and turn right, then use the pedestrian crossing to cross the main road and continue to Cross Garth. The interesting building you pass just after the crossing is Shap's old market hall, which dates back to the 17th century. Turn left here, then first right into Beck Lane (note: this looks like a disused road), and after 25m follow the signed path left, through the gate and into the field. Continue following this path, passing Goggleby Stone (pictured) until you emerge onto a small lane. Goggleby Stone is one of just a few remnants of a once-impressive avenue of stones.

Just outside the village to the north is a stone circle, now half hidden beneath the West Coast

48 BEST DAY WALKS: ENGLAND

Shap Granite

The oldest piece of local history originated 394 million years ago with the formation of Shap granite. The quarry originally opened in 1864 and after a brief closure it is again open today – you'll find it just south of Shap on the A6. This granite was once one of the most highly sought-after products in the country for builders and architects and is found in many high-status buildings, including St Paul's Cathedral and Euston Station in London. There are many outcrops along the route and the rock can be easily identified by its large pink (feldspar) crystals.

ADAMIB8789, CC BY 4.0, VIA WIKIMEDIA COMMONS

Mainline, and the stone avenue leading away from this once stretched for two miles. If you study the OS map you can pick out others nearby. The precise location of the avenue (or, as some argue, avenues) is far from certain, but a painting by Lady Lowther from 1775 shows it in all its glory. Over the years stones have been moved, buried, or broken up and recycled into gate posts, field boundaries and homes.

02 Take the signed path opposite across the field and continue on as it reaches the boundary and follows the road towards Keld. Pass over the stile at the end, continue left to Keld then fork right in front of **Keld Chapel**, a National Trust property that's kept locked but can be accessed by obtaining the key on the wall from the house opposite. It was built in the 16th century as the chantry for Shap Abbey but, over the years, has also served as a cottage and a meeting house. From the chapel remain on this road for 1 mile until you reach the farm.

03 Immediately before the farm, fork left to follow a track towards the flanks of the small hill ahead. Keep following the track as it rounds the hill and drops down to **Swindale Valley**. Cross the beck using the footbridge then turn right along the road.

The beck is the site of an important rewilding project. Headed by Lee Scholfield, the project has restored the natural twists and turns in the river that had been removed 200 years ago. This slowed the flow, improved the gravel beds and led to a dramatic increase in flora and fauna, including the return of salmon spawning in the first year.

04 Continue on along this road, passing a small car park, then a water-treatment

BEST DAY WALKS: ENGLAND   49

works. After you have passed the bridge down in the valley on your right, look for a track through the bracken leading down to the concrete road. When you reach the road, turn right to cross the bridge, then follow the old road for just over a mile.

This **old concrete road** was a 'temporary' road, built in the 1930s to transport materials from the main A6 to the site of Haweswater dam in the next valley. The whole route is still passable, bar one small section near the A6. It is open to walkers and cyclists, and while it is technically closed to general traffic, it is still a popular local shortcut, so do take care.

05 Look to your left and you will see a track leading down towards **Shap Abbey** (pictured). Follow this track down, through a gate and on through the next field until you reach the abbey. After you have explored the abbey take the track across the bridge, then remain on the road as it climbs up and reaches a four-way intersection (a footpath is available, but the road is easier on the legs!). Turn right here to follow the enclosed track. At the end turn left, then right to reach a stile leading back to Goggleby Stone, then retrace your steps back to the start of the walk.

50 BEST DAY WALKS: ENGLAND

The White Monks

Shap Abbey was founded in the year 1200 and although it was a large abbey it was home to a relatively small community. It also holds the distinction of being the last abbey to be dissolved by Henry VIII during the dissolution of the monasteries. The monks of the abbey were known as the 'white monks' due to their white woollen habits, made from the fleece of local sheep. Powerful local monasteries such as this traded in wool and created the foundations of the present day 'futures' market by agreeing multi-year deals for fleece prices. The site is now a scheduled monument.

Take a Break

While there are no refreshment stops along this route, there are a few places to pause and enjoy your sandwiches. The brow of the hill above the Swindale Valley has a pleasant rocky outcrop with great views all around or, for something more sheltered, there's a small car park on the edge of Swindale with a few shady trees.

No walk here is complete without a visit to award-winning **Shap Chippy** (shapchippy.co.uk; fish & chips £5-10) for fresh and fabulous fish and chips. It's open for lunch and evenings except Mondays.

11

Whitbarrow Scar

DURATION	DIFFICULTY	DISTANCE	START/END
4-4½hr	Moderate	6.9 miles/ 11km	X6 bus stop, Mill Side Rd
TERRAIN	Hard track and some loose scree		

South Cumbria is limestone country and there are an assortment of 'scars' dotted across the area. Typically, these are a lot lower than the Lake District fells, but what they lack in loftiness they more than make up for with their panoramic views, from Blackpool Tower in the south to Skiddaw in the far north. This walk begins in sheltered woodland before crossing the expansive limestone landscape in the nature reserve on the summit, then descending through woods teeming with butterflies and finishing along a path beneath an imposing limestone cliff in the old quarry.

Getting Here
The X6 bus offers a regular service between Kendal and Barrow-in-Furness.

Starting Point
There's ample free on-road parking along the old road near Mill Side, with plenty of space on all but the busiest days of the year.

01 Follow the road leading directly away from the A590. Continue on to a T-junction and turn right, before forking left at the next intersection. Remain on this road as it becomes a track at the **Hiker's Rest**. This rudimentary rest stop is welcome but can be unpredictable – it has a toilet and often has tea/coffee available with an honesty box, but may not always be well stocked or cleaned. Continue into the woods and after 50m bear right to follow an undulating hard track running parallel to the scar. When you reach the gate at the end go through it then turn right to cross a stile at the edge of a playing field.

Wildflowers Galore

It may look like a barren rocky desert, but the environment is unique and supports a wide range of rare plants and animals. The thin soils provide ideal growing conditions for a variety of plant species, from the spring stars of hoary rockrose, primrose, cowslip and early-purple orchid to bird's-foot trefoil, lesser meadow-rue, dropwort, limestone bedstraw and wild thyme later in the summer. And remember to peer down into the grikes (deep channels) to get a bird's-eye view of a microclimate right beneath your feet. These deep, sheltered fissures continue to throw up new species surprises for scientists and botanists.

PETE STUART/SHUTTERSTOCK ©

02 Cross the field and remain on this path as it climbs the side of the scar. This is the trickiest part of the walk as it rises steeply and crosses limestone scree, so please take care. Challenging though it is, it's also a great chance to see the **limestone** up close. This is carboniferous limestone, laid down 350 million years ago, and this location is renowned as one of the finest examples of limestone pavement in the county. If you peer closely at the rock, you may even be lucky enough to spot the odd fossil or two.

03 As you near the **summit** the distinctive large cairn (pictured) will be clearly visible – use this as your marker if you want to explore the summit ridge. Once you're ready to descend, take the clear path leading away from the cairn and down towards a dry-stone wall. Cross over the stile and continue down through the woods. Follow the waymark post leading down a short steep section to the left, then remain on this path until you reach a wooden gate.

On a clear day, you can see all the way up to Skiddaw in the far north of the Lake District and, to the south, you should be able to spot Blackpool Tower. The area between the foot of the scar and Morecambe Bay is Foulshaw Moss, which is home to a breeding pair of osprey. They have been nesting and breeding here since 2000 and you can watch their yearly progress via Cumbria Wildlife Trust's Osprey Cam.

04 Pass through the stile next to the gate and continue on the main track as it bears to the right. When you reach a junction with a larger track, turn right. The valley you see peeping in and out beyond the trees is the **Lyth Valley** and it is famed for its damsons. Damson Day is still celebrated in April each year with a fair and plenty of damson-related produce. The Victorians used to take charabancs (coaches) from Grange-over-Sands station to admire the blossom on the trees. Nowadays, during autumn, you will find roadside stalls throughout the valley with jams, chutneys and more, all for sale via honesty boxes.

05 The track you need for the final descent is usually marked with traffic cones on your left and winds down to **Rawson's Farm**. Pass the houses then turn right along the broad track. After the small car park follow the track that bears right, away from the main route – this will take you up to the old quarry. Continue along the track that follows the base of the impressive cliffs. Parts of this section can be slippery after wet weather, and you may find it easier to stick close to the woodland edge. Although once the site of heavy industry, today the woods along this section are popular with local butterfly spotters and are home to a variety of species including high brown and dark green fritillary butterflies.

06 Once the path reaches another main track turn left, then, after 20m, turn right to follow the signed route down to another **farm**. Pass through the farm, following the track out onto the lane. Turn left here to return to the start of the walk.

Nature Preserved

The summit of the scar, Lord's Seat, is 215m high. The imposing cairn monument was built by Colin Park and Michael Bowerbank in 1969 and commemorates the surrounding 250 acres being acquired by the Lake District Naturalist's Trust – better known today as Cumbria Wildlife Trust. This area was originally known as Flodder Allotment, and it was given to the trust by local philanthropists, the Argles family. Its official title is the Canon Hervey Nature Reserve, after the man who founded the trust with the aim of preventing the destruction of wildlife by acquiring reserves, campaigning, educating and advising.

Take a Break

There are plenty of limestone outcrops to perch on to enjoy both your sandwiches and the fabulous views. The area around the cairn is the most popular but, if you fancy a bit of peace and quiet, head up onto one of the nearby ridges where you will find plenty of tucked-away nooks and crannies. The **Derby Arms** (derbyarms.co.uk; mains £15-20) in Witherslack, where you'll find plenty of excellent local food and beers, is a mile down the road from the start.

Also Try...

PETE STUART/SHUTTERSTOCK ©

The Other Borrowdale

There's another Borrowdale Valley tucked away just north of Kendal. Park in the lay-by at Huck's Bridge and follow the track along the valley floor opposite. You'll need to backtrack up the hill a bit to reach the start. It's a pretty little valley, once described by Alfred Wainwright as 'the most beautiful valley outside the Lake District'.

The route follows Borrow Beck, passing old stone farms and plenty of sheep along the way. There's scope to extended it either to the end of the valley, or up and over to the deserted village of Bretherdale Head. (Note: if you try this, the path on the map leading back along Bretherdale to the road is completely overgrown and requires GPRS navigation.)

DURATION 1hr
DIFFICULTY Easy
DISTANCE 2.5 miles/4km

High Cup Nick

The first stretch of this walk forms part of the Pennine Way and is well signposted and well trodden.

The first part of the walk offers a long, slow, gentle climb to the top of High Cup Nick (pictured), which has distinctive geological formations. It's said that those quarrying here gave the word 'sill' to the world of geology to describe the unique rock formation. The second part involves descending the large scree slope, which isn't for the faint of heart but is doable if you take your time. The reward for this effort is walking along an isolated valley with huge rock walls wrapped around you. This section is not as well trodden but it's straight-forward to navigate back to the lane, and then head right, back to Dufton village.

DURATION 4-5hr
DIFFICULTY Hard
DISTANCE 8.5 miles/13.7km

NIGEL EVE/SHUTTERSTOCK ©

Lacy's Caves & Long Meg

The River Eden is the longest river in Cumbria and one of only a handful in the UK that flow north. The whole valley is a joy to explore, and this route takes in two of its most famous features.

From Little Salkeld follow the path north along the riverside, to Lacy's Caves – a quirky Victorian folly carved into the red sandstone cliffs. At Daleraven Bridge head up a short road section before taking the wide track on the right. This will bring you to the ancient Long Meg and Her Daughters (pictured). It's a neolithic construction and, if you look closely, you should be able to spot cup and ring marks on the stones, examples of ancient artwork.

DURATION 2½-3hr
DIFFICULTY Moderate
DISTANCE 4.6 miles/7.4km

Bowness-on-Solway to Drumburgh

Walk a stretch of the Hadrian's Wall path and keep going as long as your legs will take you. There are regular buses along this stretch of the coast.

This is only a short walk but there's plenty of interest along the way. At Bowness, look west along the estuary to spot a promontory that was once a bridge right across to Annan and part of a busy rail network. Port Carlisle used to be Fishers' Cross until a canal to Carlisle was dug, turning it into a busy dock, the remains of which can still be seen. And in Drumburgh the distinctive castle helps answer the question 'where did all the rocks from Hadrian's Wall go?' They were recycled into local buildings.

DURATION 2-2½hr
DIFFICULTY Easy
DISTANCE 4.2 miles/6.7km

Bodmin Moor (p73), Cornwall

Devon & Cornwall

12 Teign Gorge
Explore a stunning gorge and a work-in-progress woodland restoration. **p62**

13 Wistman's Wood
Delve into Dartmoor's oldest forest. **p64**

14 River Dart Walk
Stroll the banks of the idyllic Dart. **p66**

15 Kynance Cove & Lizard Point
Loop round Britain's southern tip. **p68**

16 St Agnes & Chapel Porth
A classic walk through Cornish mining country. **p70**

17 Brown Willy & Rough Tor
Climb Cornwall's highest and second-highest hills. **p72**

18 Porthcurno to Land's End
Look out from Britain's westerly limit. **p74**

19 Tintagel to Boscastle
Take a mythical coastal walk. **p78**

20 Isles of Scilly
Discover St Mary's, the largest Scilly isle, on a round-island adventure. **p82**

21 Combe Martin
A cove-to-cove walk for water lovers. **p86**

Explore
Devon & Cornwall

Sand, sea, surf – these are the three things that draw most people to Britain's most far-westerly counties, and for clifftop scenery and coast walks you really will be spoilt. If you like a walk by the ocean, followed by a congratulatory pint at a seaside pub, this is the corner of Britain for you. But there are other sides to Devon and Cornwall that feel different to the coast – two of Britain's great moorlands, Bodmin Moor and Dartmoor, straddle the granite spine of the counties, while a web of pretty rivers and estuaries provides tranquil waterside walks.

Truro

Dominated by the three spires of its 19th-century cathedral, Truro is Cornwall's capital and its only city. It's the county's main centre for shopping and commerce: the streets here are packed with high-street chains and independent shops, and there are regular weekly markets held on the paved piazza at Lemon Quay (opposite the Hall for Cornwall).

Traces of Truro's wealthy past remain in the smart Georgian townhouses and Victorian villas dotted around the city – especially along Strangways Tce, Walsingham Pl and Lemon St.

Penzance

Overlooking the majestic sweep of Mount's Bay, the old harbour of Penzance has a salty, sea-blown charm that feels altogether more authentic than many of Cornwall's polished-up ports. Its streets and shopping arcades still feel real and a touch ramshackle, and there's nowhere better for a windy-day walk than the town's seafront Victorian promenade, where you can also take a dip at the newly restored saltwater Jubilee Pool (jubileepool.co.uk; £7). The town is a useful base for exploring the far west of Cornwall, including Land's End and the Penwith Peninsula. Buses serve most local villages.

Exeter

Well-heeled and comfortable, Exeter exudes evidence of its centuries-old role as the spiritual and administrative heart of Devon. The city's Gothic cathedral presides over pockets of cobbled streets; medieval and Georgian buildings and fragments of the Roman city stretch out all around. A snazzy contemporary shopping centre brings bursts of the modern; thousands of university students ensure a buzzing nightlife; and the vibrant quayside acts as a launch pad for cycling or kayaking trips. Throw in some stylish places to stay and eat, and you have a relaxed but lively base for explorations of central and southern Devon.

Totnes

The market town of Totnes is a magnet for Devon's free spirits as well as for eco-conscious travellers. Set on the banks of the River Dart, Totnes is small but stuffs in organic cafes, independent shops and boutiques, and local farmers' markets that have been setting up shop for

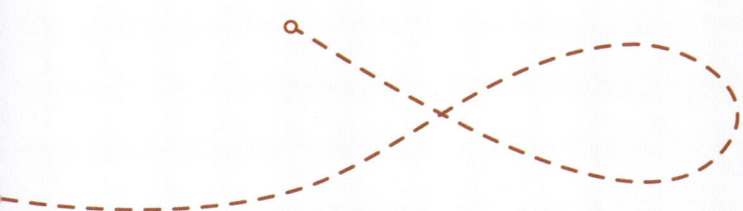

Resources

South West Coast Path (southwestcoastpath.org.uk) Excellent guide to walking the southwest's longest trail.

I Walk Cornwall (iwalkcornwall.co.uk) Good local guide to out-of-the-way Cornish walks.

Visit Dartmoor (visitdartmoor.co.uk) Walking advice, routes and guidance for Dartmoor National Park.

hundreds of years. History buffs will enjoy Totnes Castle's sweeping views, poking around in the Elizabethan House Museum and discovering the 16th-century Tudor Guildhall, while nature lovers can explore the riverside, catch a boat or a steam train down to Dartmouth or hike the wilds of nearby Dartmoor.

 ## When to Go

Spring and autumn are usually the best times for walking, with fewer crowds and settled weather. Summer is peak season in Devon and Cornwall: prices are at their highest and beaches can be crowded, but reliable sunshine mean that this can be still a good time to walk. Winter means wrapping up to battle fierce winds, but winter storms bring real drama to the landscape.

 ## Transport

Devon and Cornwall sit at the far end of England, and getting here sometimes feels like it. The main A30 runs down the centre of the counties, while the A38 travels along the southern edge via Plymouth. GWR runs trains from Bristol and London, while CrossCountry connects to the north.

 ## Where to Stay

Devon and Cornwall have a great range of places to stay, from cosy pubs to stylish B&Bs and hotels. Booking at least two months in advance for holiday periods (Easter, mid-July to early September, and Christmas) is strongly advised. A good selection of YHA hostels and rural campsites makes budget travel easy here, but again, you'll need to book ahead at the most popular times in summer. There are some real camping gems in both counties – in Devon, Little Meadows is a peaceful spot to pitch up by Watermouth Harbour, while in Cornwall, Treen Farm Campsite is right on the South West Coast Path.

 ## What's On

St Piran's Day (Mar) Processions in honour of Cornwall's patron saint.

Padstow May Day (May) Raucous 'osses (hobby horses) cavort round Padstow.

Falmouth Sea Shanty Festival (falmouthseashanty.co.uk; Jun) Sea-songs fill the harbour air.

Eden Sessions (edensessions.com; Jun & Jul) Big bands play in front of the space-age biomes.

Dartmouth Royal Regatta (dartmouthregatta.co.uk; Aug) Yachties ply the waters round Dartmouth.

British Fireworks Championships (britishfireworks.co.uk; mid-Aug) Plymouth's skies are filled with bursts of colour.

12

Teign Gorge

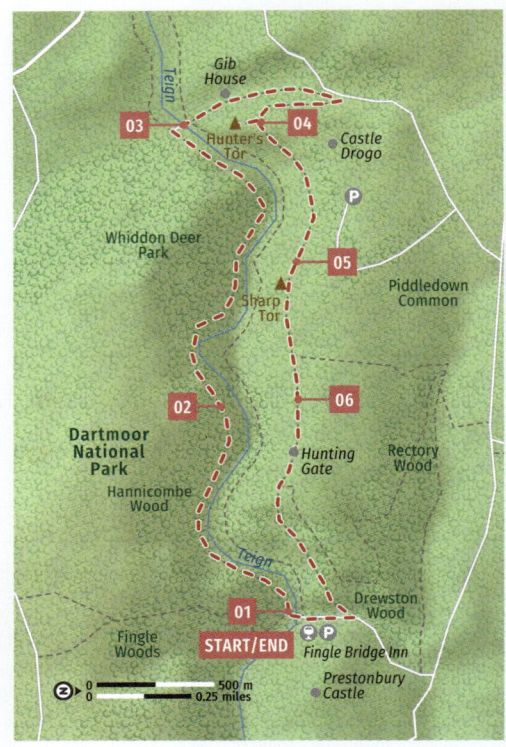

DURATION	DIFFICULTY	DISTANCE	START/END
2½-3hr	Moderate	4 miles/ 6.5km	Fingle Bridge car park
TERRAIN	Woodland and riverbank		

Skirting the cliffs of a tree-cloaked, almost Alpine-esque valley, this woodland loop offers one of the most impressive vistas on Dartmoor, and visits one of the UK's largest forest restoration projects.

Getting Here
Castle Drogo is 3.3 miles northwest of the village of Chagford. Dartline Coaches (dartline-coaches.co.uk) bus 173 stops at Castle Drogo and Drewsteignton, from where it's about a mile's walk down to Fingle Woods.

Starting Point
From the Fingle Bridge car park (free) it's a short walk into Fingle Woods.

01 The walk begins in the middle of **Fingle Woods** (NT; 01647-433356; finglewoods.org.uk), an 825-acre area of ancient woodland spanning the slopes of the River Teign. Damaged by the planting of non-native conifers, the forest was jointly acquired by the National Trust and Woodland Trust in 2013, with an aim to restore it by planting native species such as oak, ash and beech – a project that will take 200 years. It's a glorious spot for a stroll, especially on a sunny spring day, when the sunlight filters down through the trees and the woods ring with bird-song, or even better, in autumn, when the tree canopy lights up in reds, oranges and golds.

02 To begin with, a clear trail leads along the riverbanks all the way to **Whiddon Deer Park**. After around 1½ miles, you'll walk past a small hydroelectric turbine and begin to follow the course of an old drystone wall.

03 Near its end, a footbridge crosses the river, then leads up a quiet lane past Gib House.

Castle Drogo

This outlandish modern-day **castle** (NT; ☏01647-433306; nationaltrust.org.uk/castle-drogo; near Drewsteignton; adult/child £15/7.50; ⏰10am-5pm; P) – England's most recent, built between 1911 and 1931 – was an architectural flight of fancy designed by Sir Edwin Lutyens for self-made food millionaire Julius Drewe, who wanted to combine the drama of a medieval castle with the comforts of a country house.

Best for

A POST-HIKE PINT

Look out for a sign on the right leading through a gate onto the **Castle Drogo** estate. The path climbs gently through the trees.

04 Before long you'll see another sign pointing to **Hunter's Tor**, an outcrop that juts out into the gorge like the prow of an ocean-liner. Pick your way along the gorse-lined path to the tip of the promontory for an east–west panorama along the gorge, and across Chagford to the high moors. The canopy of Fingle Woods stretches out handsomely below.

05 Backtrack to the main path, and continue east along the edge of the gorge, with ever-expanding views of the deep, tree-cloaked valley (pictured). The path leads across the open ground of Piddledown Common to another viewpoint, **Sharp Tor**, with a dizzying drop straight down: vertigo sufferers beware. Listen and you'll hear the clatter of the Teign below.

06 From Sharp Tor, the path continues east, dropping gently down into the trees. Walk through **Hunting Gate** and return to the car park, where a celebratory pint at the Fingle Bridge Inn awaits. High on the hillside above the inn are the remains of an Iron Age hillfort, **Prestonbury Castle**; you can clearly see the outline of the fort as you stand on Fingle Bridge.

 **Take a Break**

A more perfect place for a riverside pint you could not find than the **Fingle Bridge Inn** (☏01647-281287; finglebridgeinn.co.uk; Fingle Woods; ⏰11am-5pm Mon-Wed, to 10pm Thu-Sat, to 6pm Sun). Nestled in the middle of the woods, on the banks of the Teign, this delightful pub is popular with ramblers exploring the trails. Light pub lunches are served daily, dinners from Thursday to Saturday. Alternatively, there's a pleasant cafe at Castle Drogo.

13

Wistman's Wood

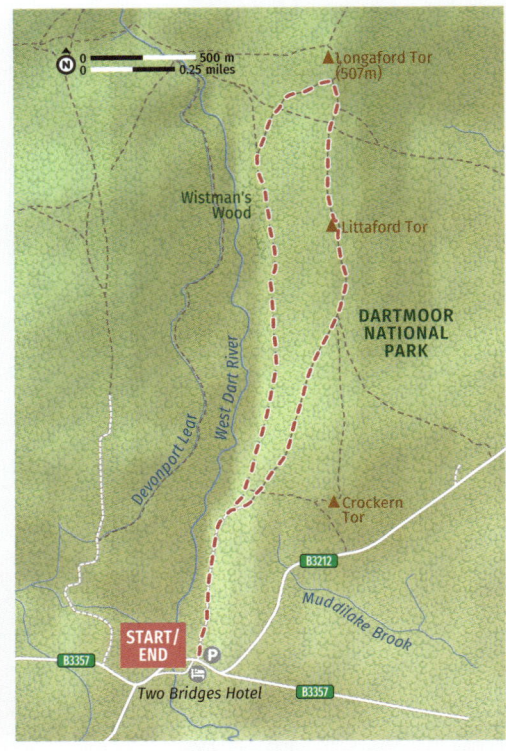

DURATION	DIFFICULTY	DISTANCE	START/END
2½hr	Moderate	4 miles/ 6.3km	Two Bridges car park

TERRAIN	Moorland and woods

This classic short walk visits one of the oldest surviving woodlands on Dartmoor, a last remnant of the mighty forest that once covered the entire moor, and much of southwest England.

Park opposite the Two Bridges Hotel, and follow the farm track north past a small white cottage. Head to the right of the cottage, climbing up onto the open moor.

After about a mile, you will come to the southern edge of the wood. The main path skirts its edge, but it's well worth taking a quick detour off the main trail just to experience the haunting, otherworldly atmosphere. There's no clear path through the trees, and it's very unstable underfoot – but the moment you enter the forest, it feels like entering a parallel world. It's a magical spot, with twisted, lichen-cloaked oaks sprouting from a chaotic jumble of moss-covered boulders (pictured). Unsurprisingly, numerous local legends surround this place: it's said to have been a sacred grove for the druids, and many people claim to have spotted fairies here. It's also rumoured to be the home of demonic 'Wisht Hounds' who race through the woods by night in search of unwary travellers.

Assuming you haven't been bewitched by fairies or devoured by hell-hounds, once you've explored the wood, head back to the main path along the edge. After a while, it bears north away from the trees, then climbs up the grassy slopes to **Longaford Tor**, a jumble of granite stacks that looks as though it's been left behind by a giant. You can pick your way up to the top if you wish. From Longaford Tor, an indistinct and occasionally rather boggy trail leads south across **Littaford Tor**, then bears southwest down the hillside, before rejoining the farm track back to the Two Bridges car park.

14

River Dart Walk

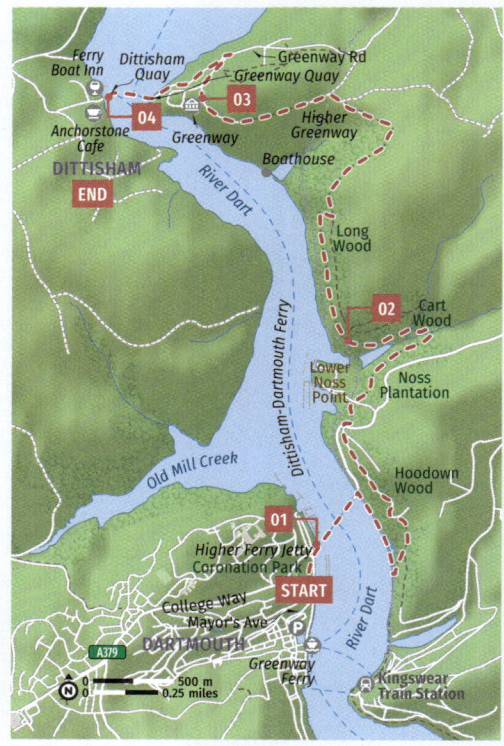

DURATION	DIFFICULTY	DISTANCE	START/END
2hr	Easy	4 miles/ 6.4km	Dartmouth/ Dittisham

TERRAIN	River path, woodland

The southwest's great estuaries were once the key to Britain's seagoing might, and few have as illustrious a history as the Dart. From the riverside town of Dartmouth, this route tracks the course of the river to Agatha Christie's summer home at Greenway.

Getting Here

Dartmouth is 13 miles south of Totnes. Stagecoach bus 92 runs every hour Monday to Saturday, twice on Sunday. You can also catch the Dartmouth Steam Railway (dartmouthrailriver.co.uk) from Paignton to Kingswear.

Starting Point

Coronation Park in Dartmouth; the nearest car park is on Mayor's Ave.

01 From Coronation Park, walk to the jetty for the **Dartmouth–Kingswear Higher Ferry** (☏ 01803-837163; dkfb.co.uk; car/pedestrian 1 way £5.60/60p; ⏱ 6.30am-10.50pm Mon-Sat, from 8am Sun), which crosses the river every six minutes. On the far side, walk up the road, and follow signs onto the permissive footpath on the right. The path leads along the river, then turns up into **Hoodown Wood**. Follow signs along the Dart Valley Trail towards Greenway Ferry and Maypool. The trail leads through the woods, turning into a lane above Lower Noss Point. Cross the road, and continue through the trees into Noss Plantation and Cart Wood.

02 The trail turns back sharply towards the river, then continues north through **Long Wood**, an important area of semi-ancient oak woodland. You're now walking on the long-distance **Dart Valley Trail**, roughly following the same course as the old Paignton and Dartmouth Steam Railway. The

🎫 Coleton Fishacre

For a glimpse of jazz-age glamour, drop by the former home of the D'Oyly Carte family of theatre impresarios, **Coleton Fishacre** (NT; 📞 01803-843325; nationaltrust.org.uk/coleton-fishacre; Brownstone Rd, near Kingswear; adult/child £15/7.50; ⏱10.30am-5pm mid-Feb-Oct, 11am-4pm Sat & Sun Nov & Dec; 🅿). Built in the 1920s, its art deco embellishments include original Lalique tulip uplighters, comic bathroom tiles and a stunning saloon – complete with tinkling piano. The subtropical gardens afford sudden vistas of the sea. A 4-mile path leads along the cliffs from Kingswear.

03 Keep following the trail though the woods. At its north end, you'll see waymarkers pointing to Greenway; turn left past Higher Greenway, then left again downhill to Maypool. The lane leads down to **Greenway** (📞 01803-843325; nationaltrust.org.uk/greenway; Greenway Rd, Galmpton; adult/child £11.60/5.80; ⏱10.30am-5pm mid-Feb-Oct, 11am-4pm Sat & Sun Nov & Dec), the captivating summer home of crime writer Agatha Christie. Christie owned the house between 1938 and 1959, and it feels frozen in time – complete with piles of hats in the lobby, a book-stocked library and a wardrobe filled with clothes (you can even listen to her speak via a replica radio in the drawing room). In Christie's book *Dead Man's Folly*, Greenway doubles as Nasse House, with the boathouse making an appearance as a macabre murder scene.

04 Once you've explored the grounds of Greenway, summon the foot ferry by ringing a ship's bell on Greenway Quay (pictured) and hop across the river to the village of Dittisham. From here, you can catch the **Dittisham-Dartmouth Ferry** (📞 01803-882811; greenwayferry.co.uk; adult/child return £13.50/11; ⏱Easter-Oct) – a picturesque way to round out the day.

 **Take a Break**

For riverside dining, it's hard to beat Dittisham's **Anchorstone Cafe** (📞 01803-722365; anchorstonecafe.co.uk; Manor St, Dittisham; mains from £9; ⏱noon-4pm Wed-Sun mid-Mar-Oct) for crab, hand-dived scallops and local Sharpham wine. Less fancy is the waterfront **Ferry Boat Inn** (📞 01803-722368; ferryboatinndittisham.pub; Manor St, Dittisham; ⏱11am-11pm).

15

Kynance Cove & Lizard Point

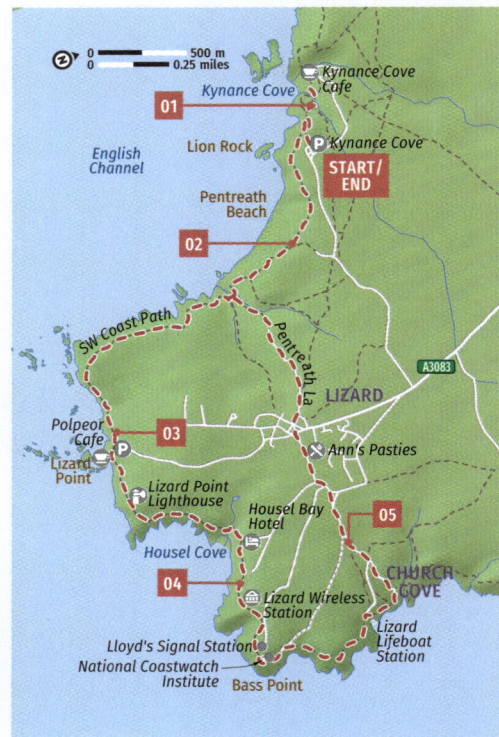

DURATION	DIFFICULTY	DISTANCE	START/END
3hr	Moderate	5.9 miles / 9.5km	Kynance Cove

TERRAIN	Coast path, clifftops

This cliff walk takes in some of southern Cornwall's most postcard-worthy views, including an island-studded cove and a historic lighthouse.

Getting Here

Kynance Cove is 12 miles south of Helston. In summer, **First Kernow** (📞customer service 0345 646 0707, timetables 0871 200 2233; firstbus.co.uk/cornwall) runs hourly services between Helston and the Lizard.

Starting Point

Kynance Cove car park. NT members can park for free, but spaces go fast in summer.

01 Park at **Kynance Cove**. Studded with craggy offshore islands rising out of seas that seem almost tropical in colour, it's one of Cornwall's most ravishing beauty spots. The cliffs around the cove are rich in serpentine, a red-green rock popular with Victorian trinket-makers.

02 From Kynance, pick up the coast path and head south past **Lion Rock** and rocky **Pentreath Beach**. This is a good area to spot choughs: a member of the crow family, identifiable by its bright orange beak, the bird features on Cornwall's coat-of-arms, but was almost wiped out by pesticides and habitat loss. Since being reintroduced and protected, choughs are now breeding here in decent numbers.

03 One-and-a-half miles south, you'll reach the craggy outcrop of **Lizard Point**, the southernmost point of mainland Britain. Historically

Poldark Country

Cornwall's ruggedly gorgeous coastline has a glamorous alternate life as a star of film and screen, perhaps most famously providing the backdrop for the swashbuckling *Poldark* adventures. The 2015 BBC adaptation of the much-loved books by Winston Graham was filmed across the county, but Kynance Cove had a starring role as Poldark's home beach of Nampara Bay, while the cliffs above the cove were used for shots of Ross Poldark galloping through yellow gorse.

Best for WILDLIFE

this is one of Britain's deadliest headlands. Hundreds of ships have come to grief around the point, and are now a hub for scuba divers. A steep track winds down to the long-disused lifeboat station and shingly cove. Nearby, the white tower of **Lizard Lighthouse** hoves into view.

04 Continue around the coast to **Housel Cove**, home to a Victorian-era hotel, then trek onwards towards **Bass Point**. You'll pass a small building which, a century ago, housed a signal station; a plaque outside is dedicated to Guglielmo Marconi, often credited as the inventor of radio. There's a small visitor centre inside. The main signal station is in a white building a little further east (you can't miss it – it's labelled in gigantic letters).

05 Trek north past the modern lifeboat station, which can be visited if you wish. A bit further north, you'll pass pretty **Church Cove**. From here, follow the main road from the cove back into the centre of **Lizard Village**. Once you've browsed around the village's souvenir shops, follow Pentreath Lane from the main car park, onto a lane which rejoins the coast path and leads back to Kynance Cove (pictured).

Take a Break

Everyone has their favourite pasty shop, but **Ann's Pasties** (01326-572282; Beacon Tce; pasties from £3.50; 9am-5pm) has the approval of many top chefs (including Rick Stein). They come in steak, cheese and vegan versions.

Alternatively, above Lizard Point, **Polpeor Cafe** (01326-290939; mains £10; 10.30am-4.30pm or 5pm) serves lunches and cream teas, and claims to be Britain's most southerly cafe, and **Kynance Cove Cafe** (01326-290436; kynancecovecafe.co.uk; mains £5-14; 9am-5.30pm) does cream teas, crab sandwiches and delicious cakes.

16

St Agnes & Chapel Porth

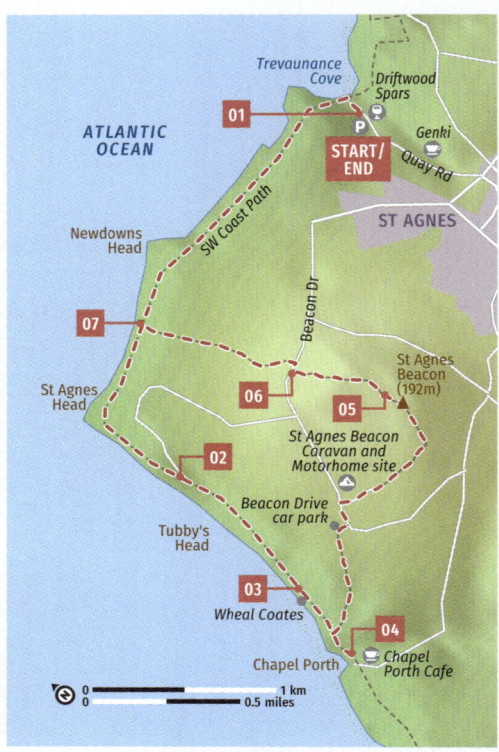

DURATION	DIFFICULTY	DISTANCE	START/END
3hr	Moderate	6.5 miles/ 10.4km	Trevaunance Cove

TERRAIN	Coast path, clifftops

This walk takes in the beautiful, windblown scenery around the old mining village of St Agnes, factoring in panoramic coastal views and a trip to the top of the area's highest point, the Beacon.

Getting Here
St Agnes is 9 miles from Truro. Bus 87 (45 minutes, hourly in summer) stops in St Agnes on its way from Newquay, via Crantock, Holywell, Perranporth and Trevellas, to Truro.

Starting Point
You can park in Trevaunance Cove opposite the pub.

01 Start at **Trevaunance Cove**. From the beach, the coast path climbs steeply around the clifftops to Newdowns Head. Offshore there are two rocks known locally as the **Bawden Rocks**, which according to local legend were hurled there by the local giant, Bolster. The coast path then tracks round to St Agnes Head, travelling through thick heather and gorse.

02 The trail then swings south, opening out onto the exposed, heather-carpeted cliffs around **Tubby's Head**. This is among the most impressive stretches of the north Cornish coastline, with huge views stretching south all the way to Godrevy Lighthouse. Once an important mining area, the clifftops all around here are littered with the remains of disused shafts, engine houses and mine workings.

03 The most picturesque mine – and possibly the most photographed in all of Cornwall – is the engine house and chimney stack at **Wheal Coates** (pictured), dramatically framed against the blue Atlantic. There are various other workings nearby to explore, and you can peer down into a capped shaft.

Mining in Cornwall

Mining runs through the Cornish landscape like a seam of copper – the industry long defined Cornwall's identity, and the stark chimneys and ruined pump houses of long-abandoned mines stand everywhere on the coastline like beacons of the past. Miners worked underground painstakingly searching for tin and copper by candlelight, while above ground were the copper-dressing floors where women and children worked to extract the prized metal. **Levant Mine** (nationaltrust.org.uk, open for pre-booked tours, adult £12) is a good place to learn more about the industry that shaped Cornwall.

04 From here it's a steep walk downhill to the cove of **Chapel Porth**, where you can fuel up with a hot tea and hedgehog ice cream from the ever-busy little **Chapel Porth Cafe** (sandwiches & cakes £2-5; 10am-5pm).

05 Backtrack towards the Wheal Coates mine ruins, this time turning inland along the uphill path (roughly northeast). You'll reach the National Trust car park beside Beacon Dr. Turn left onto the road, then immediately right through St Agnes Beacon Caravan and Motorhome site. Walk up through the farm, picking up the path out onto the fields. A well-trodden trail climbs sharply up the hilltop, giving majestic views of **St Agnes** and the coastline, and inland towards Carn Brea. In summer, it's covered in yellow gorse; by late summer, it's purple heather.

06 From the top, several trails lead back down onto Beacon Dr. It doesn't really matter which you take; when you get to the road, turn right. Walk along till you reach a bench with a rough lane opposite (if you reach a hamlet of houses, you missed the turning, so you need to backtrack).

07 Take the lane and follow it back to the coast path, turning right (east) for the last section past the old **clifftop quarries** and a stone staircase down to **Trevaunance Cove**.

 **Take a Break**

The whitewashed **Driftwood Spars** (driftwoodspars.com; Trevaunance Cove; mains £8-16; 11am-11pm; P) has served generations of St Agnes drinkers, and brews its own ales. Downstairs is a hugger-mugger wooden bar, with upturned barrels and bench seats; there's a more refined restaurant upstairs. On the road up to the village, **Genki** (Quay Rd; mains £4-8; 9am-5pm) is a simple shack cafe that's ideal for paninis, smoothie bowls and salads.

BEST DAY WALKS: ENGLAND

17

Brown Willy & Rough Tor

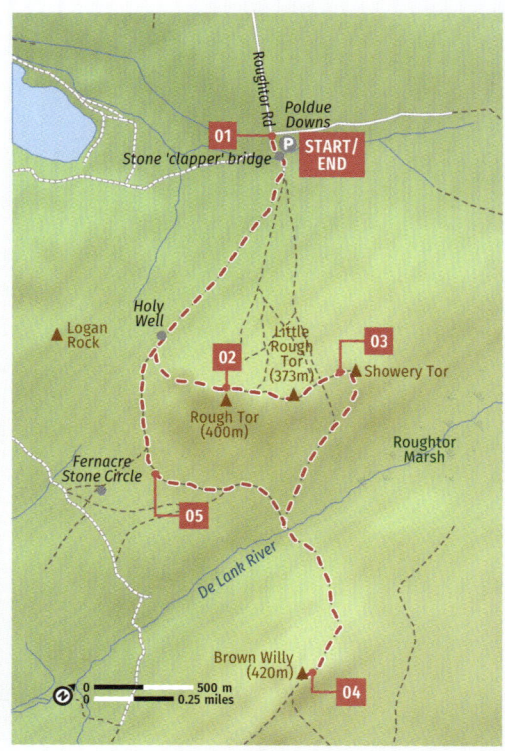

DURATION	DIFFICULTY	DISTANCE	START/END
2½-3hr	Moderate	5.2 miles/ 8.4km	Poldue Downs Car Park
TERRAIN	Moorland and rocky tors		

Alright, alright, stop sniggering at the back. A perennial source of amusement for Cornish schoolkids, Cornwall's highest hill actually gets its name from the Cornish *bronn wennili*, or 'hill of swallows' – and if it's big, bleak views you're after, nowhere else in Cornwall compares.

Getting Here

The nearest town is Camelford, served by the 95 bus from Truro, Wadebridge and Bude, operated by First Kernow. If you have wheels, follow the A39 north to Camelford, drive through the village and turn right onto Roughtor Rd.

Starting Point

There's a large, free car park at Poldue Downs at the end of Roughtor Rd. There's usually enough space for everyone. Look out for murmurations of starlings in autumn.

01 Head east from the car park and cross over the ford via the **stone 'clapper' bridge**. These rustic bridges, made of granite slabs, date back to medieval times: the one here is an unusual double span and is Grade II-listed. Follow the track south, passing through the remains of around 120 hut circles, relics of a **Bronze Age settlement** which once thrived in the shadow of the tor. Hidden among these ruins is a holy well, but you'll have to search a bit to find it.

02 From the holy well, ascend up the west side of **Rough Tor** (pronounced 'row' to rhyme with 'cow'). It's a steep hike to the summit at 400m, but the panoramic views from the top are stunning. The top of the tor (pictured) is marked by massive stacks of granite, carved out by aeons of wind and rain.

Bronze Age Bodmin Moor

Looking out over the empty wildness of Bodmin Moor, it might seem strange to find the remains of so many ancient settlements around Brown Willy. But several thousand years ago, the moor's landscape (like others in the southwest) was very different: it was covered by forest, which was cleared over the centuries for cultivation and agriculture, resulting in the barren landscape we see today. It's perhaps the earliest example in Britain of manmade climate change.

03 Brown Willy's bulk looms to the southeast, but for now, follow the ridgeline north towards **Showery Tor**, another granite stack at the far northern end of Rough Tor's ridge. At the end of the rocks, bear east down into the valley, following the De Lank River (it can be boggy round here). You'll reach a bridge; cross it and begin the slog up **Brown Willy**. You'll cross a couple of stiles en route to the summit; it's pretty obvious when you've reached the top, but a trig point marks the official spot.

04 Congratulations: you're standing on Cornwall's highest point, 420m above sea level. Take a breather and admire the views: on a clear day you can see all the way to the north coast. More **Bronze Age cairns** are littered around the summit, which may mark burial sites or even solstice calendars.

05 Double back down to the bridge, cross the ford, then follow the path along the fence-line, before turning west towards **Fernacre Stone Circle**. It's one of the largest in Cornwall, measuring 44m across and consisting of around 60 standing stones. Skirt round the southwest side of Rough Tor, and return north to the car park.

Take a Break

Run by well-known chef Emily Scott, the **St Tudy Inn** (01208-850656; sttudyinn.com; St Tudy; mains £19-30; meals noon-2.30pm & 6.30-9pm Mon-Sat, noon-2.30pm Sun) is one of East Cornwall's top gastropubs, blending big British flavours with seasonal Cornish ingredients. It's in St Tudy, 6 miles southwest of Camelford.

Alternatively, for picnic supplies, the friendly **Hilltop Farm Shop** (01840-211518; hilltopfarmshop.co.uk; teas £3-9) in Slaughterbridge, 2 miles north of Camelford, is known for its Cornish fudge, pasties, cheeses and excellent cream teas.

18

Porthcurno to Land's End

DURATION	DIFFICULTY	DISTANCE	START/END
3½-4hr	Moderate	7.2 miles/ 11.5km	Treen/ Land's End

TERRAIN	Cliffs and coast

Is this the finest coast walk in all of Britain? Many a seasoned rambler might say so – and there are few who would sensibly argue. This walk really has it all: booming surf, massive cliffs, historic lighthouses and wild Atlantic vistas that will sear themselves onto your retinas.

Getting Here

Treen is about 7½ miles southwest of Penzance. The village is easily reached by bus: Land's End Coaster operated by First Kernow runs four to nine times daily. Some buses are open-top in summer.

Starting Point

There is a small car park near the Logan Rock Inn. Theoretically this could be done as a return walk, but it'll make for a long day – an easier option is to take the Land's End Coaster back from Land's End to Treen. A shorter option is just to follow the walk as far as St Levan, then circle back along the same route – it's about 3.8 miles return this way, but you'll be missing out on some serious coast views if you do.

01 This is a long walk, so starting out as early as possible is an extremely good idea – not least since the small private car park just past the Logan Rock Inn fills up fast. Once you've got your gear together, head out of the car park and turn left up the lane past the white building (a former chapel). Soon after, another narrow, easy-to-miss **lane** (signed for Logan Rock) turns left under the trees. If you miss it, don't worry, as you can just follow the main lane along to the coast path.

02 Either way, you'll eventually end up on the coast path, looking out towards a distinctive, fortress-like headland (pictured). This was the site of a large Iron Age hillfort, Treryn Dinas, but it's better known as the home of the **Logan Rock**. This massive boulder once famously rocked back and forth on its own natural pivot with only the slightest pressure; its name supposedly derives from the Cornish verb 'log', meaning 'to rock', used to denote the motion of a drunken man. Unfortunately, in 1871 a young naval lieutenant by the name of Hugh Goldsmith (the nephew of the Restoration playwright Oliver Goldsmith) commandeered his crew and knocked the rock off its perch. The locals were so incensed, Goldsmith was forced to restore the rock to its original position under threat of his naval commission – a task that required the efforts of 60 men, winches borrowed from Devonport Dockyard and a total cost of £130 8s 6d (a copy of the bill can be seen in the Logan Rock Inn). The path out to it involves traversing narrow cliff paths and sheer drops, so take care if you want a closer look.

03 Turn west along the coast path. Before long, you'll pass the perfect little cove of **Treen Cove**, also known as Pedn Vounder, one of Cornwall's few nudist-friendly patches of sand. It can be accessed via a formidably steep cliff path, but it's very easy to miss the turning – ideally you need someone to show you where it starts. It's followed soon after by the famed crescent of **Porthcurno**, as perfect a beach as you'll find in west Cornwall (and accordingly busy). It's a great place to swim, with a deep drop-off, although the waves can be rough. From the beach, look up: carved into the crags is Cornwall's celebrated clifftop theatre, the **Minack** (pictured; ☎01736-810181; minack.com; tickets from £10). Overlooking Porthcurno and the azure-blue Atlantic, it looks like a relic from ancient Greece, but it was actually built in the 20th

PK Porthcurno

This fascinating **museum** (☎01736-810966; pkporthcurno.com; adult/child £12/6; ⏰10am-5pm) charts the unlikely tale of Porthcurno's role in transatlantic telecommunications. In 1870 an underwater cable was laid here, which enabled telegraph messages to be sent as far as Bombay in less than a minute. Over the next century, 14 cables ran into Porthcurno, carrying much of Britain's global telecommunications before being decommissioned in 1970. The museum features interactive morse-code kits, vintage equipment, archive footage and so on, plus a network of WWII-era tunnels.

BEST DAY WALKS: ENGLAND   75

century; it was the lifelong passion of theatre-lover Rowena Cade, who dreamt up the idea in the 1930s. It's still a hugely popular place for al fresco theatre, with plays staged from mid-May to mid-September. A steep path leads up the cliff past the visitor centre.

04 Continue across the Minack car park, following the coast path around the headland of **Pedn-mên-an-mere** (Headland of the Great Stone). Just around the headland nestles another lovely beach, **Porth Chapel**, which usually stays a good deal quieter than its neighbour. Just off the path above the beach is **St Levan's Holy Well**, one of several such sacred springs in this part of West Penwith. The waters are said to have healing powers, but it would be a brave soul indeed who drinks the mucky water. Best stick to the water in your canteen.

05 A little further west hides the fishing cove of **Porthgwarra**, with a steep slipway leading down to the sheltered beach. It's another good spot for a dip, but take care not to swim out past the headland, where the sea currents can be strong. The little **Porthgwarra Cove Cafe** (☎01736-871754) serves snacks, sandwiches, pasties and ice creams, and has a pleasant little garden to sit out in.

06 Next looms **Gwennap Head**, the southernmost point of the Penwith Peninsula. A coastguard lookout station sits out on the point, and makes a good place to take a break and enjoy the incredible Atlantic views. On a clear day, you might just about be able to spot the profile of Wolf Rock Lighthouse, 9 miles out to sea, a lonely beacon rising from a spur of rock jutting out of the Atlantic Ocean. Forty-one metres high, the granite lighthouse took eight years to build, from 1861 to 1869. Given its location, and the storms that regularly lash this stretch of coast, that it was ever built at all is something of an engineering marvel.

07 From Gwennap Head, the coast ducks and dips, passing Pendower Cove, before reaching the broad, boulder-strewn expanse of **Mill Bay** (pictured; known locally as Nanjizal). There are plenty of sand and rock pools to investigate, and on one side of the beach is a natural arch called **Zawn Pyg** (from the Cornish for 'pointed chasm'), where the sea has worn a passage through the cliffs. Many locals know it as the Song of the Sea cave. There are many other zawns, or steep-sided inlets, pockmarking the surrounding coastline.

08 Beyond Nanjizal, you're within striking distance of the most westerly point of mainland Britain. The coast path opens up as you stride over wide cliffs all the way to **Land's End**. Famous as the last port of call for charity walkers on the 874-mile slog from John O'Groats in Scotland, this wild,

🗼 Longships Lighthouse

Perched on a rocky reef, 1.25 miles out to sea from Land's End, this photogenic lighthouse is one of Cornwall's most upstanding feats of maritime engineering. Built to warn ships away from this infamously dangerous stretch of coastline, the first structure was built in 1795 but was swamped by waves, and subsequently replaced in 1873 at the considerable cost of £43,870. Since then it's somehow withstood even the worst of the Atlantic storms, and has been unmanned since 1988.

craggy headland is where Cornwall (and, by extension, the rest of Britain) comes to a screeching halt, and the black granite cliffs fall away into thundering white surf and sea spray. The views are epic: the restless Atlantic seems to wrap itself around the horizon, shimmering and flashing in the late-afternoon light, and when the weather's clear you can often glimpse the faint outlines of the Isles of Scilly, 28 miles out to sea. It's a special spot – which makes the decision to build a tacky theme park here in the 1980s utterly inexplicable. Still, once you bypass the tat – and there's plenty of it here – the coast regains its wild splendour. The curiously named Doctor Syntax's Head was named after a fictitious schoolmaster who featured in a series of popular books in the early 1800s.

The signpost at Land's End marks the official end of the trail (unless you still have the legs to push on to Sennen, another 1½ miles further along the coast path). According to the signpost, it's 3147 miles to New York, 874 miles to John O' Groats, 1½ miles to the Longships Lighthouse and 28 miles to Scilly.

09 Heading back to Treen, it's a rather more manageable 4 miles; Land's End Coaster buses run four to nine times a day. The last bus of the day is usually between 7pm and 8pm, but double-check the First Kernow website to confirm timings.

☕ Take a Break

A mile inland from Land's End, the **Apple Tree Cafe** (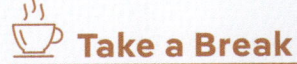01736-872753; Trevescan; mains £6-12; ⏱10am-4pm Thu-Sat) is a real community hang-out – there are paintings and crafts by local artists, a menu of sandwiches, soups and wholefood salads, and a counter lined with sinful-looking cakes.

Alternatively, the 400 year-old **Logan Rock Inn** (📞01736-810495; theloganrock.co.uk; Treen; mains £6-14; ⏱11am-11pm, closes mid-afternoon winter) brims with old-time atmosphere – head-scraping ceilings, wooden seats, a crackling hearth and brassy trinkets.

19
Tintagel to Boscastle

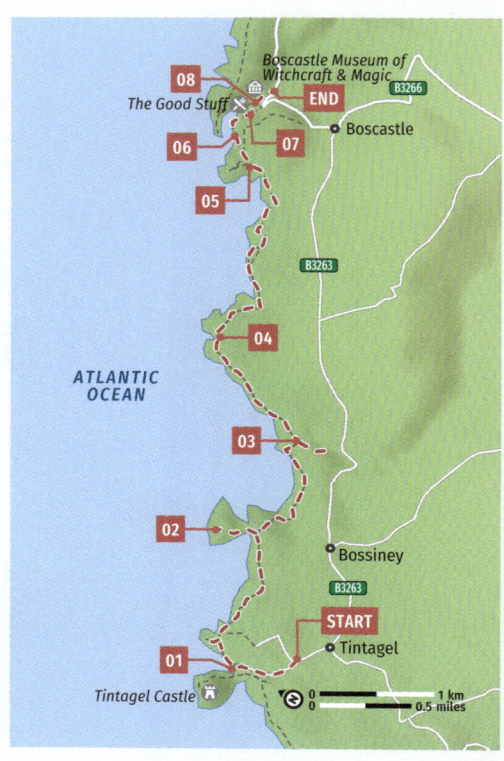

DURATION	DIFFICULTY	DISTANCE	START/END
3hr	Moderate	5 miles/ 8km	Tintagel/ Boscastle

TERRAIN	Grassed coastal path, steep steps

If you like a hike steeped in myths and legends, it doesn't get better than this stroll along Cornwall's storied northern coast. Start in Tintagel, which legend has it was the birthplace of King Arthur, and search for Merlin's Cave on the beach here. The route then follows a jaw-droppingly scenic section of coast path to reach Rocky Valley, a deep coastal gorge where a river has formed a string of plunge pools and where there are ancient maze-like stone carvings hidden in the rocks. It then reaches the spookily good fishing village of Boscastle, rumoured to be home to a witches' coven.

Getting Here
There is car parking in Tintagel and in Boscastle, and bus 95 from Newquay connects both villages every two hours.

Starting Point
The route starts in Tintagel at the Glebe Cliff National Trust car park.

01 From Glebe Cliff car park, follow the South West Coast Path to the right along the cliffs; this route sticks to the path with the sea on your left all the way to Boscastle. Here there are wonderful views back to eerie **Tintagel Castle** (english-heritage.org.uk/visit/places/tintagel-castle; 10am-6pm, adult/child £18.10/11.30). The castle ruins that remain were built in the 13th century, long after the time when Arthur is said to have lived, by Richard, Earl of Cornwall, who likely chose the site because of its legendary associations. Below is Tintagel Haven, a small cove where Merlin's Cave (free to access) is revealed at each low tide.

02 Carry on around the rocky promontories of Barras Nose and Lye Rock. At Lye Rock there

King Arthur

This slice of Cornwall's coastline is forever linked to tales of King Arthur, the mythical monarch of Britain. According to legend, Tintagel Castle is the birthplace of Arthur, conjured into the world by the wizard Merlin. There are a few reasons why Tintagel is linked to his myth, including the 12th-century writing of Geoffrey of Monmouth and the discovered remains of a 5th-century settlement. However, some historians argue that Tintagel deserves to be remembered for more provable historical reasons – as the seat of Cornwall and Devon's dark-age rulers and as a key trading settlement that linked the region with the Byzantine world.

Best for

ANCIENT HISTORY

are the remains of a settlement and views out to the **Sisters** sea rocks. Continue along a grassy path above **Bossiney Haven** (pictured), surely one of Britain's most beautiful beaches – the path down to the sands was closed at the time of research due to unstable conditions. The route continues high on the breezy bluff, passing gorse bushes that turn bright gold in spring, before descending down stone steps to the aptly named Rocky Valley.

03 **Rocky Valley** is a deep and narrow coastal gorge where the Trevillet River has carved its way through rocks to reach the sea, forming a necklace of plunge pools. Leave the coast path at the bottom of the valley and follow a footpath to the right to reach a wooded glade where there are ancient, mysterious maze-like stone carvings in the rocks – these labyrinths may date back to the Bronze Age and be up to 4000 years old.

04 Retrace your steps back to Rocky Valley and follow the coast path as it climbs steeply upwards again – this is a short, sharp climb but the route levels out on top of the cliff and offers undulating walking and amazing views of the sparkling blue sea dotted with islets. Take a breather while gazing out at **Ladies Window**, a stone archway framing dramatic cliffscapes next to the squat island of Grower Rock.

05 The last stop before Boscastle is **Willapark Lookout Station**. This striking whitewashed building looks like a fortified castle tower and is now used as a coastguard lookout, but it was originally built by a 19th-century merchant as a 'pleasure house' (a place to sit and watch the sea) and was later leased to the Board of Trade and used to watch for smugglers. The bay below the southern cliffs of Willapark is known as Western

Blackapit and was a notorious spot for shipwrecks.

06 The route then descends into **Boscastle Harbour** and follows along one side of the River Valency as it flows out to meet the sea. As you approach the storied harbour, keep your ears and eyes peeled for a glimpse of Satan himself – he sends out streams of foam from a blowhole known as the Devil's Bellows in the rocky walls of Penally Point, opposite the path, when the tide is just right.

07 The coast path reaches a snug inlet lined by old fishermen's cottages and the beginning of **Boscastle village** (pictured). Boscastle has been an important natural harbour since the 12th century, when clever local witches used to sell 'wind' in the form of magical knotted ropes to the captains of becalmed ships waiting in the harbour for better sailing weather.

08 Seek out the witches at the curious **Boscastle Museum of Witchcraft and Magic** (museumofwitchcraftandmagic.co.uk; 10am-5pm; adult/child £7/5). This warren-like museum is one of Britain's most fascinating, taking visitors through the weird and wonderful history of the occult. Boscastle is also the perfect place to refuel after a hike – try the Good Stuff cafe on the harbour, the National Trust Pilchard Cellar cafe, which does a cracking cream tea, or the cosy Cobweb Inn for a pint. To return to Tintagel hop on bus 95.

Magic & Witches

Boscastle's crowning glory has to be seen to believed – in a world of slick, modern museums, the Museum of Witchcraft and Magic's collection is a spooky, slightly creepy treat. Established in 1960, it houses a plethora of witchcraft-related artefacts including spell books, charms and tools of the craft. Beginning with the apparatus used to torture medieval enchantresses, the museum progresses past a wise woman's cottage, an exhibition of witches from vintage Hollywood, a huge display of herbal ointments and potions, and information on the rites and rituals of modern-day Wiccans. Don't miss the depictions of the witches of Boscastle, who sold 'wind' to the captains of becalmed ships.

Take a Break

The **Good Stuff** (thegoodstuffcafe.co.uk; Harbour Light; 9.30am-3pm Mon, Thu & Fri, to 4.30pm Sat & Sun) is a friendly indie cafe serving coffee, snacks and seriously good smoothies from a snug whitewashed cottage right on the harbourside. For the owners, the 'good stuff' means seasonal, local and ever-changing produce magicked up into fresh salads and home-baked cakes – perfect for the end of a hike. Sit outside when it's sunny to keep an eye on Boscastle's medley of fishing boats, lobster pots and fellow hikers.

20

Isles of Scilly

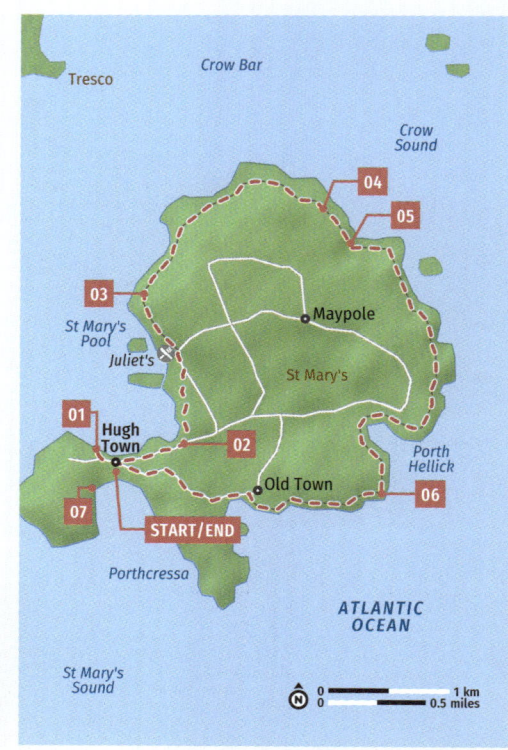

DURATION	DIFFICULTY	DISTANCE	START/END
4-5hr	Moderate	8 miles/ 12.9km	Hugh Town

TERRAIN	Coast path, pavement

Journey from the British mainland to the Isles of Scilly, a subtropical archipelago 28 miles off the coast of Cornwall, and you may well feel as though you're arriving in another world. Reached only by ferry or tiny prop plane, this scattering of five inhabited and 140 uninhabited islands are a world apart from the rest of England. The largest island, St Mary's, is a wonderful place to explore on foot, as it's completely encircled by a coast path with big views of the other islands, plus fascinating Bronze Age burial sites, lunch stops and swimming spots in the archipelago's famously clear turquoise waters.

Starting Point

This route starts and finishes at St Mary's Hugh Town quay and follows roads and the coastal path. All the islands except St Mary's are car-free, but even St Mary's doesn't exactly have busy traffic.

01 Begin at the **quay** in Hugh Town, the island's central hub – this is where you'll get off the ferry from the mainland, and taxis can drop you here from the tiny airport.

02 Walk through town, passing the Mermaid Inn, walking along Hugh Rd and then Lower Strand with the sea on your left. At **Porthmellon Beach** the route leaves the road and follows signs for the coastal footpath. Continue along the path to **Porthloo Beach**, where the path cuts through a working boatyard and then joins Porthloo Lane for a short, steep climb uphill. At the top of the hill is

Getting Here

The Isles of Scilly are a bit trickier to reach than most of the mainland walks in this book, but they are well worth the journey for a few days of laid-back island walking. Get to St Mary's, the largest of the isles, by plane from Land's End or Newquay airports in Cornwall, or Exeter airport in Devon, or by ferry from Penzance in Cornwall with Isles of Scilly Travel. From St Mary's, reach the four other inhabited islands on small interisland boats – buy tickets on the pier or on board.

the wonderful Juliet's restaurant, a Scilly institution where you can stop for lunch or a cream tea in a bucolic terraced garden with a view back to Hugh Town and the harbour.

03 Rejoin the coast path behind Juliet's and continue onwards around **Carn Morval Point**, where there are the remains of a battery from the Civil War. Keep an eye out for the wild seabirds that visit the islands as you walk onwards past Halangy Down to find Bant's Carn (pictured), one of two well-preserved Bronze Age tombs along this route, and Bar Point, where there's a beautiful sand

bar at low tide. The land tapers off to a narrow point, offering views of Samson Island. Once inhabited, this minute island is now a wildlife sanctuary.

04 Follow the path as it passes Innisidgen Hill and a second ancient burial site, **Innisidgen Upper and Lower Burial Chambers** (free). These ancient tombs date back to around 2000 BCE and were used as communal 'entrance' graves and possibly for rituals, providing a fascinating glimpse into the island's prehistoric past. Where the path forks, follow the right-hand coastal path, passing a copse of pine trees and reaching

Helvear Down. Here you can also leave the coast path and detour along shady lanes inland, past flower farms and vineyards that flourish in the islands' temperate climate (the islands are the warmest place in Britain).

05 Further along the coast path you'll round a corner and come to **Watermill Cove**. The small beach here is sometimes hard to access due to seaweed building up on the shore but it's well worth picking your way down to have this cove's pure white sand and crystalline water all to yourself. This idyllic little beach looks more like a postcard from the

BEST DAY WALKS: ENGLAND

Caribbean than an island off the Cornish coast, and is a great place to stop at for a mid-walk picnic or swim.

06 You'll pass Pelistry Bay, an unspoiled beach with views of the Eastern Isles, and Carn Vean Cafe, before circling Porth Hellick, a tidal inlet watched over by a headland known as the **Giant's Castle** and home to an Iron Age cliff fort. Pass the island's pocket-sized airport before walking back into the outskirts of Hugh Town – **Old Town Bay** is another good spot for a swim and you may spot seals lolling out by Gull Rock. Finish your walk here in town or cut through Hugh Town along Church Rd to reach the Garrison.

07 The **Garrison** is a sprawling fortification constructed in the 16th century as a defensive stronghold to protect the Isles of Scilly from potential invaders. The old walls are crowned by Star Castle, an eight-pointed star-shaped fort built in 1593 during the reign of Queen Elizabeth I as a defence against the Spanish Armada. The castle is now a hotel, but much of its original structure has been preserved. The Garrison Campsite also sits inside the defensive walls and you can pitch your tent in gardens dotted with palm trees. The coast path passes outside the walls of the Garrison – if you time your walk to end on a clear evening, this side of the island is the perfect place to watch a pink sunset over the rocks before walking through a stone archway and back into Hugh Town.

Island-Hopping

The Isles of Scilly archipelago is made up of four more inhabited 'off-islands', home to sandy beaches, flower farms, coastal pubs and shady lanes. Small boats leave from St Mary's quay to these four islands: St Martin's, Tresco, St Agnes and Bryher. Head to St Martin's for a 6-mile round-island walk and a pint at the Seven Stones Inn. St Agnes is home to Troytown Farm Campsite, a wonderful place to pitch a tent with a view of the ocean. The Tresco Abbey Gardens on Tresco are full of subtropical plants, while charming Bryher, the smallest of the inhabited islands, also has a good campsite.

Take a Break

You'll be forgiven for thinking you've gone on a Mediterranean holiday if you spend a balmy summer's afternoon at **Juliet's** (julietsgarden restaurant.co.uk; 10am-5pm plus some evenings), a tearoom-turned-restaurant with a series of stone terraces looking out over Hugh Town harbour. Come for a cream tea – but order extras, as the wild birds here are so friendly they'll eat cake crumbs from your fingers – or sit indoors for an autumnal supper of freshly landed fish under beams strung with fairy lights.

21

Combe Martin

DURATION	DIFFICULTY	DISTANCE	START/END
3-4hr	Moderate	6 miles/ 9.7km	Ilfracombe/ Combe Martin
TERRAIN	Coast path, steep ascents		

Stroll along 6 miles of undulating green cliffs and stop at a string of glorious beaches on this North Devon coastal walk, including Hele Bay, a popular bathing spot since Victorian times, and Broadsands, a crescent-shaped cove that's surely one of the most beautiful stretches of sand in Britain. You'll also pass Ilfracombe's working harbour as well as some of Devon's old smuggling haunts and sheltered Watermouth Cove, where you can refuel at a charming boat cafe and explore a mysterious tower. Don't forget your swimsuit for this one – the water's lovely.

Getting Here
Bus 301 runs from Ilfracombe to Combe Martin and back once an hour and parking is available at Pier Car Park and Cove Car Park.

Starting Point
Start in Ilfracombe harbour.

01 **Ilfracombe** is a lively coastal village with a working harbour dominated by the towering 20m-high figure of *Verity*, artist Damien Hirst's controversial sculpture of a pregnant woman holding a set of scales and a sword. Nearby is St Nicholas Chapel, perched on Lantern Hill overlooking Ilfracombe Harbour. First built in the 14th century and so-named for St Nicholas, the patron saint of sailors, the chapel is still a working lighthouse today, making it the oldest in the country.

02 Follow the South West Coast Path from the right-hand side of the harbour, passing Verity and **Fort Hillsborough**, where there are the remains of an Iron Age hill fort, on your way out of the village. Below you is Rapparee Cove, where the 1796

Smugglers on the Shore

The rugged cliffs and hidden coves of North Devon's coastline were a haven for smugglers during the 18th and 19th centuries, with secluded beaches and remote caves providing the perfect cover for illicit activities. Smugglers would secretly land contraband goods such as brandy, tea and tobacco ashore, evading the excise men, and villages including Ilfracombe, Clovelly and Combe Martin played key roles in these clandestine operations. One of the most famous smuggling routes passed right through Combe Martin, where the village's narrow streets and hidden paths made it difficult for customs officers to intercept goods.

Best for COASTAL SCENERY

shipwreck of the *London* lies somewhere in the depths, and shortly the route will reach Hele Bay. Once a smuggler's haven, this is now a peaceful beach of shingle and sand with rock pools and caves uncovered at low tide. The coast path rises up again and as you keep the ocean on your left you'll walk along open grassy stretches and through copses of trees and yellow gorse.

03 Pass through the sheltered harbour of **Watermouth**, where the charming Storm in a Teacup cafe, a beached boat by the water's edge, makes the perfect place for a restorative slice of cake. A spit of land called the Warren stretches protectively around the right-hand side of the harbour, with the enigmatic **Round Tower** standing sentinel atop it – it's a 10-minute detour from the route to walk out to the tower and back along a narrow path. The history of this squat stone tower is debated, but it was likely a lookout built in the 19th century to keep an eye out for ships and smugglers.

04 The coast path goes right through **Watermouth Valley Caravan Park** – follow signposts and head uphill on a tarmac path passing tents and caravan pitches – before passing through a wooden gate and out onto the cliffs. The grassy coast path continues to climb, passing a fenced meadow on your right. When you come to the top of the hill you'll find a bench with a photo-worthy view of Broadsands Beach framed perfectly below you.

05 Pass through a metal gate and turn left onto a lane (the Old Coast Road) shaded by trees. Shortly you'll come to a signpost on the left indicating the way down to **Broadsands**. Reaching this half-moon of sand requires a stiff, steep walk down no less than 240 steps, so it's not for the faint of heart (or faint of

BEST DAY WALKS: ENGLAND

knee joint), but it's well worth the slog to reach this wide sweep of the bay, surrounded by green cliffs and enclosing beryl-green water perfect for a cooling dip. This is one of the most beautiful coves in Britain, and the strenuous descent means it's never overly busy.

06 Once you've puffed your way back up to the lane, continue onwards along the track, passing the Sandy Cove Hotel on your left. After a short distance the coast path briefly joins the A399 road – there is pavement on the left-hand side but be mindful of traffic. Take the left-hand turn down Berry Lane to descend into the village of **Combe Martin**. At the T-junction, a wooden signpost points the way left down the hill on Newberry Rd to reach the village's harbour beach (pictured).

07 From Combe Martin you can catch bus 301 back to Ilfracombe. Or for a final beach stop, continue along the coast path, climbing up a hilly section on the other side of the village and looking out for the half-hidden wooden signpost (pictured previous page) to **Wild Pear Beach**. Wild Pear is remote and hard to access – reaching the beach requires a scramble – but that means it's often wonderfully deserted. It's also a known naturist haven if you fancy a skinny-dip.

Exploring Exmoor

Combe Martin is also a great jumping-off point for exploring Exmoor, a pocket-sized national park made up of rugged moorland and wooded valleys as well as the slice of dramatic coastline from this walk. Hiking trails such as Tarr Steps and Dunkery Beacon provide panoramic views and a chance to spot red deer or the famed dusky Exmoor ponies that graze freely here. Moorland villages like Dulverton and coastal Porlock are great bases for a day or two's walking, and by night, Exmoor's skies are bright with stars – this was Europe's first International Dark Sky Reserve, so bring your telescope.

Take a Break

Come aboard the good ship **Storm in a Teacup** (facebook.com/storminateacup18). This beached former rescue boat may not actually sail anywhere these days, but it's a lovely spot for lunch by the sea in Watermouth Harbour. The cafe built on deck serves fresh coffee and doorstop-sized slices of homemade cake, plus hearty breakfasts and freshly landed fish, with smoked mackerel and crab sandwiches. If you go for a cream tea, remember it's always cream first, jam second in Devon.

Also Try...

WEWI-PHOTOGRAPHY/SHUTTERSTOCK ©

Hartland Point

A rugged right-angle of land, the Hartland Peninsula marks the edge of Devon.

In the late 19th century, this was among the most treacherous headlands anywhere in England – a macabre fact summed up by the local seamen's refrain 'From Pentire Point to Hartland Light, a watery grave by day or night'. The rusting fragments of the coaster *Johanna*, driven ashore on New Year's Eve 1982, can still be seen near Hartland Point Lighthouse (pictured). The cliffs reach their highest point at 107m near Hartland Quay.

Nearby Hartland Abbey was founded in the 12th century, but is now a grand private house, known for the ornate Alhambra Passage and a Regency library designed in the Strawberry Hill Gothic style.

DURATION 3hr
DIFFICULTY Moderate
DISTANCE 6.4 miles/10.3km

Hound Tor & Haytor

Probably the best-known tor walk on Dartmoor.

From the Haytor visitor centre, the route heads northwest past the prehistoric settlements around Smallacombe Rocks, then climbs the spookily named Hound Tor (414m), which some people claim inspired the title of Arthur Conan Doyle's classic Dartmoor-set Sherlock Holmes caper *The Hound of the Baskervilles*. Legend has it that the rocks were hounds turned to stone by a vengeful witch. From here, the path loops back across Becka Brook over Haytor (454m), with spectacular views to the South Devon coast, then visits an old flooded quarry, before following the line of a disused tramway that was built to transport granite to the port at Teignmouth. It now forms part of the 18-mile Templer Way.

DURATION 3hr
DIFFICULTY Moderate
DISTANCE 5.5 miles/8.9km

Start Point

Start Bay curves in an elongated crescent towards Devon's most southerly tip.

This loop walk begins at the abandoned village of Hallsands, which was literally swept out to sea by a great storm in 1917 (the ruins themselves are off-limits). It then circles round the dramatic Start Point Lighthouse, which was built in 1836 to protect ships from the notorious shallow rocks of the Start Point peninsula and is open to the public in the summer months. The walk then passes the beaches of Great Mattiscombe (pictured), a secluded sandy stretch, and Lannacombe and Woodcombe, peaceful and lesser-visited bays, returning via inland paths to the village of Hallsands. The area is home to a grey seal colony that you may spot lolling on the rocks.

DURATION 3½-4hr
DIFFICULTY Moderate
DISTANCE 6.8 miles/11km

Botallack & Cape Cornwall

The mineral seams around the Penwith coastline were once among the richest in Cornwall, a legacy that's still visible in the evocative mine workings around Botallack.

The Crowns engine house was one of the most productive tin-mining sites in Cornwall and has featured in many a costume drama (including the BBC's award-winning adaptation of *Poldark*), as well as becoming part of the Cornwall and West Devon Mining Landscape UNESCO World Heritage Site. To the south lies the ruined hillfort of Kenidjack Castle, an Iron Age structure, and rocky Cape Cornwall – once believed to be Cornwall's most westerly point, it's topped by one of Cornwall's earliest Christian chapels and has incredible views of the Atlantic.

DURATION 3hr
DIFFICULTY Easy
DISTANCE 4 miles/6.4km

Stonehenge (p120)

Southwest England

22 Bath Skyline
Get a grandstand view of Britain's most beautiful city. **p96**

23 Glastonbury Tor
Take a dawn walk to watch the sunrise over the Somerset Levels. **p98**

24 Avebury & Silbury Hill
Commune with ancient Britons as you circumnavigate the world's largest stone circle. **p100**

25 Tarr Steps
An Exmoor classic: a woodland walk to a venerable clapper bridge. **p104**

26 The New Forest
Shaggy ponies, ancient trees, rare creatures and wild moorland. **p106**

27 The Ridgeway
The country's oldest trail takes in some stunning prehistoric sites. **p108**

28 Corfe Castle to Langton Matravers
Castles, poets, wild cliffs and a great pub – a perfect introduction to Dorset. **p112**

29 Lulworth Cove to Durdle Door
A stunning walk along the Jurassic Coast to an iconic natural wonder. **p116**

Explore
Southwest England

'Southwest is best', or so say the locals. This corner of Britain is a treasure trove of natural beauty and urban history, all tucked into folds of charming countryside and edged by the Jurassic Coast. In Somerset, explore rolling hills, mystical Glastonbury and the city of Bath's Georgian grandeur. Wiltshire boasts the ancient wonders of Stonehenge and Avebury, while Dorset has the stunning Jurassic Coast's dramatic cliffs and fossil-filled beaches. Quaint coastal towns like Lyme Regis and vibrant, culture-mad cities such as Bristol help create the perfect blend of rural peace and urban buzz, and walkers can tread coast paths, chalk plains, old woodlands and hilly heaths.

Bath

Bath is one of Britain's most appealing cities. Famous for its Georgian architecture, it's also a lovely place to base yourself in for exploring Somerset and Wiltshire – although it's worth noting that accommodation can be pricey and parking is difficult. There is a decent YHA hostel and a huge number of hotels and B&Bs to choose from, however, and the city is well connected by bus and train to most parts of Somerset. When in town, visit the famous Roman Baths after dark for the candlelit Summer Lates, walk around the Royal Crescent and the Circus, two gorgeous examples of Georgian architecture, and pop into the Jane Austen Centre to discover more about how the city influenced the life and works of Britain's best-loved author.

Bristol

The southwest's biggest and buzziest city, Bristol is known for its alternative and slightly anti-establishment nature: it's a dynamic city with a creative edge. There are plenty of chain hotels to choose from as well as a modern YHA right by the harbour – other interesting options include Brooks Guesthouse, where a cluster of silver Airstream caravans have taken over the roof, and the Artist Residence, a smart boot factory turned hotel. Short-term rentals and self-catering are also good options here, and you're well placed for Somerset and Wiltshire walks as well as for hopping north to the Cotswolds. Walk around Bristol's iconic harbour to visit the SS Great Britain, designed by Isambard Kingdom Brunel, or head to Stokes Croft to spy out street art by Bristol's other famous creator, the graffiti artist Banksy.

Salisbury

Centred on a majestic cathedral that's topped by the tallest spire in England, Salisbury makes an appealing Wiltshire base. It's been an important provincial city for more than a thousand years, and its streets form an architectural timeline ranging from medieval walls and half-timbered Tudor town houses to Georgian mansions and Victorian villas. It's ideal for exploring Wiltshire, Hampshire, Dorset and the New Forest.

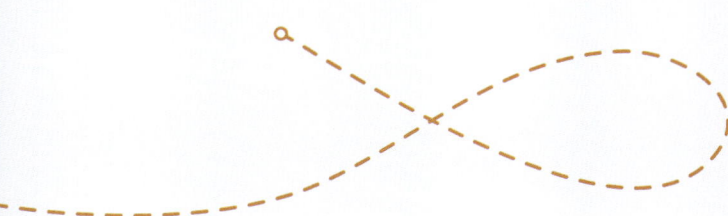

Bournemouth

A resort town since Victorian days, Bournemouth remains a popular beach retreat, but it's also a sensible launchpad for forays along the Dorset coast. The nearby town of Poole offers a slightly more chilled vibe. The town has good transport links and plenty of accommodation, especially a supply of budget-friendly B&Bs.

 ## When to Go

Spring brings colour and fragrance to the southwest, and in late spring bluebells carpet the woods. Summer holidays bring a swathe of visitors, and the end of school holidays in September brings cheaper sleeps, quieter beaches and warmer seas. Autumn is a wonderful time for walking, particularly on Exmoor, when the deer rut begins, and on the Dorset coast, where the sea looks spectacular from the limestone cliffs.

 ## Transport

The main motorway to the southwest is the M4, which runs west from London to Bristol, linking to the M5, which runs as far as Exeter. From here the road connects to the A30 dual carriageway. An alternative route is along the A303 dual carriageway, which famously runs past Stonehenge. The southwest is well served by trains to mainline stations including at Bristol, Bath, Salisbury, Bournemouth and Southampton.

 ## Where to Stay

Whatever style or budget you prefer, the West Country can accommodate you. From bare-bones clifftop campsites to clusters of hip eco-yurts; from seaside resorts thick with B&Bs to beam-heavy rural inns, and from slick city crashpads to improbably plush country-house hotels – you can sleep in them all here. Standouts include the B&B at foodie hot spot and cookery school River Cottage and bucolic Farr's Meadow campsite, both in Dorset. For a treat, book a stay at At The Chapel in Bruton, a destination restaurant with smart minimalist rooms, or The Pig Near Bath, a hip country house near town.

Resources

Visit Bristol (visitbristol.co.uk) Info on attractions, accommodation and the city's many festivals.

Bath Tourist Office (visitbath.co.uk) Accommodation booking and advice for Bath and Somerset.

Exmoor NPA (exmoor-national park.gov.uk) National park authority site, including info on walking routes.

Jurassic Coast (jurassiccoast.org) Information on Dorset's World Heritage coast and tips for fossil hunting and places to stay.

 ## What's On

Bath Festival (01225-463362; bathfestivals.org.uk; May) A multi-arts festival spanning music, literature, science and politics.

Glastonbury Festival (glastonburyfestivals.co.uk; tickets from £335; Jun or Jul) The UK's biggest and best musical mudfest takes over a Somerset farm for a wild weekend.

Upfest (upfest.co.uk; Jul) Grand celebration of street art in Banksy's home city of Bristol.

Bristol International Balloon Fiesta (bristolballoonfiesta.co.uk; Aug) Hot-air balloons fill Bristol's skies.

Jane Austen Festival (janeausten.co.uk; Sep) Bath's 10-day celebration of its beloved writer.

22

Bath Skyline

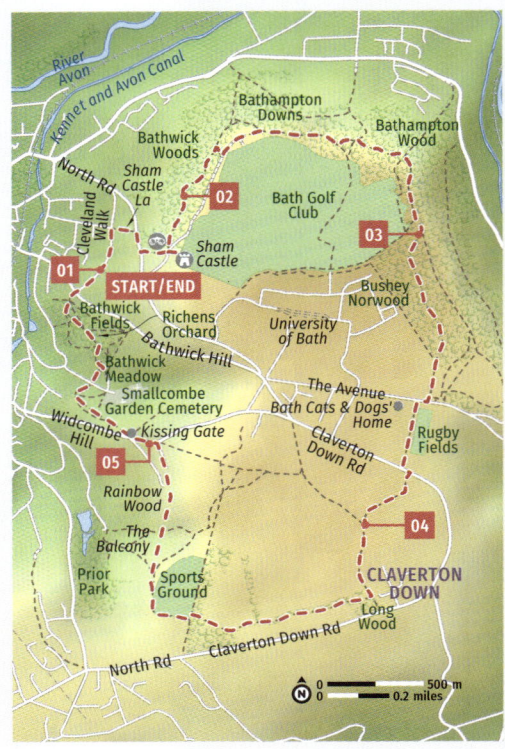

DURATION	DIFFICULTY	DISTANCE	START/END
3-3½hr	Moderate	5.9 miles/ 9.5km	Bathwick Hill

TERRAIN	Woodland, grassy fields

The belle of British cities, Bath is rightly famous for its Georgian architecture – but has some surprisingly green spaces nearby, too. This walk explores the hills and woods east of the city, ending with an eye-popping rooftop view.

Getting Here

Trains link Bath to London Paddington, Cardiff Central and Bristol. Several buses head up Bathwick Hill from the bus and train stations, including the U1 and U3, which run multiple times an hour. Parking along Bathwick Hill is permit-controlled, so leave the car in a city-centre public car park.

Starting Point

Start at Bathwick Hill, near the entrance to Bathwick Fields.

01 Take Cleveland Walk. Follow it along to a footpath on the right opposite Sham Castle Lane. The path climbs up through a small wooded area to North Rd. Turn right, then take the gate on the left which leads up through another area of woodland. At the top near a bench, there's a quick view of Bath's rooftops, and you can take a quick detour to see **Sham Castle**, a mock-medieval folly built by the entrepreneur Ralph Allen.

02 Backtrack to the bench, from where the trail enters **Bathwick Woods**, a surprisingly dense area of native woodland. There are several trails through the trees: take care to follow the waymarkers for Bath Skyline, indicated by a yellow arrow. Keep bearing right; eventually you'll turn uphill out of the trees, past some radio masts and onto the open fields of Bathampton Down. Walk along the slope, bearing slightly downhill towards the woods.

Prior Park

Prior Park (NT; 01225-833977; nationaltrust.org.uk; Ralph Allen Dr; adult/child £10/5; 10am-5pm daily Feb-Oct, 10am-4pm Sat & Sun Nov-Jan) was established by Ralph Allen, who made his fortune founding Britain's first postal service, and owned many of the quarries from which the city's amber-coloured Bath stone was mined. The gardens were partly designed by the landscape architect Lancelot 'Capability' Brown, and include cascading lakes and a graceful Palladian bridge, one of only four such structures in the world. The house itself is now a private school.

OLIVER BERRY/LONELY PLANET ©

03 A gate leads down into **Bathampton Wood**. The trail is easy to follow; you'll pass several small abandoned quarries where stone was extracted, then enter another area of open fields, Bushey Norwood; the campus of Bath University is on your left. Follow waymarkers to The Avenue; turn left here, taking the path just before the Cats & Dogs' Home. Continue to Claverton Down Rd; cross over, turn left, and look out for the trail on the right past the rugby fields.

04 You'll cross Claverton Down, then enter **Long Wood**. Continue through the trees, turning north past playing fields.

You'll pass the edge of Prior Park, then walk along a lovely section of the woodland path called **the Balcony**, with rolling valley views away to your left. The trail leads through Rainbow Wood, emerging onto Widcombe Hill.

05 Walk down Widcombe Hill, then through a **kissing gate** on your right. Cross the field and walk down into the valley: Smallcombe Garden Cemetery is on your right. Climb steeply up the other side, passing the community-run Richens Orchard and coming out onto **Bathwick Fields**. This is where the views get really grand: as you cross the sloping hill, the rooftops of Bath open up in front of you like a diorama from a Disney movie. Walk across the fields to where you began on Bathwick Hill.

 **Take a Break**

Lodged above a vintage boating station, the **Bathwick Boatman** (bathwickboatman.com) serves lunches with lovely river views; afterwards, you can steer a wooden rowboat along the River Avon. On Walcot St, the olde-worlde **Star Inn** (01225-425072; abbeyales.co.uk) still has many of its 19th-century pub fittings. It's the brewery tap for Bath-based Abbey Ales; some are served in traditional jugs.

23

Glastonbury Tor

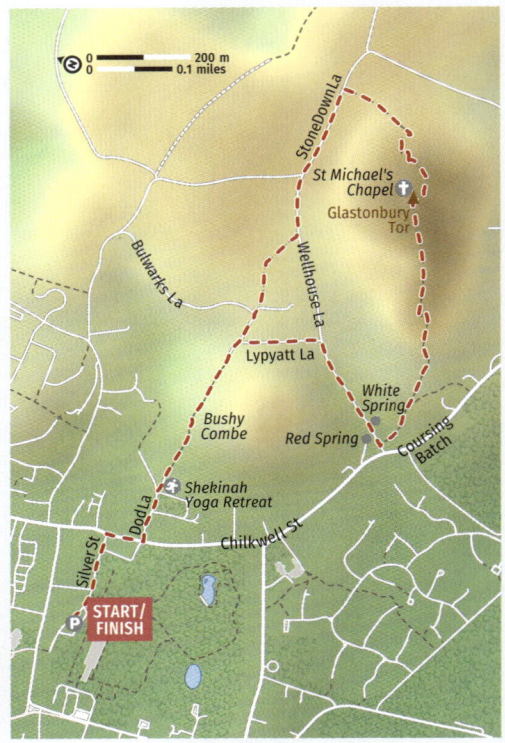

DURATION	DIFFICULTY	DISTANCE	START/END
1–1½hr	Easy	2.2 miles/ 3.6km	Silver St car park

TERRAIN	Country lanes, grassy hill

Myths and legends swirl around the strange hillock of Glastonbury Tor. Visible for miles around, it's one of Somerset's most unmistakable landmarks – and arguably its most unmissable view.

Depending on which legend you believe, the tor is either the home of the faerie king of the underworld, the last resting place of King Arthur or a mystical node where many ley lines converge. It's also a cracking short walk: steep but easygoing. Hike early or late in the day to avoid the crowds; at dawn or dusk, its mystical power is impossible to deny.

Walk up Glastonbury's main street, turning right onto Chilkwell St, then left up Dod Lane past the Shekinah Yoga Retreat. The path leads through a gate uphill across the fields of **Bushy Combe**. You'll cross Bulwarks Lane, then more fields to Wellhouse Lane. Continue uphill to the National Trust gate.

A steep, switchbacking path leads up the tor's north-east side.

The views across the Somerset Levels are breathtaking. In ancient times (when the Levels were often flooded), the tor would have appeared as an island, cut off by impassable marshes and bogs; this perhaps explains its legendary status as the Isle of Avalon. At the summit, the tower of **St Michael's Chapel** (pictured) spikes skywards; in 1539, the last abbot of Glastonbury Abbey, Richard Whiting, was hung, drawn and quartered here for refusing to denounce the pope.

Walk down the other side of the tor to Wellhouse Lane. Nearby, one of Glastonbury's sacred springs, the **White Spring,** bubbles up underground; the other, the **Red Spring,** emerges in Chalice Well & Gardens. Turn right (uphill) along Wellhouse Lane, left onto Lypyatt Lane, and back down Bushy Combe to the town centre.

24

Avebury & Silbury Hill

Best for

ANCIENT HISTORY

DURATION	DIFFICULTY	DISTANCE	START/END
2–2½hr	Easy	4 miles/ 6.4km	Avebury National Trust car park

TERRAIN	Grassy fields

Everyone's heard of Stonehenge, but far fewer people know much about Avebury – Britain's largest stone circle, so enormous they plonked a village right in the middle of it. It forms part of a vast ancient landscape whose exact purpose still remains shrouded in mystery.

Getting Here

Avebury is about 9 miles northeast of Devizes, 7 miles west of Marlborough. Bus 49 runs hourly to Swindon (30 minutes) and Devizes (15 minutes). There are six services on Sunday.

Starting Point

The National Trust has built a large car park (£7 per day) outside Avebury's village centre.

01 Around the same time the ancient Egyptians were building the pyramids, neolithic Britons were hard at work creating their very own wonders of the ancient world. Unlike the circle at Stonehenge, with its distinctive upright trilithons, the stone circle of Avebury takes imagination to decipher – not least because Avebury's stones are half-hidden among the buildings of its namesake village. But in terms of scale alone, Avebury dwarfs its better-known neighbour on Salisbury Plain – it's nearly 10 times the diameter of Stonehenge, and forms part of a sprawling complex of prehistoric monuments that must have taken decades, if not centuries, to construct. All of which suggests that, at least to its builders, Avebury may have been at least as sacred a site as Stonehenge – and perhaps, given its size, even more important.

Carrying a satellite map of the Avebury landscape is a good way to get your bearings, as it can be hard to make sense of the geography of the site from the ground alone. From the National Trust car park, cross the road and follow the signed track along the edge of the River Kennet. It's easy to follow, but can be gloopy in wet weather.

02 About half a mile south of the car park, you'll catch sight of your first ancient wonder of the day. To the southwest, a conical green hill rises up in the middle of a nearby field. Unremarkable, you might think – until you realise it's too smooth, too uniform, too perfect to be a natural feature. And you'd be right. This is **Silbury Hill** (pictured), perhaps the strangest of all the monuments around Avebury. Forty metres high, this hill is the largest artificial earthwork in Europe, comparable in height and volume to the Egyptian pyramids. It was built in stages from around 2500 BCE. Incredibly, it's been estimated that it would have taken 500 men roughly 15 years to build, but despite countless theories, no-one really has any idea what its purpose was – a ceremonial platform, perhaps? A monument to the dead? Some kind of celestial marker? No one knows. Several tunnels have been bored into the middle over the decades, but so far, other than a few tools and bones, no significant archaeological artefacts have been found. Why did they feel building their own hill was so important? We'll probably never know – and since the tunnels have now been filled with concrete to avoid the hill's collapse, the secret of Silbury Hill is likely to remain a mystery, perhaps forever.

03 It's not permitted to climb the hill – it looks solid, but is surprisingly delicate – but you'll get fine views as you walk south along the fields towards the A4. When you reach the busy main road, carefully cross over (look out for fast-moving traffic), and follow signs across the fields pointing to **West Kennet Long Barrow**. There is a clear path to follow; you'll head slightly uphill, reaching the barrow after about 10 minutes' walk.

The Restoration of Avebury

In the Middle Ages, when Britain's pagan past was an embarrassment to the Church, many of Avebury's stones were buried, removed or broken up. In 1934 wealthy businessman and archaeologist Alexander Keiller supervised the re-erection of the stones; he later bought the site for posterity using funds from his family's marmalade fortune. The small **Alexander Keiller Museum** on the High St documents his history and contains prehistoric finds.

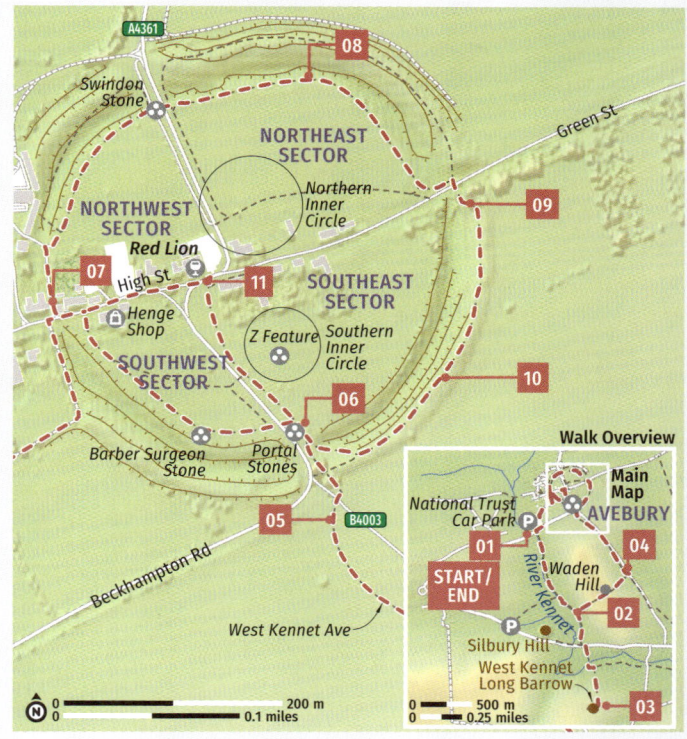

BEST DAY WALKS: ENGLAND

Like Silbury, it's an improbably massive structure: 100m long and 20m wide, far bigger than most other ancient barrows of its kind. Dating from around 3500 BCE, its entrance is guarded by huge sarsen stones, and its roof is made out of gigantic overlapping capstones. Inside, several circular chambers have been excavated; about 50 skeletons were found interred here, but for some reason, at a later date, it appears the barrow was deliberately abandoned and infilled several centuries after its construction. Again, no-one really knows who was buried here, or why the monument is quite so enormous, or why it was abandoned. Another similar burial mound, **East Kennett Long Barrow**, sits on private land nearby, but is not as well preserved and is sadly off-limits to the public. The people who built Avebury are believed to have occupied a site at **Windmill Hill**, about 1 mile northwest of the circle.

04 Backtrack down the hill, cross the road and follow the Kennet River north until you reach a hedgerow fence leading away to your right. Here, a permissive path leads northeast over **Waden Hill**, offering superb views of both Silbury Hill and West Kennet Long Barrow. It's a fairly steep but short climb, which then drops down over the other side of the hill. As you approach the road, a double line of massive standing stones appears, leading away to the northwest: this is the **West Kennet Avenue**, a sacred processional route which ancient Britons used to approach the circle. It's hard not to get a haunting feeling as you walk through the massive stones, just as our ancestors of old would have done. A second avenue is also once believed to have existed, leading to another site at Beckhampton.

05 The Avenue ends near Beckhampton Rd. Here, you'll get your first real glimpse of the great **stone circle** itself, although its scale is obscured by buildings and trees, so you'll have to use your imagination to picture how it must have originally appeared. With a diameter of approximately 330m at its widest point, Avebury is the largest stone circle in the world. It's also one of the oldest, dating from 2500 to 2200 BCE. Originally, it's believed the henge consisted of an outer circle of around 100 standing stones of up to 6m in length, many weighing 20 tonnes. The stones were surrounded by another circle delineated by a 5m-high earth bank and a ditch up to 9m deep. Inside were smaller stone circles to the north (27 stones) and south (29 stones). Today, around 30 stones remain in place; the others were plundered or smashed up for stone long ago. Pillars now show where missing stones would have been.

06 Across Beckhampton Rd, you enter the circle through two huge **portal stones**. From the portal stones, walk in a clockwise direction around the circle. Modern roads into Avebury neatly dissect the circle into four sectors: the southwest sector between Beckhampton Rd and the High St contains 11 stones, including the **Barber Surgeon Stone**, named after the skeleton of a man found buried under it (the equipment interred with him suggests he was a barber-cum-surgeon).

The Sanctuary

A lost stone circle called **The Sanctuary** can be visited just south of the busy A4 road. Many human bones and food remains have been excavated here, suggesting the circle may have hosted sacred ceremonies and perhaps death rites. The stones have long since disappeared, but their location is marked by concrete slabs.

07 Cross High St and continue into the northwest sector, perhaps the most complete. Note how different the shapes are here: at Stonehenge, they were crafted into uniform pillars, but at Avebury, they're much more free-form. This sector contains the massive 65-tonne **Swindon Stone**, one of the few never to have been toppled: it's the one nearest the A4361.

08 Cross the main road into the northeast sector, where fewer stones have survived. Three sarsens remain of what would have been a rectangular cove.

09 Cross Green St, passing under a great oak tree into the southwest sector. This is the best place to appreciate the scale of the ditch around the circle: the amount of work required to excavate this channel from the bone-hard chalk underfoot is hard to comprehend even today, let alone with only stone tools. Aerial photos suggest that the ditch may originally have been filled with other structures, probably made of timber. One theory has suggested that the white chalk under Avebury and Stonehenge may have been important; originally, perhaps the monuments were completely cleared of grass and vegetation, so that they might have appeared as shining, white otherworldly platforms.

10 The path circles back to the portal stones. Once, a southern inner circle stood in this sector and within this ring was an obelisk, now marked by a stone plinth. Nearby, a curious line of stones, known as the Z Feature, may have served an important sacred purpose, as the row appears to be orientated to face the sunrise and sunset.

11 Follow High St to the **Henge Shop** (hengeshop.com; 9.30am-5.30pm) to pick up souvenirs, then head back to the National Trust car park.

Take a Break

It's worth stopping in at the **Red Lion** (chefandbrewer.com; High St; 9am-11pm), if only to say you've had a pint in the world's only pub inside a stone circle. One seat covers a 26m-deep well dating from the 17th century. There's a hearty menu of pies, puds and other pub classics.

25

Tarr Steps

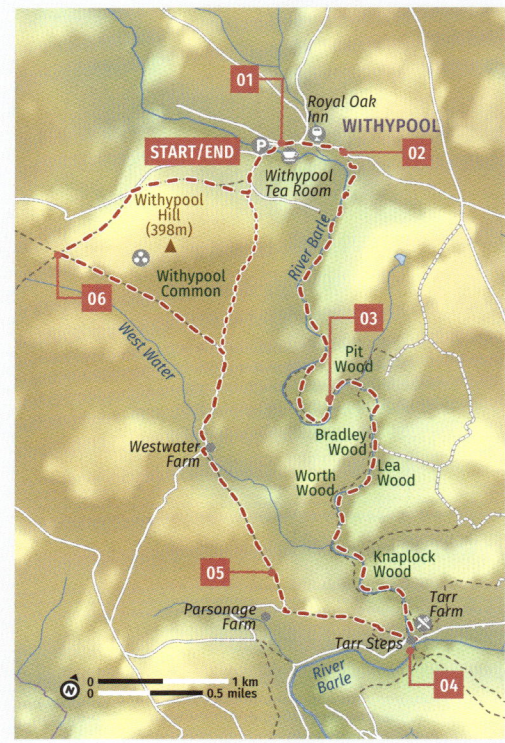

DURATION	DIFFICULTY	DISTANCE	START/END
3½–4hr	Moderate	8.3 miles/ 13.4km	Withypool

TERRAIN	Riverside trail, woodland, heath

Many walkers overlook Exmoor, but that's a mistake. This hike encapsulates all that's lovely about the UK's smallest national park: dappled woodland, peaceful fields, fast-running rivers and rural architecture – in this case, a famous stone clapper bridge.

Getting Here

Withypool is 9 miles northwest of Dulverton. There's no regular bus service so you'll need your own car; alternatively, Exmoor is good (albeit hilly) cycling country.

Starting Point

There is a small car park in Withypool, but spaces are limited.

01 Exmoor has a special, sleepy magic that's uniquely its own, and this hike along the banks of the River Barle explores some of the national park's loveliest countryside. The woodland cover makes this a particularly good autumn walk, but it's good in any season, even midwinter. The walk begins in the village of **Withypool**, where you can stock up on supplies from the village shop.

02 Walk east along the main road past the Royal Oak Inn. The road dips, then heads uphill; cross a stile on your right over a drystone wall and walk down towards the woods.

03 Follow the path south along the river, crossing the boggy meadows before rounding an oxbow bend and entering **Pit Wood**. Continue on through the trees, through Lea Wood, and across fords; waymarkers provide guidance at key points.

Exmoor's Red Deer

Exmoor supports one of England's largest wild red deer populations. In autumn during 'rutting' season, stags bellow and clash horns to impress prospective mates. The Exmoor National Park Authority runs regular free wildlife walks, which include evening deer-spotting hikes, or you can go on 4WD safaris: try **Red Stag Safari** (01643-841831; redstagsafari.co.uk; safaris £45) or **Barle Valley Safaris** (07977 571494; exmoorwildlifesafaris.co.uk; adult/child £50/35; tours 9am & 2pm).

Much of the riverside path is very rooty and rocky, so watch your step.

04 After climbing briefly, the path drops back down to the river, entering the gnarled trees of Knaplock Wood before reaching **Tarr Steps** (pictured). This is the largest and possibly oldest 'clapper' bridge on Exmoor, made of stone slabs propped on supporting columns embedded in the River Barle. Folklore claims the Devil used it for sunbathing; it first appears in the historical record in the 1600s, and recently had to be rebuilt after 21st-century floods.

05 Cross the bridge, then take the side trail uphill towards Parsonage Farm. You'll follow the hedgerows across the muddy fields, with views over the river valley. Continue across Parsonage Down to Westwater Farm, emerging onto a minor road. You can follow this road all the way back to Withypool, but it's worth detouring across Withypool Common; a waymarker points left after a cattlegrid.

06 The faint path peters out as you cross the down. Continue west till you pick up another faint footpath; turn right (northeast). You can sidetrack to the top of the hill, where the remains of a vanished **stone circle** and a **Stone Age tumulus** can be seen. If not, skirt the northern edge of the down before dropping back down to Withypool.

Take a Break

Beside the clapper bridge, **Tarr Farm** (01643-851507; tarrfarm.co.uk; 11am-11pm) is fab for cream teas and hearty lunches. Baked spuds, cakes and sandwiches are on offer at the little **Withypool Tea Room** (01643-831279; withypoolexmoor.co.uk/tea-rooms; 9am-5pm spring-autumn), while the **Royal Oak Inn** (01643-831506; royaloakwithypool.co.uk) pulls a decent pint.

26

The New Forest

DURATION	DIFFICULTY	DISTANCE	START/END
3hr	Moderate	6 miles/ 11km	Lymington/ Brocken- hurst

TERRAIN	Boggy paths, woodland

The New Forest is a world apart, with a very distinct atmosphere, and even its own court and system of local law, drawn up in 1217 to counter oppression from William the Conqueror's descendants. Despite the name, its not all about trees here – there's a lot of open moorland, populated by small shaggy ponies that roam free. This plus a large deer population and otters in the Lymington River make it a special place for wildlife lovers.

Getting Here
This walk is ideal for those using public transport, as it starts at one train station and ends at another, a little way down the line. If you're driving you could park at Lymington and return by train from Brockenhurst.

Starting Point
The route starts at Lymington Town Station, which sits on the banks of the Lymington River on the eastern edge of the town. From here you're straight into a country walk, so detour if you want to buy any supplies.

01 From Lymington Station, turn right onto Waterloo Rd and then right again at the T-junction to cross the railway line and estuary. Over the bridge, turn left and, after 100m where there's a bend in the road, go straight ahead on the path signed for the **Lymington Beds Nature Reserve**. The path hugs the right-hand bank of the Lymington River, across land that can be wet and boggy. From here, start looking out for ponies.

02 At the end of the Reserve go ahead on the paved path and then turn right towards Pilley. Past Spinner's Garden (you pay a small fee to

106   BEST DAY WALKS: ENGLAND

Watch Out for Wildlife

Best for WILDLIFE

The adorable wee ponies are only the most visible of the New Forest's natural inhabitants. Varied habitats here – valley bogs, wet and dry heaths and deciduous woodland – support some rare and wonderful creatures. Among the wild gentian flowers and wild gladioli, you might spot southern damselflies and large marsh grasshoppers. Adders, grass snakes and rare smooth snakes slither around at ground level, while look up and you might spot woodlarks and wood warblers. Fallow, roe and red deer inhabit the woodland, while one of the most extraordinary sights is during autumn 'pannage' when scurrying pigs are set free to root around for acorns.

see the magnolias, azaleas and irises) you come into the village of **Pilley**, where the thatched **Fleur de Lys** pub – an amazing 1000 years old – has an upmarket restaurant as well as bar (a better bet for muddy boots).

03 Continuing through the village past the pub, you come to the wild expanses of **Beaulieu Heath**, which can be treacherously boggy and very hard to navigate without a detailed OS map.

04 Instead, follow footpaths which lead via clearings and patches of woodland past the Church of St John the Baptist.

Then head past Haywards Farm and round the back of Dilton Farm, eventually entering the **Roydon Wood Nature Reserve**. Some of the broad-leafed trees here are classified 'ancient'. Continue downhill to cross the Lymington River, and pass Roydon Manor to your right.

05 A sinuous network of bridleways lead out of the woods, past an avenue of trees (pictured) and onto a road. Turn right and you come to the **Church of St Nicholas**, where 'Brusher' Mills (see right) is buried. Carry on down the road to reach Brockenhurst station.

Take a Break

At the end of the walk and handily near the station you'll find the **Snakecatcher** (01590-622348; thesnakecatcher.co.uk; Lyndhurst Road, Brockenhurst; mains £13-18) pub. It serves five local real ales plus craft beers and ciders. There's a range of meals, but the big deal is the burgers, which include veggie and mushroom varieties. The pub is named for local character Harry 'Brusher' Mills, who drank in the pub when it was the Railway Inn; born in 1840, he spent a lifetime living in the woods here catching grass snakes and adders.

27

The Ridgeway

DURATION	DIFFICULTY	DISTANCE	START/END
5hr	Hard	11 miles/ 18km	Foxhill/ Wantage

TERRAIN	Steep tracks and fields

The Ridgway is one of the most ancient walkways in the country. It runs for 87 miles, from Overton Hill in Wiltshire to Ivinghoe Beacon in Buckinghamshire. We've chosen a longish stretch – it's a little difficult to access, meaning you need an early start, and you'll probably want to stay at the hostel at the end. But it's well worth the effort to follow in the footsteps of some of England's first hikers, and the prehistoric sites you'll encounter – the tomb of Wayland's Smithy, the earthworks of Uffington Castle and the graceful White Horse – are some of the most mesmerising anywhere.

Getting Here

First take a train to the somewhat uninspiring town of Swindon, reached in an hour from London Paddington. From Swindon Station, head up Wellington St and turn left on Manchester Rd to reach the bus station. Take bus 46 or 48a to Foxhill, which will take around 20 minutes.

Starting Point

Once at Foxhill, head up the minor road following signs to Hinton Parva. Soon after this, follow the Ridgeway sign which leads off to the right.

01 The route starts with a steepish climb up to the ridge of a hill, which gives views of **Lammy Down**, a tumulus (burial mound) which is the first of the ancient sites you'll spot along the way. Ahead you'll see the swelling mound of Uffington Castle. There's a signed detour here to the **Strip Lynchets**, medieval earth banks cut into the fields to create terraces for growing crops; the terraces may also have had a role in ceremonies. The route cuts across two narrow country lanes; down the second, en route to Idstone, is a fort known as **Alfred's Castle** where the heroic king is said to have defeated the Danes at the Battle of Ashdown at the age of just 22. Despite its possible epic place in English history, you may not want to make the 3-mile round-trip detour to the site with so many stunning attractions ahead. Alfred's Castle is a visually modest site, with low oval-shaped earthworks.

02 The Ridgeway runs on to a patch of woodland, emerging at one of its most thrilling sights: a Neolithic long barrow tomb fronted by tall stones, known as **Wayland's Smithy** (pictured). The tomb's antiquity is astounding: the original chamber was constructed between 3590 and 3550 BCE and held 14 bodies, then around 3400 another burial chamber was built on top. The name was given to the tomb in the early Middle Ages by the Saxons, who appropriated it for the mythical Wayland.

03 Continue on the route for around 30 minutes more, and you come to more exceptional sights: ascend a hill and then turn left at the gate where you'll see a National Trust sign. You emerge into the great sweeping earthwork known as **Uffington Castle** – not, in fact, a castle at all, but a high hill fort dating back to the early Iron Age. Aside from the still-dramatic earth banks, no evidence of building was found here, but excavations have revealed pottery and loom weights. The Manger valley which falls below the fort has steep undulating banks, which were formed by retreating Ice Age permafrost. Nearby sits Dragon Hill, a natural conical hill with a flattened top which is poetically said to be the spot where St George slew the dragon. No grass grows on the top of the hill, something which is traditionally ascribed to the poisonous blood of the

🥾 Walkers on the Ridgeway

Set high on a long crest, the Ridgeway is often described as the oldest road in England; it has been tramped by drovers, itinerants and soldiers for at least 5000 years. Its elevation was a protection against attack – this was where the Saxons under Alfred the Great clashed with invading Vikings – as well as providing less boggy terrain for people and animals. Ancient hill forts along the way suggest that the Ridgeway was used as a secure trading corridor in ancient times. The route became formalised after the 18th-century enclosure act, but up until then it would have been a looser network of tracks and trails.

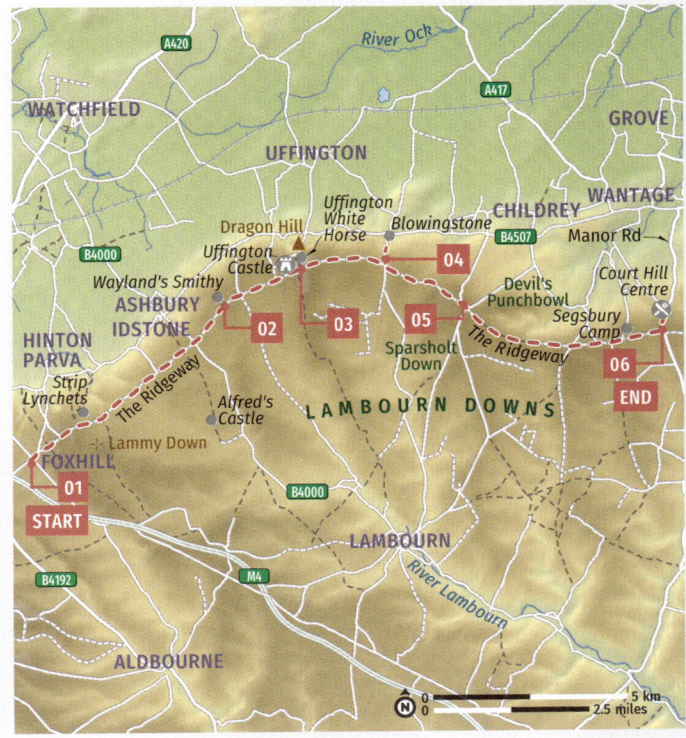

BEST DAY WALKS: ENGLAND 109

slaughtered dragon. Only slightly more prosaically, high levels of potash have been found here, suggestive of pagan ceremonies involving fire. Dragon Hill has clearly been a significant site for centuries: 46 Roman burials and eight Saxon ones were discovered here in the mid-19th century. Beyond the fort, on the slope of the glacial valley is the wonderfully artistic White Horse of Uffington, whose 3000-year-old, 110m-long form is stretched across the hillside.

04 Walk for another 2 miles or so, and you come to a minor road leading left down **Blowingstone Hill**. It's possible to make a detour here (2 miles in total, with a steep ascent back to the Ridgeway) to the Blowingstone itself, a weathered and rugged chunk of sarsen which, according to legend, is what King Alfred used to summon his army to battle. You can try yourself to emit a battle cry – a booming sound – by blowing into one of the holes in the stone.

05 Back on the route, you walk along fenced 'gallops' used for exercising race horses. The path climbs up to Sparsholt Down with a radio mast to the right. Turn right onto the paved road and then follow signs to where the Ridgeway resumes its course. Below you to the left is the steep green valley known as the Devil's Punchbowl. After around 20 minutes' walk, there's another detour by some farm buildings to Iron Age **Segsbury Camp**, an earthwork which was excavated

The White Horse

It is just one of the mysteries of the White Horse at Uffington (pictured) that it can only be clearly seen from the air. The horse is famously minimal and modern in appearance, a few bold lines cut deep into the chalk – the lines were dug up to a metre in depth around 2500 years ago. Indeed the jury is out on whether it does actually represent a horse – some claim the chalk lines may depict a sabre-toothed cat or a dog. Maintenance of the figure is now carried out by a group of National Trust volunteers, but until the late 19th century this work was done at hugely popular country fairs held on the hillside, with thousands in attendance.

in 1871 and was found to contain a Saxon burial, with human bones, a shield boss and urn fragments.

06 Another 15 minutes' walk brings you to Manor Rd, where you should turn left: here this stage of the Ridgeway walk ends at the **Court Hill Centre**. The centre is a great spot to get a simple meal and an equally simple bed for the night. Alternatively, call for a taxi, which can take you down the hill to Wantage.

Take a Break

The independent **Court Hill Centre** (01235-760253; courthill.org.uk; Wantage; dorms £20, meals £8.50) was created out of five old barns, and enjoys a picturesque setting at the end of this route. It contains bunk beds and a few private rooms, and is a little spartan but very attractive. There's a lovely wood-beamed tea room, and simple but tasty meals are served for people staying overnight. It also provides breakfast and packed lunches for Ridgeway walkers.

28

Corfe Castle to Langton Matravers

DURATION	DIFFICULTY	DISTANCE	START/END
4hr	Moderate	7 miles/ 11.2km	Corfe Castle/ Langton Matravers

TERRAIN	Grassed paths and roads

Welcome to the Isle of Purbeck, a rather mystical peninsula (and not in fact an island at all) at Dorset's southern tip. Purbeck is crowned in the middle by the 11th-century ruins of Corfe Castle, built by William the Conqueror and now managed by the National Trust. The eerie ruins rise from an outcrop in a gap in the Purbeck Ridge, and are the perfect place to start for a walk across country to reach the sea and the sheer limestone cliffs that characterise this coastline, plus there's a great pub for a mid-walk pint and a pasty.

Getting Here

Purbeck's narrow roads can be congested, so catch a train to Wareham then hop on the hourly Purbeck Breezer 40 bus to Corfe Castle, which also runs to Langton Matravers.

Starting Point

Start at Corfe Castle in the same-named village.

01 Built in the 11th century by William the Conqueror to consolidate control over England, **Corfe Castle** (nationaltrust.org.uk/corfe-castle) was regarded as one of Britain's most impregnable fortresses, with its lofty location on a hilltop providing a strategic vantage point to protect the surrounding area, including important trade routes. All was well until Oliver Cromwell got his hands on the castle, partially destroying it in 1646 and leaving the dramatic ruins of Purbeck limestone that rise up from the landscape today.

02 From the grounds of the castle follow the **Hardy Way**, so named for poet Thomas Hardy, who wandered the southwest of England with his wife Emma, finding inspiration for his novels of love and tragedy. The 216-mile long-distance route

Try Climbing

If you fancy really getting to grips with the Isle of Purbeck, try your hand (literally) at sport climbing – this is one of the best spots in the country for rock climbing with a view of the sea. **Cumulus Outdoors** (cumulusoutdoors.com/activity/climbing-abseiling) runs climbing and abseiling lessons at Dancing Ledge and nearby Hedbury Quarry that are suitable for beginners and families, and also runs sessions aimed at seasoned indoor climbers keen to tackle rock outdoors. For experienced climbers, **UK Climbing** (ukclimbing.com) lists sport and trad climbing routes across Purbeck; the shelter of the cliffs means that climbing is possible year-round.

named for him is signposted and follows West St through Corfe Castle village and then, where the lane meets Corfe Common, continues across a series of fields for 2 miles to reach the hamlet of Kingston.

03 Sleepy **Kingston** is perhaps most famous for the delightful Purbeck Ice Cream, made on a village farm using Dorset cream, although you'll have to wait until you reach Worth Matravers further along the walk to sample some. From Kingston, the route leaves the Hardy Way (follow the yellow arrow signs through the village) and continues towards the sea along a quiet lane (South St). Where the lane ends, take the left-hand grassy path through meadows and around Hill Bottom. Here the route joins the South West Coast Path and briefly takes you out onto the cliffs before turning left and crossing fields to enter Worth Matravers via Renscombe Rd.

04 Here, limestone cottages cluster around a picturesque duck pond and village green, but the real gem worth seeking out in **Worth Matravers** is the Square & Compass (pictured), a proper Dorset pub that serves just two things: pies and pasties, all washed down with homemade cider. Allow plenty of time for a lunch stop at this laid-back spot or come back after your walk to catch live music of an evening.

05 Leave Worth Matravers, passing to the left of the village green and turning left at the wooden signpost. The footpath slopes down towards the sea past strip lynchets (ancient field systems) and rejoins the South West Coast Path at **Seacombe Cliff**. Turn left and walk along the cliff's edge, keeping the huge expanse of sea on your right until the route reaches Dancing Ledge.

06 A wooden sign on the footpath marks the way down to **Dancing Ledge** (pictured) – it's a bit of a scramble down to reach these flat rocks framed by soaring cliffs. This area was used for quarrying of Purbeck stone and the ledge is a straight drop off into the sea, which is deep enough here for small ships to come right up to the ledge so local quarrymen could transport the stone away from the area. It may be human-made, but Dancing Ledge is now a pleasingly sunny spot for a picnic, and is so-called because at certain stages of the tide, waves wash over the horizontal rock surface and undulations cause the water to bob about. At low tide, a delightful rectangular sea pool is revealed – perfect for a cooling dip on a hot summer's day. In dry weather you'll also spot climbers tackling the best of Purbeck's limestone on the upper long quarry wall above the pool.

07 Turn away from the sea and head uphill again towards **Langton Matravers**. Stone steps lead up the hill and the path continues through two fields where at dusk you may be lucky enough to spot glowworms twinkling green in the grass. Pass Spyway Barn and enter the village of Langton Matravers. Catch a bus back to Corfe Castle, or if you fancy spending the night here, a pleasant little spot to pitch a tent is **Tom's Field** (tomsfieldcamping.co.uk), a meadow campsite that feeds its happy campers hearty breakfasts and homemade pizzas.

ADRIAN BAKER / SHUTTERSTOCK

Swanage Railway

Fancy puffing in leisure back to the starting point of this walk on a vintage steam train? Hike from Dancing Ledge to Swanage, 3 miles further along the coast path, to catch the **Swanage Railway** (swanagerailway.co.uk; Apr-Oct), a charming stream train that trundles back to Corfe Castle during summer, as well as special periods such as Christmastime. The railway's heritage steam and diesel locomotives, now run mostly by volunteers, provide an authentic glimpse into English mid-20th-century rail travel. When Enid Blyton, author of much-loved children's book series *The Famous Five*, holidayed in Dorset, she used the railway and would often include the train journey in her books.

Take a Break

The **Square & Compass** (squareandcompasspub.co.uk; noon-late; pies £5) is a proper old-fashioned pub with a sunny beer garden where huge stone tables, usually thronging with a cheery crowd of locals, climbers and walkers, look out to sea. Don't expect posh grub – the pub serves pies, pasties and pints from a hatchway. Come instead for the relaxed vibe, the home-pressed cider and live music in the summer, or a seat by the log fire and a nose around the pub's fascinating fossil museum in winter.

BEST DAY WALKS: ENGLAND

29

Lulworth Cove to Durdle Door

DURATION	DIFFICULTY	DISTANCE	START/END
3hr	Hard	5 miles/ 8km	Lulworth Cove

TERRAIN	Steep coastal path and grassy tracks

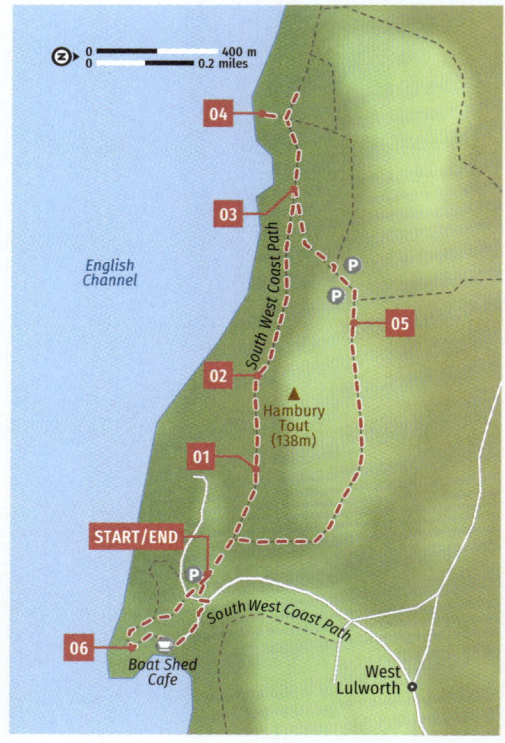

There are few coastal spots in Britain as dramatically gorgeous as Durdle Door, where a huge limestone arch rears away from Dorset's Jurassic coastline and plunges back into the blue. The path from the horseshoe bay of Lulworth Cove to the Door and back again is steep in places, but rewards with huge views and some incredible spots to stop off for a sea swim. This is a popular and crowded hike in summer, but it's worth it – plan to hike early in the morning or out of season if you want that photo-worthy view or a dip under the Door all for yourself.

Getting Here
The hourly Jurassic Breezer 30 and 31 buses stop at West Lulworth and Durdle Door. If driving, park in West Lulworth village or at Lulworth Cove.

Starting Point
Start in Lulworth Cove car park.

01 From the chocolate-box-pretty village of West Lulworth and its clutch of thatched cottages, follow signs for the South West Coast Path. At **Lulworth Cove** take the track heading up the hill, away from the large car park. Wide stone steps head straight up – this is the steepest part of the route and requires some puff, but once you're at the top you're rewarded with views of the sea in front and, behind you, of the turquoise horseshoe of Lulworth Cove.

02 You're standing above **Stair Hole** (pictured), a small and lesser-visited cove reputed to be the inspiration for the location of Enid Blyton's book *The Rubadub Mystery*, a ripping children's yarn of blowholes, whirlpools and submarines. The Hole is an example of the Jurassic Coast's folded limestone

Fossil Hunting

Countless fossils lie hidden in the soft clay of Dorset's Jurassic Coast and make a fascinating window into 185 million years of the Earth's history. You're free to hunt for ammonites, ichthyosaurs and plesiosaurs as you hike – winter is the best time, as the beaches are quiet, and fossils are brought in to shore with rough weather. You'll be following in the footsteps of trailblazing collectors such as Mary Anning (1799–1847) of Lyme Regis, who discovered the first correctly identified ichthyosaur skeleton when she was aged 12, and went on to work as a paleontologist even though, as a woman, she was not eligible to join the London Geological Society.

Best for

COASTAL SCENERY

strata known rather charmingly as the 'Lulworth crumple'. The path will reach a wooden gate at a T-junction with a wooden fingerpost. Pass through the gate and turn left to continue following the coast path to Durdle Door.

03 The pathway opens out at the cliff edge with stairs leading down, on your left, to **Man O'War Beach** (not named after the painful man-of-war jellyfish, but because the shape of the rocks standing like sentinels out to sea are said to resemble the cannon-carrying warships). This sheltered cove is a peaceful, pebbly spot to stop off at for a swim in water that turns turquoise when the sun is out – on the clearest days you can see down to the seabed. The coast path curves away along the cliffs to the right and leads to a fabulous view of the famous Durdle Door archway.

04 A set of steep wooden steps zigzags down to **Durdle Door Beach** (pictured following page). There are regular rock falls along this coastline so it's worth checking online that the beach and all pathways are accessible before you start off. Down on the golden sand and shingle, admire the white limestone arch sometimes nicknamed the 'drinking dragon', as it frames the far-off Isle of Portland. To the right you can walk all the way along the adjoining beach at Bat's Head at low tide. At high tide you'll need to take the coastal path along the cliffs and scale the stiff walk up Swyre Head to get here, climbing above the brilliantly named Scratchy Bottom (voted the seventh-rudest place name in the UK).

05 From Durdle Door, follow the coast path back the way you came until you reach a fork above Man O'War Beach. Follow the higher, left-hand path to reach Durdle Door car park. Continue straight through the car park to a metal gate leading to the footpath. This lesser-walked route continues inland past fields and below **Hambury Tout** (you can detour to climb this chalk hill, which hides an ancient burial mount, for far-reaching views). Even on the busiest days of the summer holidays you're likely to have this peaceful section of the walk all to yourself. At Hambury Farm follow the right-hand footpath through hedges – keep your eyes peeled for the rare butterflies found here, including the Lulworth Skipper and the Adonis Blue. Pass through the car park again and into Lulworth Cove.

06 At the water's edge in **Lulworth Cove** the Boat Shed Cafe does cream teas on a balcony looking out over the water and the Castle Inn pulls a decent pint. You can also continue along the coast path to encircle Lulworth Cove, one of only a handful of perfect half-moon coves in the world and a UNESCO World Heritage Site. At the time of research a large rockfall had cut off the clifftop coast path but an alternative route above the village is easy to follow.

A PHOTON BOUNCE CREATION/SHUTTERSTOCK ©

Old Forests & Footsteps

The Fossil Forest near Lulworth Cove offers a fascinating glimpse into Earth's ancient past. Formed over 145 million years ago during the Late Jurassic period, it contains the remains of prehistoric trees encased in limestone that once stood tall when dinosaurs roamed this landscape. These unique 'burrs' are fossilised tree bases, surrounded by ripple patterns from an ancient swampy lagoon – today it also provides breathtaking views back to Lulworth Cove. For more of a Jurassic Park vibe, head to Langton Matravers, where 100 fossilised dinosaur tracks are preserved in rock at Spyway.

 Take a Break

The **Boat Shed Cafe** (lulworth.com/visit/food-drink/boat-shed-cafe; 8am-6pm; sandwiches £10), once a fishermen's lockup and now managed by the Lulworth Estate, looks out over the bobbing fishing boats and the swimmers splashing in sparkling Lulworth Cove. Grab an outdoor table to refuel with freshly landed seafood or a cream tea in the summer months, or sit inside the small but snug space in winter to warm up with a steaming bowl of seafood chowder. They also serve local beer.

Also Try...

NICOLA PULHAM/SHUTTERSTOCK ©

Avon Gorge & Leigh Woods

Slicing right through the centre of Bristol, and spanned by one of the great monuments of Victorian engineering, Isambard Kingdom Brunel's mighty Clifton Suspension Bridge (pictured; cliftonbridge.org.uk), the Avon Gorge makes for a super city walk.

Start in Leigh Woods, home to the Stokeleigh Camp hill fort, then cross the bridge to Clifton to visit the gorge-side lookout known as the Giant's Cave, at the Clifton Observatory, for one of the best vistas of the bridge. The observatory is also home to a museum featuring a rare Victorian-era camera obscura. A grassy area next to the bridge is perfect for a mid-hike picnic. Return via the bridge, walking down through Nightingale Valley for a stroll along the edge of the River Avon, then a final climb back to the car park.

DURATION 3hr
DIFFICULTY Moderate
DISTANCE 4.6 miles/7.4km

Stonehenge

Like Avebury, Stonehenge is much more than just a stone circle: it's part of a huge prehistoric landscape comprised of many different monuments. Built 4000 years ago for mysterious reasons, it was originally made up of standing stones called 'sarsens' and two circles made of smaller 'bluestones'.

North of Stonehenge is the Cursus, an elongated embanked oval; the smaller Lesser Cursus is nearby. Two clusters of burial mounds, the Old and New Kings Barrows, sit beside the ceremonial pathway (the Avenue), which originally linked Stonehenge with the River Avon, 2 miles away. Trails connect all these monuments together – you can't even begin to understand Stonehenge without seeing how it sits within the context of this wider landscape. Few walks in Britain feel as moving, or as mysterious.

DURATION 2½-3hr
DIFFICULTY Easy
DISTANCE 6.4 miles/10.3km

CHRISNOE/SHUTTERSTOCK ©

Old Harry Rocks

This is a classic Dorset walk along the World Heritage–listed Jurassic Coast, celebrated for its crimson cliffs and copious fossil deposits.

From the small village of Studland, the walk heads out around Handfast Point, affording sweeping views of the tall chalk rock pillars known as Old Harry Rocks (pictured), sculpted into shape by the sea. On sunny days, they blaze white against the ocean. Look out for the remains of fields used by Celtic farmers. The walk then heads west over Ballard Down, before looping round over Godlingston Heath and Agglestone Rock – the jury is out on how the 'devil's anvil', a huge, iron-rich sandstone block, came to be sitting in solitude on a small hill.

DURATION 3-3½hr
DIFFICULTY Moderate
DISTANCE 6.4 miles/10.3km

The Quantocks

The 12-mile range of red sandstone hills known as the Quantocks are a mix of moors, carpeted in purple heather in autumn, lush green valleys and ancient woods, home to Exmoor ponies, roe and red deer and the mythical nightjar.

They offer stirring views across the Bristol Channel: when the weather's fine, you can see across to the Gower coastline in South Wales. A route travels west across Alfoxton Park from the beautiful village of Holford, whose landscape inspired Coleridge and Wordsworth when strolling over this section of the hills, to the Bicknoller Post hill summit. The route then loops round to climb back up the wooded Holford Combe.

DURATION 2½-3hr
DIFFICULTY Moderate
DISTANCE 6.5 miles/10.5km

Gordale Scar (p139)

Northern England

30 Ingleborough
Conquer the summit of one of Yorkshire's famous Three Peaks. **p126**

31 Pendle Hill
Soak up an incredible hilltop view. **p130**

32 Dunstanburgh Castle
Coastal riches and a medieval ruin. **p132**

33 Hadrian's Wall
Hike along the famous fortification. **p134**

34 Malham Landscape Trail
Discover the limestone crags and gorges of the Yorkshire Dales. **p138**

35 Robin Hood's Bay
Walk to a storybook village by the sea. **p140**

36 Rievaulx
Explore the ruins of this ancient abbey. **p142**

37 Berwick-upon-Tweed
Take a tour of this border town. **p144**

38 Blyth to Tynemouth
Lighthouses, watch houses, towering monuments and sandy beaches. **p148**

39 York
Patrol the walls and explore the alleyways of this distinguished city. **p152**

Explore

Northern England

Some of the most popular walking spots in England can be found among the rolling hills and lush green valleys of the Yorkshire Dales and North Yorks National Parks, but so can some of the finest tucked-away spots, often just around the corner from the main routes – it's all a question of knowing where to look. Northumberland's cinematic landscape is filled with vast empty beaches, rugged clifftop castles and artistic inspiration. It offers an intriguing 'no nonsense' landscape built on top of an eventful history and a proud industrial past, coupled with views that will surprise and delight any visitor.

Newcastle

Many of the routes included here are easy to connect to using public transport, with Newcastle providing an excellent base to reach York, Blyth, Haltwhistle, Berwick-upon-Tweed and Whitby. Other spots require the use of a car, but parking is generally less of an issue in this area than it is in busier places such as the Lake District.

Newcastle and the other main cities of Leeds, York and Darlington may lack the chocolate-box charm of the more rural areas, but you're more likely to find cheaper accommodation here, particularly during the busier times of year. It's also worth remembering that this region attracts a lot of visitors from Scotland, where the school summer holidays are offset from the English ones and run from late June to early August, meaning late August is generally less busy here than further south.

York

The sprawling landscape of northeastern England remains largely undiscovered by many, but those who do visit always appreciate the warm welcome, the sandy beaches, and the striking wide-open landscape. It's a place of contrast and contradictions. The ancient city walls of York surround a modern and vibrant city, and the dramatic, pre-historic scenery of Malham and the Yorkshire Dales has provided the backdrop to many Hollywood blockbusters.

Yorkshire Dales National Park

The popular spots in the heart of the Yorkshire Dales National Park are perfect starting points for exploring the surrounding landscape and many are well connected by road, rail and canal – a cycle ride along the local canals is a great way to explore on a non-walking day.

When to Go

This region is prone to a coastal fog known as the 'Fret', and it's most common through late spring and early summer, so late summer and early autumn are the perfect times to visit. Winter, with its northerly winds, can be bitter but breathtaking – in every sense

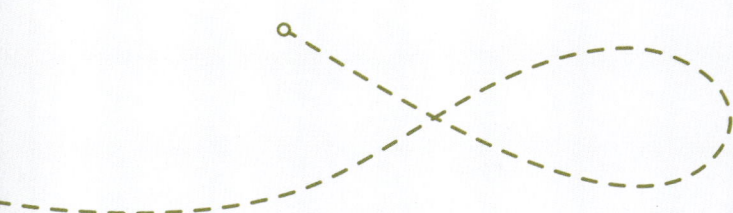

Resources

Visit Northumberland (visit northumberland.com) For everything that's going on in the county.

Northumberland Coastal Path (northumberlandcoastpath.org) If you're inspired to visit more of this wonderful coastline.

Welcome to Yorkshire (yorkshire.com) A full listing of what's happening and where.

Tideschart (tideschart.com/United-Kingdom/England/East-Riding-of-Yorkshire) Tide times for Yorkshire, to stay safe on your coastal walks.

of the word – with the ice and snow accentuating the dramatic landscape.

 ## Transport

London to Newcastle by train takes under three hours, and there are regular trains from Manchester and Carlisle. The A1 is the main arterial road running through the centre of the region but it can be very prone to delays. The central region around Malham and Grassington suffers from heavy traffic during the summer months.

 ## Where to Stay

For a larger group, the medieval Lendal Tower (lendaltower.com) in York offers a truly unique way to experience the ancient city; it oozes with history and overlooks the river and city walls. The Yorkshire Dales National Park offers many perfect camping spots for tents and tourers. Silloth House Campsite (silloth-house.co.uk) is in the heart of the dales and is an excellent base for tackling the Ingleborough and Malham walks. Jesmond Dene House (jesmonddenehouse.co.uk) is a unique hotel tucked away in peaceful grounds but still close to Newcastle's city centre. The Walls B&B (thewallsberwick.com) offers warm and welcoming accommodation right on Berwick's town walls.

What's On

Northumberland Dark Skies Festival (northumberlandnationalpark.org.uk/northumberland-dark-skies-festival; Feb) Be blown away by the Milky Way.

Wakefield Rhubarb Festival (experiencewakefield.co.uk/event/rhubarb-festival; Feb) A chance to celebrate Wakefield's most famous vegetable.

Berwick Film & Media Arts Festival (bfmaf.org; Mar) Explore cinematic history, past, present and future.

Doncaster Balloon Festival (doncasterballoonfestival.co.uk; Jul) Up, up and away in a host of beautiful balloons.

Druridge Bay Festival (druridgebay.co.uk; Sep) An intimate musical festival and camping experience.

30
Ingleborough

Best for

WILD VIEWS

DURATION	DIFFICULTY	DISTANCE	START/END
6-7hr	Hard	11 miles/ 18km	Clapham

TERRAIN	Rough, stony paths, often steep

Scenic Ribblesdale cuts through the southwestern corner of the Yorkshire Dales National Park, where the skyline is dominated by a trio of distinctive hills known as the Three Peaks: Whernside, Ingleborough and Pen-y-ghent. The ascent of Ingleborough (724m) from Clapham village is a classic Dales hike, full of interest and rewarded with fantastic and far-rainging views from the summit.

Getting Here
Clapham is 50 miles northwest of Leeds, and 57 miles north of Manchester. In addition to the train station, there is a regular bus service between Settle (served by trains from Leeds) and Clapham (20 minutes, every two hours, daily except Sunday). See dalesbus.org for timetables.

Starting Point
The National Park car park in the middle of Clapham village (£4.50 per car all day) has public toilets. About 120,000 people climb this hill every year, but don't let that lull you into a false sense of security. This is a proper hill walk, so pack waterproofs, food, water, a map and a compass.

01 Head north along Church Avenue, bear left past the church and cross the little bridge over Clapham Beck. The first half of the walk will be following the waters of this little stream almost to their source. Turn right on the far side of the bridge.

02 Where the street bends to the left, the gateway in front of you is the entrance to **Ingleborough Estate Nature Trail** (admission adult/child £2.50/1), a scenic lakeside route to Ingleborough Cave. The estate was home to botanist Reginald Farrer (1880–1920), whose obsession with alpine plants led to the publication in 1907 of his book *My Rock-Garden*, which kicked off a British fashion for garden rockeries that persists to this day. Many of the features along the nature trail celebrate Farrer's contribution to botany and horticulture. An alternative route (which avoids paying the entrance fee) continues along the street for 80m and turns right on a gravel road (wooden signpost to Ingleborough Cave, Gaping Gill and Ingleborough). Another sign says Private Road, but walkers are welcome. Follow this road, keeping right at two forks, to reach Clapdale Farm.

03 Pass through the farmyard and turn right, heading downhill to join the gravel drive on the valley floor (the exit from Ingleborough Estate Nature Trail) where you turn left and follow the road alongside Clapham Beck to the entrance to Ingleborough Cave.

04 **Ingleborough Cave** is a show cave (adult/child £16/8) that has been open to the public since 1837. Easy concrete paths lead you for just over half a mile through floodlit passages and chambers filled with beautiful flowstone formations. This is where the waters that flow into Gaping Gill high on the hillside above emerge into daylight once again as Clapham Beck. The walk continues past the cave entrance on a stony path, then turns sharp left and passes through a gate into the dramatic limestone canyon of Trow Gill.

05 Clamber up the boulder-strewn base of **Trow Gill** (pictured), which steepens and narrows before emerging into a narrow valley. The path hugs a stone wall on the left, and finally crosses the wall via a ladder stile to easier angled moorland with a view ahead to the summit of Ingleborough. A clump of bushes to the left of the path

The Three Peaks

Since 1968 more than 200,000 hikers have taken up the challenge of climbing Yorkshire's Three Peaks in less than 12 hours. The circular 24-mile route begins and ends at the Pen-y-Ghent Cafe in Horton-in-Ribblesdale (where you clock in and clock out to verify your time) and takes in the summits of Pen-y-ghent, Whernside and Ingleborough. Succeed and you become a member of the cafe's Three Peaks of Yorkshire Club.

Fancy a more gruelling test of your endurance? Then join the fell-runners in the annual Three Peaks Race (threepeaksrace.org.uk) on the last Saturday in April, and run the route instead of walking it.

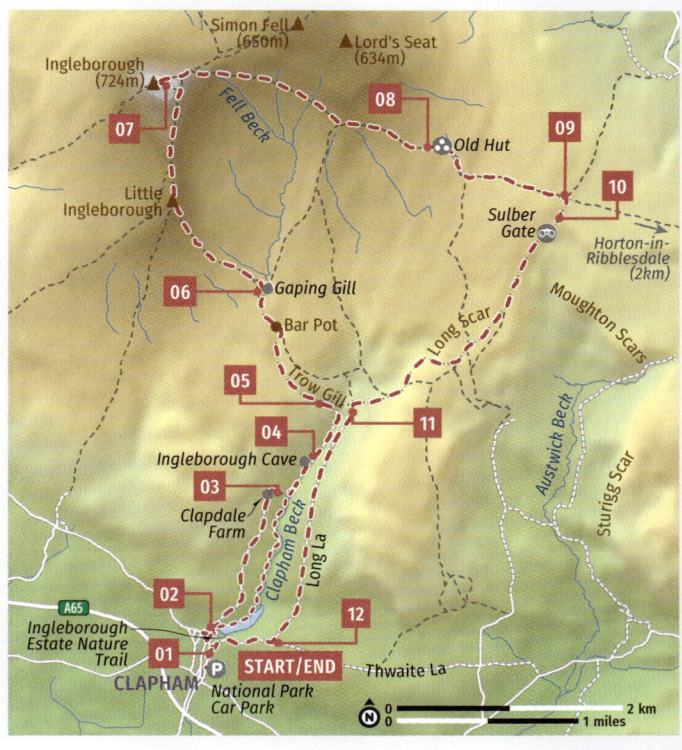

BEST DAY WALKS: ENGLAND

about 40m after the stile marks Bar Pot, one of the entrances to the Gaping Gill cave system. A short distance ahead fork right to view Gaping Gill itself, where the waters of Fell Beck plunge underground and flow through subterranean passages to Ingleborough Cave.

06 **Gaping Gill** (pictured) is one of the most famous caves in England. A huge vertical pothole 105m deep, it was the largest known cave shaft in Britain until the discovery of Titan in Derbyshire in 1999. Gaping Gill is normally off limits to noncavers, but twice a year, on the late May and August bank holiday weekends, local caving clubs hold the Gaping Gill Winch Meet when a winch is set up so that members of the public can descend into the depths in a special chair (£20 per person). For details, see bpc-cave.org.uk and cravenpotholeclub.org, and click on the Gaping Gill link. Return to the main path, which begins to climb more steeply, via stone steps in places, onto the southern ridge of Ingleborough. It then traverses to the right before a final short, steep section leads onto the summit.

DUNCAN ANDISON/SHUTTERSTOCK ©

07 The summit of **Ingleborough** is a flat, featureless plateau about 300m across, marked at the highest point by a trig pillar, a huge pile of stones, and a cross-shaped drystone shelter. The view is stupendous, looking north across Ribblehead Viaduct to the Howgill Fells, northwest to the hills of the Lake District and south to Pendle Hill. In really clear weather you can make out the peaks of Snowdonia, 100 miles to the southwest. In pre-Roman times the summit of Ingleborough was occupied by a hill-fort settlement – you can still see the remains of a wall and some hut circles on the southern part of the plateau. Leave the summit in an east-northeasterly direction (towards Horton-in-Ribblesdale) past a prominent cairn on the edge of the plateau. Shortly after dropping down off the edge of the plateau bear right on a good footpath that leads steadily downhill, crossing a wall via a stile, to reach a small ruined building.

08 This old hut once served as a shelter for hunters shooting grouse on the nearby moor. Continue downhill with the wall on your left, cross another stile and bear left where the path forks. Soon you reach an area of **limestone pavement**, where the bare limestone bedrock is exposed at the surface. The path squeezes through a trench between wall and bedrock before crossing another stile and descending to a four-way junction of footpaths.

09 A prominent signpost marks **Sulber Crossroads**. This is where the footpath from Ingleborough to Horton-in-Ribblesdale intersects with the Pennine Bridleway. Turn right here on the bridleway, heading towards Clapham, and after 400m pass through a gap in yet another drystone wall.

Ingleton Waterfalls Trail

The village of Ingleton, perched precariously above a river gorge, is the caving capital of England. It sits at the foot of one of the country's most extensive areas of limestone, crowned by the dominating peak of Ingleborough and riddled with countless potholes and cave systems. The village is the starting point for a famous Dales hike, the circular, 4.5-mile **Waterfalls Trail** (ingletonwaterfallstrail.co.uk; adult/child £10/5), which passes through native oak woodland on its way past a series of spectacular waterfalls on the Rivers Twiss and Doe. Note that the walk involves a lot of uphill climbing, but in summer you can often find an ice-cream van at the highest point of the trail.

10 On your left is **Sulber Gate** – go through the gate for an impressive view of Moughton Scars, a sweeping curve of limestone escarpment with a large expanse of limestone pavement in the hollow below. Return through the gate and continue south with the stone wall on your left. The path forks three times in the next 0.75 miles – keep right at all three junctions. The last fork leads north on a grassy track around the outcrop of Long Scar, then curves back south and downhill to a ladder stile over a wall.

11 Turn left through a gate in the wall further downhill, where your path meets several other trails coming from the right. The wooded cleft on the far side of the valley is Trow Gill, where you clambered up during the first half of the walk. Follow this walled farm track (known as **Long Lane**) for 1.5 miles, with good views to the right across the valley. At its end is a T-junction.

12 Turn right and follow Thwaite Lane downhill, through woodlands and then tunnels beneath Ingleborough Estate (built in the 19th century to provide privacy for the estate gardens), to emerge in Clapham village beside the church. Turn left down Church Ave to return to the car park.

Take a Break

There are several tearooms in Clapham, but for something a bit different head just 5km southeast on the A65 to the **Courtyard Dairy** (01729-823291; thecourtyarddairy.co.uk; Crows Nest Barn, Austwick, near Settle; 9.30am–5.30pm Mon-Sat, 10am–5pm Sun), a combined cheesemonger and cafe where you can try inventive grilled cheese sandwich wedges such as Wensleydale and caramelised carrot chutney. Don't miss the delicious rich fruit cake with a slab of local Dales cheese: a Yorkshire tradition.

BEST DAY WALKS: ENGLAND

31

Pendle Hill

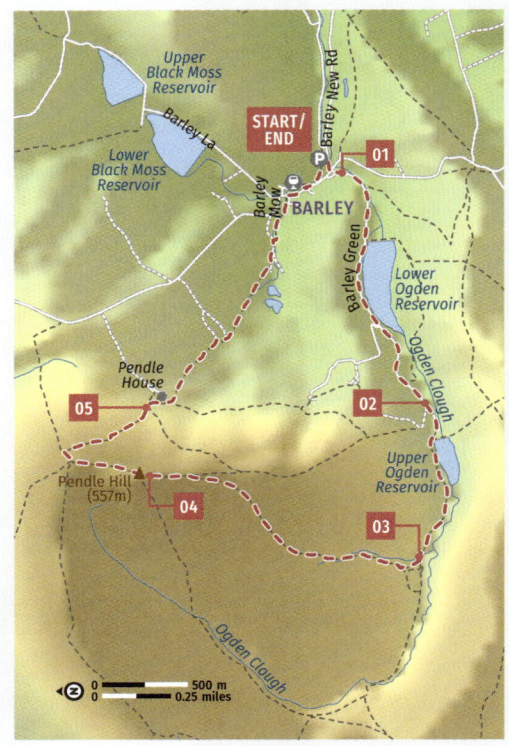

DURATION	DIFFICULTY	DISTANCE	START/END
3-4hr	Moderate	5 miles/ 8km	Barley

TERRAIN	Rough, stony paths, steep descent

Just east of Clitheroe in Lancashire lies one of England's most famous summits. Pendle Hill, forever associated with 17th-century witch trials, rises above the pretty village of Barley, commanding stupendous views that range from the Three Peaks of the Yorkshire Dales to the Isle of Man.

Getting Here

Barley is 32 miles (50 minutes' drive) north of Manchester, and 40 miles (1¼ hours' drive) west of Leeds. Bus 67 runs every two hours (Monday to Saturday) between Nelson and Clitheroe (both of which have train stations), stopping at Barley (20 minutes from Nelson, 40 minutes from Clitheroe).

Starting Point

The village of Barley has a large car park (£3 for over 3 hours) with public toilets and a cafe. Nearby you will find a couple of pubs.

01 Turn right out of the car park entrance, cross the main road and head along the cul-de-sac opposite (signposted Barley Green). Follow the private road as it climbs to the right of the dam at **Lower Ogden Reservoir** and continues along its north bank. From its far end you are following part of the 45-mile Pendle Way, indicated by waymarks with a yellow arrow and a witch's silhouette.

02 The road leads along a narrow valley to a fork. Keep straight on, through a gate and up to the dam at **Upper Ogden Reservoir**. The way ahead now is on a rough and occasionally boggy footpath which leads to a wooden gate in a stone

Quakers & Witches

In 1652 George Fox had a vision atop the summit of Pendle Hill that would lead him to found the Religious Society of Friends, or Quakers. By then, the hill had become infamous as a centre of witchcraft: 40 years earlier, in 1612, 12 local women, some of whom were village healers in accordance with ancient traditions, were caught up in the religious tensions of the time and charged with witchcraft. On 18–19 August the women were put on trial in Lancaster and all but two were found guilty: the unlucky ones were executed on Lancaster Moor, where the Ashcroft Memorial in Lancaster's Williamson Park now stands.

wall with close-cropped grass on the near side and rough heather-and-bracken moorland beyond. Go through the gate and turn right immediately (not the carved stone Pendle Way marker at your feet), heading uphill and then leftwards across the slope.

03 After the path crosses a small stream, head uphill to the right (look out for two more stone markers). Follow the path as it climbs steadily past small cairns and crosses over the stream to merge with another, much more prominent, gravel path coming from the right.

04 The summit of **Pendle Hill** (557m) is marked by a trig pillar, and commands a fantastic view of the surrounding countryside – on a clear day you can pick out Blackpool Tower, 40 miles away on the western horizon. Walk north from the summit towards a stone wall, then turn right and head downhill on a stone-paved path that slants steeply down to meet and follow another wall.

05 Go through the gate just above Pendle House, and pass to the right of the house. Continue downhill, following the Pendle Way signposts back to Barley village. At the road, turn right past the Barley Mow pub, and take the path inside the stone wall by the swings to return to the car park.

 **Take a Break**

The **Barley Mow** (01282-690868; barleymowpendle.co.uk; Barley Village; mains £15-20; 7.30am-11pm Mon-Fri, 8.30am-midnight Sat, 8.30am-10pm Sun;), a pub in the middle of the village, is a cosy rural retreat serving hearty breakfast, lunch and dinner menus aimed at refuelling weary walkers, from a full-on fry-up to fish and chips, Lancashire hotpot and Sunday roast with all the trimmings.

32

Dunstanburgh Castle

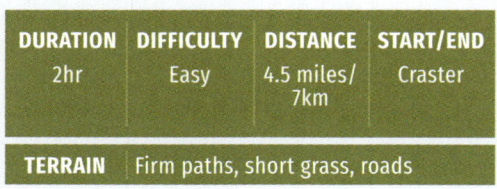

DURATION	DIFFICULTY	DISTANCE	START/END
2hr	Easy	4.5 miles/ 7km	Craster

TERRAIN	Firm paths, short grass, roads

Salty little Craster, famous for its kippers, is the starting point for one of northern England's finest coastal walks, following a sward of close-cropped turf northwards to the dramatic ruined towers of Dunstanburgh Castle and the golden sweep of Embleton Bay. It's an ideal hike to take young children on – easy going, no big hills, and a sandy beach to play on.

Getting Here

Craster is 40 miles (a one-hour drive) north of Newcastle-upon-Tyne, and 31 miles (45 minutes' drive) south of Berwick-upon-Tweed. Bus X18 runs to Craster from Berwick-upon-Tweed (1½ hours, three daily) and from Newcastle (2½ hours, three daily). From Monday to Saturday, bus 418 also links Craster to Alnwick (30 minutes, four daily).

Starting Point

Craster is a small fishing village on the Northumberland coast. The main car park is behind the tourist information office (£4 per car all day) – do not try to park in the village centre. There are toilets here (but none at Dunstanburgh Castle), and there's a pub, a tea room and a restaurant in the village.

01 From the tourist information office walk along the road to the harbour and turn left along Dunstanburgh Rd to its end. Pass through through two wooden gates and follow the grassy path along the coast.

02 After passing through another two gates, note the little bay on your right, which was once used as the harbour for Dunstanburgh Castle. At low tide you might be able to spot some rusting iron framework with scraps of timber still attached –

Craster Kippers

Craster, along with Seahouses further up the coast, is famous for its kippers (smoked herring) – in fact, the village is said to have invented the kipper. In the early 20th century, when the British herring fishery was at its height, around 25,000 herring were smoked here daily. Today only one traditional smokery remains in the village. Four generations of the same family have operated **Robson & Sons** (01665-576223; kipper.co.uk; Haven Hill; kippers per pair from £11.50; 9am-4.30pm Mon-Fri, 9am-3.30pm Sat, 11am-3.30pm Sun) for more than 120 years, smoking around 7000 fish a day over oak sawdust; loyal customers include the Royal Family.

the wreckage of a Polish trawler that ran aground here in the 1960s. The path kinks to the left and rises up across a grassy field towards the castle.

03 **Dunstanburgh Castle** (pictured) was once one of the largest and most impressive fortresses in northern England, but fell into ruin by 1550. Follow the path along the inland side of the fortifications, and continue between the sea and a golf course.

04 At the southeastern end of **Embleton Bay** the coastal rocks give way to a magnificent sweep of golden sand.

Walk along the beach for 400m then turn left on a path through the dunes beside two concrete blocks, and continue along the road ahead.

05 At the first houses, turn left through a farmyard (signposted Public Bridleway), and continue for a mile to Dunstan Square farm, with views of the castle to your left.

06 At Dunstan Square turn left through a gate (signposted Craster), and follow the path through the gap in the ridge, then turn right before another gate and follow the grassy path back to Craster.

Take a Break

The **Jolly Fisherman** (016650-576461; thejollyfishermancraster.co.uk; Haven Hill; mains lunch £8-19, dinner £18-30; kitchen 11am-3pm & 5-8.30pm Mon-Sat, noon-5pm Sun, bar 11am-11pm Mon-Sat, to 11pm Sun) is a gastropub with a beer garden at the back, which enjoys a view across the harbour to the distant towers of Dunstanburgh Castle. Crab (in soup, sandwiches, fish platters and more) is the speciality of the menu, but it also has a variety of fish dishes, as well as a house burger and steaks served with beef-dripping chips. A strong wine list complements its wonderful real ales.

33

Hadrian's Wall

Best for

ANCIENT HISTORY

DURATION	DIFFICULTY	DISTANCE	START/END
4hr	Moderate	7.5 miles/ 12km	Sill visitor centre

TERRAIN	Roads, stony paths, steep steps

Hadrian's Wall is the most dramatic and extensive legacy of the Roman occupation of Britain, stretching for more than 70 miles across northern England. This walk follows part of the famous Pennine Way along the most scenic stretch of the wall, as well as visiting the two best-preserved Roman forts in the country (the time given is for walking; allow at least two hours extra for exploring at Housesteads and Vindolanda).

Getting Here

The Sill visitor centre is 35 miles (a 50-minute drive) west of Newcastle-upon-Tyne, and 25 miles (a 40-minute drive) northeast of Carlisle. The AD122 Hadrian's Wall bus (hourly Easter to September) is a hail-and-ride service that runs between Hexham and Haltwhistle, calling at the Sill and other Hadrian's Wall sites.

Starting Point

The **Sill National Landscape Discovery Centre** (01434-341200; thesill.org.uk; Military Rd, Once Brewed; 9.30am-6pm Apr-early Nov) was built in 2017 as a state-of-the-art visitor centre, with grasses and wildflowers growing on the roof to help it blend in with the landscape. It has a permanent exhibition on the landscape, culture and history of Northumberland alongside various temporary exhibitions. The car park charges £5 for all-day parking.

01 Head across the main B6318 road (be careful of traffic) and go north along the roadside path leading towards Steel Rigg viewpoint (signpost pictured), steadily gaining height as you climb towards the rocky ridge of the Great Whin Sill.

02 Turn right through a wooden kissing gate at the far side of Peel Cottage (signposted Public Footpath to Hadrian's Wall). Bear left across the field to another gate in a stone wall and join a larger footpath on the other side. You are now on part of the **Pennine Way** national trail (note the acorn symbol waymarks). The path descends into a dip with rocky outcrops to the left, and then climbs steeply up stone steps to the crest of the ridge.

03 Looking back to the west, the pointed hill is **Winshield Crags** (345m), the highest point of the Great Whin Sill. The sill is one of northern England's most significant geological features, a layer of black dolerite (hard, erosion-resistant igneous rock) that stretches from Holy Island and Dunstanburgh Castle on the Northumberland coast to the western flank of the Pennines and the northern fringes of the Yorkshire Dales. Wherever it outcrops it creates prominent crags and ridges, including those at High Cup Nick, and much of Hadrian's Wall was built along its top. The path continues to the east along a well-preserved section of Roman wall, with broad views south across the valley of the River South Tyne to the high moors of the northern Pennines.

04 After another dip with a kissing gate, the wall on your left now little more than a low, turf-covered mound, you reach **Castle Nick**, a hollow in the ridge housing the stone outline of Milecastle 39. Every Roman mile (0.95 modern miles) along Hadrian's Wall there was a gateway guarded by a small fort (called a milecastle), and between each milecastle were two observation turrets (these are less well preserved and not usually visible).

05 A steep descent leads into **Sycamore Gap**, a hollow in the ridge that was previously the dramatic site

The Roman Wall

Named in honour of the emperor who ordered it to be built, Hadrian's Wall was one of Rome's greatest engineering projects. The 73-mile-long wall was built between 122 and 128 CE to protect against attacks from the Pictish tribes to the north. Today, the awe-inspiring sections that remain are testament to Roman ambition and tenacity. When completed, the mammoth structure ran across northern Britain's narrow neck from the Solway Firth in the west almost to the mouth of the Tyne in the east. A series of forts was built some distance south (and may predate the wall), and 16 lie astride it, including the impressive sites of Housesteads and Vindolanda.

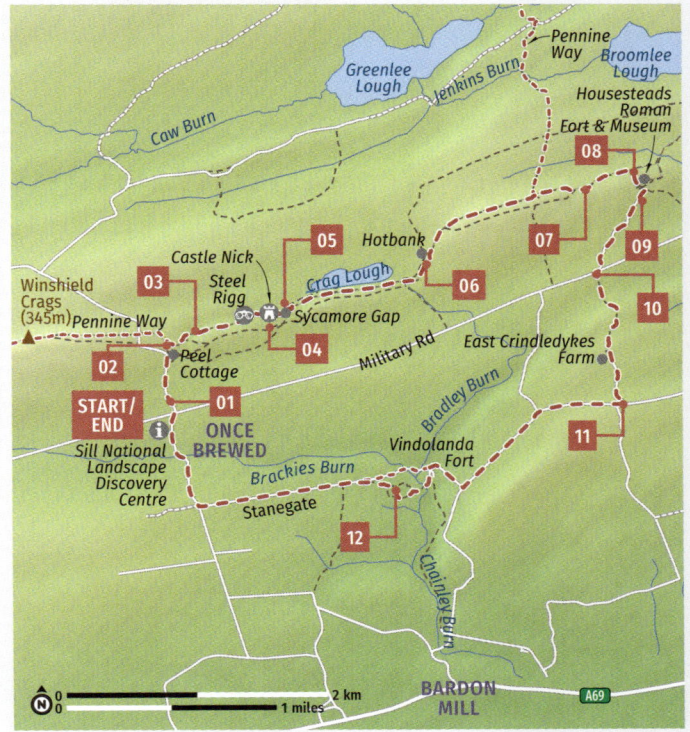

BEST DAY WALKS: ENGLAND

of a famous sycamore tree, before it was illegally felled in September 2023. The path now crosses the line of the wall and climbs gradually onto the crest of Highshields Crags, crossing a drystone dyke via a ladder stile (keep dogs and children close by here, as there is a vertical drop to the left); you may see rock climbers here. The little lake of Crag Lough lies at the foot of the cliffs as the path enters a picturesque stretch where it is lined with Scots pine trees. Another ladder stile over a wall marks the end of the woodland.

06 After crossing a farm road, easy going on a grassy path leads to a section of trail paved with stone slabs curving away from Hotbank farmhouse and back again, marking the site of **Milecastle 38**. Pass through a kissing gate and climb up past woods on the left. A section of rebuilt drystone wall runs along the crest of the ridge, with Greenlee and Broomlee loughs off to the left. At the next dip, the Pennine Way diverges to the north across a ladder stile on the left. Your route keeps straight on, through the small gate just ahead.

07 Another rise leads lead to **Milecastle 37** (pictured), which contains some well-preserved structures. You can see the remains of an arched gateway in the main wall, and the remains of barracks or storerooms in the eastern part (each milecastle was garrisoned by 20 to 30 Roman soldiers). Beyond the milecastle a gate leads into an area of woodland. At the far end of the woods go through a gate in the wall on your right into a grassy field. The stone structure ahead is Housesteads Roman Fort.

08 The most dramatic site on Hadrian's Wall – and the best-preserved Roman fort in the whole country – is at **Housesteads** (EH; 01434-344363; english-heritage.org.uk; Haydon Bridge; adult/child £11.50/6.50; 10am-6pm Apr-Sep, to 5pm Oct, to 4pm Nov-Mar). Set high on a ridge and covering 2 hectares – up to 800 troops were based at Housesteads at any one time – the fort commands the moors of Northumberland National Park to the north. Its remains include an impressive hospital, granaries with a carefully worked out ventilation system, and barrack blocks. There's a scale model of the entire fort in the small museum at the far side of the field.

09 Descend past the museum and turn right along the tarred access road that leads southwest from the old farmhouse next to the museum (don't take the gravel path that leads to the museum car park, where most visitors will be heading).

10 When you reach the main B6138 road, turn right for only 20m and cross the ladder stile beside the gate (signposted Public Bridleway). Follow the grassy path across the field then slant left up the hillside to a

Hadrian's Wall Path

The **Hadrian's Wall Path** (nationaltrail.co.uk/hadrians-wall-path) is an 84-mile national trail that runs the length of the wall from Wallsend in the east to Bowness-on-Solway in the west. The entire route should take about seven days on foot, giving plenty of time to explore the rich archaeological heritage along the way. Preserved remains of forts and garrisons and intriguing museums punctuate the route, along with sections of the wall you can freely access. Another coast-to-coast option is **Hadrian's Cycleway** (hadrian-guide.co.uk), a 174-mile route between South Shields or Tynemouth and Ravenglass in Cumbria along the general line of Hadrian's Wall.

marker post. Bear right across a muddy dip and rise past two more marker posts, and pass to the left of East Crindledykes Farm via a pair of gates. Continue along the farm access road to reach a minor road.

11 Turn right and follow this road for a mile past two junctions, one to the left, and then one to the right. Turn right at the next junction (signposted Roman Vindolanda), and follow the road downhill past the car park to reach the site of Vindolanda Roman Fort. Turn left at the museum if you plan to visit the site; otherwise keep straight on along the minor road, passing an original Roman milestone (on the right, just after crossing the stream).

12 The extensive site of **Vindolanda** (01434-344277; vindolanda.com; Bardon Mill; adult/child £12.50/6, with Roman Army Museum £16/9; 10am-6pm Apr-Sep, to 5pm early Feb-Mar & Oct, to 4pm Nov-early Feb) offers a fascinating glimpse into the daily life of a Roman garrison town. The time-capsule museum is just one part of this large, extensively excavated site, which includes impressive parts of the fort and town (excavations continue) and reconstructed turrets and temple. Exit the site via the turnstile at the western end (or reach this point via the minor road) and continue west on the country lane for 0.75 miles. At a T-junction, turn right – another 0.5 miles leads back to your starting point.

 **Take a Break**

Just west of The Sill is the **Twice Brewed Inn** (01434-344534; twicebrewedinn.co.uk; Military Rd, Once Brewed; 10am-11pm;), the ideal spot for a post-walk pint. Beer was first made on this site over half a millennium ago. Today, the pub's own brews include Ceres (wheat beer), Sycamore Gap (pale ale) and the brilliantly named Ale Caesar (American amber ale). There's a large beer garden with live music in summer, a roaring open fire in winter, and hearty food made with local Northumberland produce.

BEST DAY WALKS: ENGLAND

34

Malham Landscape Trail

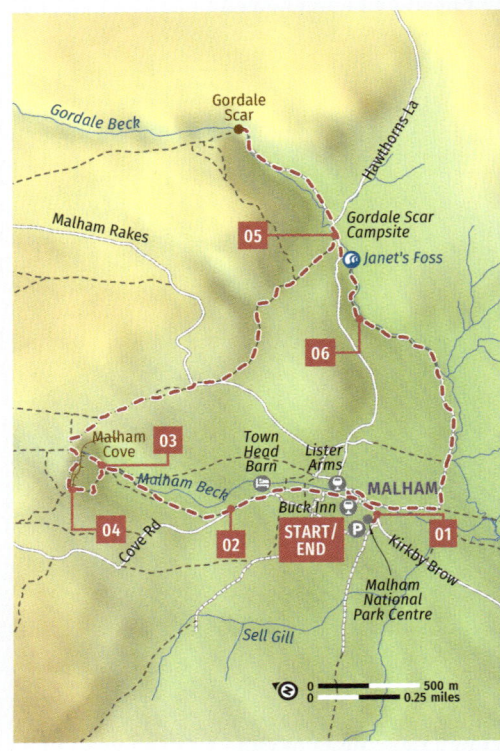

DURATION	DIFFICULTY	DISTANCE	START/END
2-3hr	Moderate	4.5miles/ 7 km	Malham

TERRAIN	Roads, rough paths, steep steps

Even in the Yorkshire Dales, where competition is fierce, Malham stands out as a strikingly attractive village. It sits within the largest area of limestone country in Britain, stretching west from Grassington to Ingleton – a distinctive landscape pockmarked with potholes, dry valleys, limestone pavements and gorges. This walk takes in two of the most spectacular features – Malham Cove and Gordale Scar.

Getting Here

Malham is 38 miles northwest of Leeds, and 52 miles north of Manchester. There are at least two buses a day Monday to Saturday year-round from Skipton to Malham (35 minutes). The scenic Malham Tarn Shuttle bus route links Settle with Malham (30 minutes), Malham Tarn and Ingleton six times daily on Sundays and bank holidays only, Easter to October. Check the DalesBus website (dalesbus.org).

Starting Point

The car park at Malham National Park Centre (£4.50 per car all day) has an information centre and public toilets. Note that Malham is reached via narrow roads that can get very congested in summer, especially at weekends.

01 Turn left out of the car park and follow the road through Malham village, keeping left at the fork in front of the Buck Inn.

02 About 150m after passing Town Head Barn, go through the double gate on the right (signposted Pennine Way) and continue on the well-made hardpacked path through rolling pastures (there may be sheep and cattle grazing here). Pass

138 BEST DAY WALKS: ENGLAND

Malham Cove

Malham Cove (pictured) is a huge rock amphitheatre lined with 80m-high vertical cliffs, a playground for local rock climbers. A large glacial waterfall once tumbled over this cliff, but it dried up thousands of years ago. You can hike up the steep steps on the left-hand side of the cove (follow Pennine Way signs) to see the limestone pavement above the cliffs – a filming location in *Harry Potter and the Deathly Hallows*.

Peregrine falcons nest on the cliffs in spring, when the Royal Society for the Protection of Birds (RSPB) sets up a birdwatching lookout with telescopes near the base of the cliff – consult the national park centre for the schedule as it changes every year.

Best for

A POST-HIKE PINT

through two more gates to reach a fork in the path.

03 Take the right fork to visit the base of **Malham Cove**, where the waters of Malham Beck reappear after their underground journey from Malham Tarn up above (the trail as far as the bottom of Malham Cove is accessible for all-terrain wheelchairs). Retrace your steps and bear right to reach the foot of a long flight of stone stairs that lead to the top of the Cove.

04 At the top of the stairs go through the gate and turn right to wander across the rugged limestone pavement and soak up the view. At the far side of the pavement, go through the gate in the stone wall and bear right uphill. Follow this path for just over a mile, crossing a road halfway, to emerge onto another road at a layby (there may be a snack bar here in summer).

05 At the road turn left, then left again along a level path that leads into the spectacular gorge of **Gordale Scar**. Return to the road and turn right, past the layby. Just as the road begins to climb uphill, go left through a gate (National Trust signpost) and along a wooded path to the pretty waterfall of **Janet's Foss**.

06 From Janet's Foss, follow the waymarked path along the river, across two stiles and through fields back to Malham village.

 Take a Break

The **Lister Arms** (01729-830444; thwaites.co.uk; Cove Rd; mains £15-26; 8am-11pm Mon-Sat, to 10.30pm Sun;) is the best spot in Malham to kick back after a walk, with open fires for chilly days, a beer garden out back and classic pub meals plus chalkboard specials. In the busy summer months drinkers lounge out on the grass in front of the pub.

BEST DAY WALKS: ENGLAND 139

35

Robin Hood's Bay

DURATION	DIFFICULTY	DISTANCE	START/END
4-5hr	Moderate	9 miles/ 14.5km	Hawsker

TERRAIN	Grass, gravel paths, can be muddy

The North Yorkshire coast is famous for its dramatic scenery and picturesque fishing harbours, and this walk makes the most of both, following part of the Cleveland Way national trail along the fossil-rich seacliffs south of Whitby to visit the storybook village of Robin Hood's Bay.

Getting Here

Hawsker is a small village on the A171 road, 3 miles southeast of Whitby. It's 75 miles southeast of Newcastle-upon-Tyne, and 51 miles northeast of York. Bus 93 runs hourly between Whitby and Scarborough via Hawsker and Robin Hood's Bay.

Starting Point

There is a car park (free) beside the village hall at the north end of Hawsker village. There are no facilities here, but there are toilets and cafes at Robin Hood's Bay. From Hawsker village hall, head along the B1447, turn left at the bus stop (signpost for Swan Farm), and follow the track across the old railway line towards the coast.

01 At the entrance to Gnipe Howe farm, go through a gate on the right and aim for the corner of an old stone wall. Head downhill with the wall on your left and cross a stile to reach the **Cleveland Way** coastal path. Turn right.

02 Beneath the caravans of Northcliffe holiday park, the seacliffs of **Maw Wyke** are home to nesting seabirds in late spring and summer, notably a colony of kittiwakes – delicate-looking seagulls with black wingtips and a distinctive call that echoes their name.

03 As the path rounds Clock Case Nab there is a grand view back along the cliffs of

Robin Hood's Bay

Picturesque Robin Hood's Bay (pictured) has nothing to do with the hero of Sherwood Forest – the origin of its name is a mystery, and the locals call it Bay Town. But there's no denying that this fishing village is one of the prettiest spots on the Yorkshire coast. Its maze of narrow lanes and passages is dotted with tearooms, pubs, craft shops and artists' studios (there's even a tiny cinema), and at low tide you can go down onto the beach and fossick around in the rock pools. The **National Trust visitor centre** (nationaltrust.org.uk; The Dock; 10am-5pm Apr-Oct, to 4pm Sat & Sun Nov-Mar;) houses an exhibition about local geology and natural history, with pamphlets on local walks.

Best for
COASTAL SCENERY

Far Jetticks. These layered rocks are part of Yorkshire's famous Jurassic Coast, which has yielded many of Britain's most important dinosaur fossils.

04 A tall wooden post to the right of the path marks the National Trust's **'Rocket Post Field'**. This is a replica of the original post used to practise rescuing shipwrecked sailors from the sea below the cliffs – a line was fired by rocket to the stranded ship, and the survivors winched ashore (an information board provides details). There is a fantastic view across the bay from the bench opposite the Rocket Post.

05 As you pass through a gate into the village of **Robin Hood's Bay**, note the signpost marked 'Cinder Track' – this indicates the start of your return route. Meanwhile, go straight ahead and turn left at the main street, then steeply downhill to explore the village.

06 The old coastguard station above the shoreline marks the end point of the famous Coast to Coast Walk. Retrace your steps uphill to the Cinder Track sign, and follow this track (an old railway line) for 4 miles back to Hawsker.

Take a Break

It's debatable who wins the contest for most atmospheric pub; the Laurel Inn is a snug spot, while the Bay Hotel is the only pub with sea views.

The delightfully named **Tea, Toast and Post** (facebook.com/TeaToastandPost) mixes the quirky with the traditional right down on the shore, and the **Galley on the Quarterdeck** (galleyinthebay.co.uk), behind the Old Coastguard Station, is the perfect place to take in the bay on sunny days, with its outdoor seating and freshly made doughnuts.

36
Rievaulx

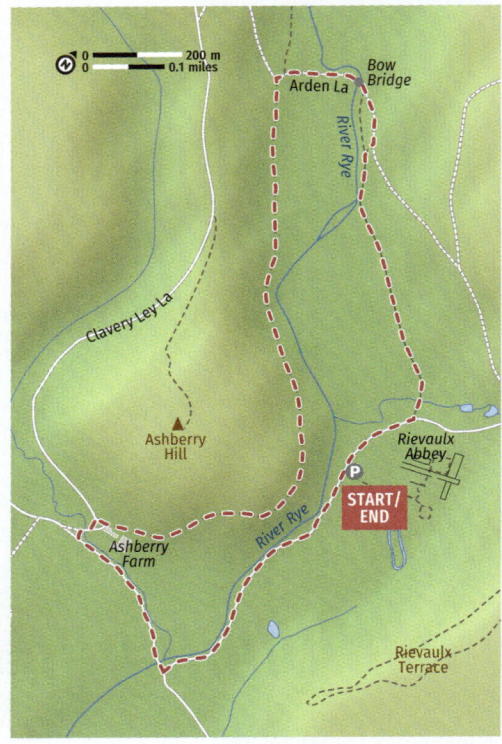

DURATION	DIFFICULTY	DISTANCE	START/END
1-2hr	Easy	2.5 miles/ 4km	Rievaulx Abbey

TERRAIN	Grassy paths, some uphill, muddy

In the secluded valley of the River Rye stand the magnificent ruins of Rievaulx Abbey. This idyllic spot was chosen by Cistercian monks in 1132 as a base for their missionary activity in northern Britain. St Aelred, the third abbot, famously described the abbey's setting as 'everywhere peace, everywhere serenity, and a marvellous freedom from the tumult of the world' – an atmosphere well captured by this woodland and riverside walk.

Head north from the abbey entrance (car parking £5) and turn left through a wooden gate beside a stable (signposted Bow Bridge). Cross a small stream, pass through another gate and follow the path alongside the hedge. The ditch to the right was originally a channel cut by the monks to supply water to the abbey. Follow the path for 800m along the banks of the River Rye.

Go through a gate at a marker post and turn left along a country lane. Cross the 18th-century stone arch of Bow Bridge and follow the lane ahead for 120m before turning left through a wooden gate (signposted Ashberry). Bear right through another gate, and as the path climbs steadily through the woods there are glimpses through the trees of the abbey and the mock temples of Rievaulx Terrace on the hillside above.

The path emerges from the woods at Ashberry Farm. Turn left, cross the red brick bridge and go left along the road. After 300m you cross a bridge over the River Rye – turn left to return to your starting point. The romantic ruins of the **abbey** (pictured; EH; english-heritage.org.uk; adult/child £12.50/7.50; 10am-6pm Apr-Sep, to 5pm Oct, to 4pm Sat & Sun Nov–mid-Feb, daily Mar; P) are well worth a visit before or after your walk.

37

Berwick-upon-Tweed

DURATION	DIFFICULTY	DISTANCE	START/END
3-3½hr	Moderate	7.3 miles/ 11.7km	Berwick train station
TERRAIN	Tarmac and hard track		

Sitting right on the border between England and Scotland, the tiny seaside town of Berwick-upon-Tweed hasn't had the most peaceful of pasts. It's changed hands between these countries 13 times over the years and its colourful history is woven into every hidden nook of today's town. Arriving by train from the south is a real treat, with magnificent views of the town as you cross the Royal Border Bridge, with the Royal Tweed Bridge and 17th-century Berwick Bridge far below. With all this history it's easy to forget that Berwick also has beautiful sandy beaches and artistic royalty in its veins.

Getting Here

Berwick train station has regular services from north and south and a full range of facilities. It also has a good-sized pay-and-display car park.

01 From the station entrance turn hard left, up steps to the road and cross the bridge over the railway. Turn left to follow a signed route down to 'Public Park and Riverside'. At the bottom, turn left along the riverside path and continue on towards the high road bridge. Just prior to the bridge take the steps leading up towards 'Golden Square'. At the top cross the road and turn right over the bridge.

Take the time to admire the elegant arches of the **Royal Border Bridge** (pictured). It was designed by Robert Stephenson and opened by Queen Victoria in 1850 and was, at that time, one of the largest bridges in the world. Although its construction was

➡️ LS Lowry Connection

The artist LS Lowry is well known for his images of industrial scenes in northern England, but he also has a deep connection with Berwick-upon-Tweed. He first visited the town on holiday in the 1930s and continued to return up to his death in 1976. He loved the clear sea air and the varied architecture of the town, and he produced a range of images, quite different to the images he is most often associated with. There are a number of information boards plus a Lowry Trail around the town dedicated to his work and our walk visits several of them.

a remarkable feat of engineering, it did result in a lot of damage to the remains of the castle.

02 Take the enclosed path on the left just before the small park and continue over the next road and into Yard Heads; follow this to a small road. Turn right here to the main road, then immediately left then right to reach **Brewery Lane**. Follow this lane, continuing in the same direction passing a church. Just beyond here keep right to follow a path up to a road.

The name 'Berwick' derives from 'Barley Farm' so it's no surprise that a brewery played a vital role in the growth of the town. At one point it produced 400 barrels per week but, as with many old breweries, it went through several changes of ownership before finally closing in the 1950s.

03 Turn left, then right up steps to a path through woodland. When you reach a path junction, turn right and continue up to a road. Turn left to follow the road down and around in front of the campsite. Where the road bears sharp left, turn right, up steps into Spittal Banks and remain on this path until it passes under a railway arch. Immediately after the arch turn hard left along a grassy path then continue in the same direction along a quiet road that turns into a farm track. Remain on this to Seaview Farm then follow it left, down and under the railway, and continue on down to the **Spittal promenade**.

04 Turn left to follow the prom back towards Berwick and follow the path around the headland dunes until it rejoins the road. Continue on towards **Berwick Old Bridge**, then turn right to cross it. This beautiful old bridge was built in the 17th century on the orders of King James VI of Scotland

BEST DAY WALKS: ENGLAND

who saw it as uniting his two kingdoms. Look closely and you'll notice that the sixth pillar out from Berwick is larger than the others: this is because it originally formed the border between Berwick and North Durham (now Northumberland). Turn right onto the Quay Walls (the higher of the two paths) and remain on the town walls until you pass the cannon. Fork left here down onto the road, then turn right, under the walls, and continue along the coastal path to the jetty.

05 Take the waymarked route along the road to the left and continue on to the **golf course**, sticking to the clifftop path around the edge of the course. When you reach a hard track turn left towards the town, passing under the wall, then right, through a gate and back up onto the wall path leading left. After the wall crosses the road drop down left and double back to reach the road.

06 Turn left through the arch, then left again into **Castle Vale Park**. Turn right at the end and emerge onto Tweed St. Turn left before the cream building to follow Castle Parks Trail, then follow the signed route through the park and back to the station. At the top of the path pause and say hello to **'Bari' the Berwick Bear**, created in 2017 as part of the Sculpture Trails project.

Iconic Town Walls

The Elizabethan Town Walls (pictured) were completed in the 1550s at a cost of £126,000 – equivalent to over £56 million today. They were built to protect the town from Scottish invaders, with gates that would have controlled access. The gun emplacements meant every part of the wall was covered, and water-filled ditches beyond the walls offered further protection. Today they are the only example of bastioned town walls in the UK, and one of the best surviving examples in Europe. There are also remains of an earlier set of walls, built by Edward I, whose existence is another indicator of Berwick's turbulent past.

Take a Break

The **Corner House** (facebook.com/thecornerhouseberwick) in Church St offers a good selection of well-priced scones, soups and sandwiches and **Lowry's at the Chandlery** (facebook.com/Lowrysatthechandlery) has sandwiches, hot meals (including plenty of seafood and vegetarian options) and cakes, right on the quayside. There's also a cafe on the promenade at Spittal that offers basic refreshments. Both along the prom and around the town walls you'll find a good choice of benches if you prefer to eat outdoors, but be sure to tuck yourself out of the wind.

38

Blyth to Tynemouth

DURATION	DIFFICULTY	DISTANCE	START/END
4-5hr	Hard	10.2 miles/ 16.5km	Blyth/ Tynemouth

TERRAIN	Tarmac, hard track, dunes, farmland

The coastline along this stretch of Northumberland takes most people by surprise with its long sandy beaches and tiny, tucked-away coves. This route is well served by public transport with plenty of buses to the start point and options along the way to shorten the walk by hopping back on a bus if needed. The metro station at Tynemouth dates to 1882 and has cafes and local stalls to enjoy as you await your train back to Newcastle. The route is easy to follow and could be summarised as 'keep the sea on your left until you reach the monument'.

Getting Here

Blyth has ample parking, including a large car park on the quayside. The X10 and X11 buses run from Newcastle. At the end catch the Metro to Newcastle and bus back to the start.

01 This route passes many large bays where, tides permitting, you could walk along the beaches, which run parallel to the stages described here. With your back to the bus station head left along Bridge St, then over the roundabout to the quayside. Turn right to follow the England Coast Path. At the RNLI (Royal National Lifeboat Institution) station the path joins the road. Continue on to reach **Ridley Park** then turn left to enter the park, continuing south until you emerge back onto the road. Turn left to follow the road past the docks until you reach Beachway. Blyth is still a working port so watch for ships coming and going along the bay. When viewed from the correct angle, the seemingly abstract statue along the quay forms the shape of a train pulling a coal truck.

St Mary's Lighthouse

It's worth a detour to visit this local landmark, which has served as a lighthouse since medieval times. Back then it was known as Bate's Island and had a small chapel dedicated to St Helen, which burned a light in the window to warn ships away from the rocks. The lighthouse we see today was built using 645 stone blocks and 750,000 bricks. It first lit its beacon in August 1898 and was converted to electricity in 1977. It was decommissioned in 1984 and converted into a museum and visitor centre. In 2024 it underwent a major renovation to preserve and protect it.

Best for COASTAL SCENERY

02 Take the short road to the beach then turn right to follow the coastal path again. When you reach the gun emplacements turn right then left to remain on the England Coast Path and follow this down to **Seaton Sluice**. The pretty watch house here has a fascinating history and forms part of the origins of today's RNLI. The vast number of shipwrecks along this coast in the 18th century prompted the formation of the Volunteer Life Saving Company. This watch house was opened on 14 January 1880 and was involved in two major rescues just a few months later.

03 When the path joins the road follow it to cross a bridge, then turn left along Collywell Bay Rd. Remain on this road through the village until you reach a broad, hard track, leading off left at right angles to the road. Continue along this path, passing a campsite. It is here where you have the option to detour left to visit **St Mary's Lighthouse** (pictured). If you wish to do so, follow the signed route there and back (note: check tide times before crossing to the lighthouse).

04 Once back on the main track, follow it to emerge at a car park. Cross the road to follow the path along the cliff tops of Whitley Bay. The **Spanish City** is a large white building with a complex and intriguing history, involving a troupe known as the North East Toreadors (hence the name), who used to perform here in tents with brightly painted scenery. The building first opened in 1908 and grew into a popular theme park. After an eventful past, including time as a military base, a ballroom and a bingo hall, it fell into disrepair before undergoing renovations and reopening in 2018 to offer everything from fish and chips to champagne. At the Spanish City remain on the prom and follow the footpath up and around the headland to the next bay.

05 Look for the sign on the left leading away from the road and around a small promontory to reach **Cullercoats Beach** (pictured). Keep going around this bay to Long Sands Beach and finally around to King Edwards Bay and the **Tynemouth Priory**.

06 To reach the Collingwood Monument continue past the priory and down towards the car park. Take the gravel track between to two tarmac lanes and follow it up. The **Collingwood Monument** offers bird's-eye views of the estuary, especially for those brave enough to climb all the steps. It is dedicated to Vice Admiral Lord Cuthbert Collingwood, born in nearby Newcastle, who was second in command to Admiral Lord Nelson during the Battle of Trafalgar. The monument opened in 1845 (apart from the cannons, which were added a few years later) and was positioned so that it could be seen from the Tyne. When you're ready to return, retrace your steps back to the priory, then turn left along Front St, over to Huntingdon Pl, then continue as it sweeps left and around to the station.

Priory & Castle

Three kings are buried in Tynemouth Priory: Oswin, Osred II and Malcolm III of Scotland. This led to it becoming a place of pilgrimage and three crowns being included in the Tynemouth coat of arms. The prominent headland has seen fortifications since Roman times, and the priory was founded in the 7th century. It remained active until it was dissolved by Henry VIII in January 1539. The nearby castle was built in the 14th century and saw action in the English Civil War, before a lighthouse was added, which was used until 1898 when St Mary's Lighthouse was completed.

Take a Break

You are never going to be short of somewhere to pause and take a break on this walk. In Blyth, **14 Stanley Street** (14stanleystreet.co.uk) is a great place to stock your rucksack with local food for a picnic. Along the route there are a plethora of cafes to choose from, but **Rendezvous** in Whitley Bay is a perennial favourite (and has popped up in a few episodes of TV show *Vera*). There are also plenty of benches along the route to rest and enjoy your lunch.

BEST DAY WALKS: ENGLAND

39
York

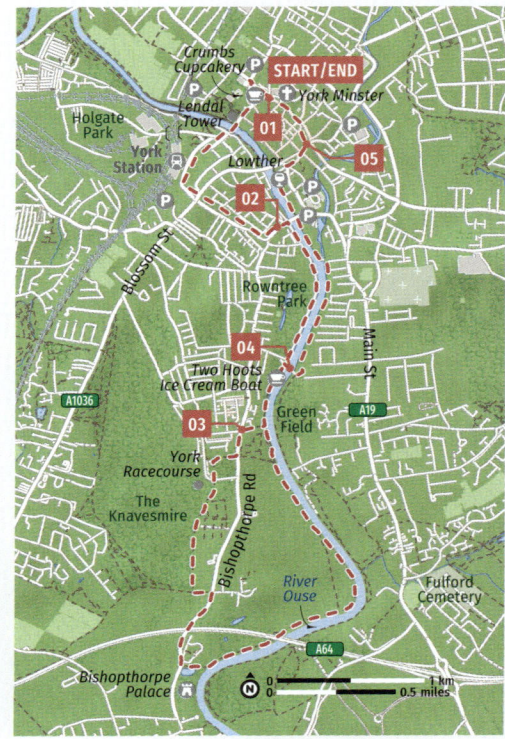

DURATION	DIFFICULTY	DISTANCE	START/END
3-3½hr	Moderate	7 miles/ 11.3km	York Minster

TERRAIN	Tarmac, hard track, dunes, farmland

No matter which era of history fascinates you the most, York will have something for you, from Roman ruins to Viking museums and from the elegant towers of the Minster to cobbled Tudor lanes. The city is at the heart of the northeastern rail network and, if you arrive by train, the history lesson begins when you step onto the platform with the Zero Mile Post and the spacious 19th-century architecture of the station building. When you emerge from the building the city walls opposite await, ready to transport you back into the past of this distinguished city.

Getting Here

The main entrance to York Minster is a 10-minute walk from the station. City parking is busy and pricey but there are a range of park-and-ride schemes available (itravelyork.info/park-and-ride).

01 In Precentor's Court, with the main entrance behind you, follow the street leading directly away from the Minster (High Petergate). Continue on through an arch and turn left to walk alongside the walls. Keep going until you reach a large road junction and turn right along Museum St, continuing on until you reach the library archive and **Lendal Tower**. Built around 1300, the tower would have originally been a circular building, but it has had extra walls added to give it additional support over the years. An iron chain would have stretched across the river from here to North Street Postern Tower on the opposite bank. This would have been used to control river traffic and ensure all tolls were paid. From the 17th century right through to the early 20th century its functions were connected to water pumping and distribution, and it was enlarged

York Racecourse

This is one of the oldest racecourses in the world and it's thought that the Romans raced horses in this area 2000 years ago. It was originally known as Knavesmire and was simply a large, flat, albeit somewhat boggy area that became popular for racing horses (when it wasn't being used for public hangings). After a lot of draining and levelling work the first official race was held here in 1731. In December 1753 the York Corporation authorised a grandstand to be built on the site. It opened in 1754 and was one of the first modern grandstands in the world.

and strengthened several times during this period. It's now private holiday accommodation. From here, cross over the river then turn immediately right onto the City Wall path.

02 Remain on the city walls all the way around to Baile Hill. Exit here and cross the road parallel to the wall (do not cross the river). Take the slip road on the far side (Tanners Moat) leading down to the river, then turn right to follow the riverside road and path. Keep following the river, past **Millennium Bridge**, until the tarmac path swings sharp right up an alley.

The **city walls** (pictured) offer you the chance to view the city from every angle, and it's worth completing a full lap if you have the time. From this section, there are excellent views of the railway station. The one we see today was built in the 1870s, but there has been a station on this site since 1841. Look for the plaque in the path that marks the site of the old signal box. The Zero Mile Post in the station would have been used as a starting point to calculate fares across the network.

03 Follow the path to the top of the alley then turn left along the road, before crossing over to reach the entrance to **York Racecourse**. Remain on the waymarked path as it leads into the racecourse and winds along the edge of the racetrack until you reach a trail junction. Turn left here and continue on to the road. Cross the road and turn right, over a road bridge, and head past the crematorium. Immediately after the Bishopthorpe sign, turn left along an enclosed track to the river. Remain on this path all the way back to Millennium Bridge.

The enclosed track runs alongside the gardens of **Bishopthorpe Palace**, which has been the residence for the

Archbishops of York since 1241. The village was originally known as St Andrewthorpe until Archbishop Walter de Grey bought the manor house and gave it to the church. It underwent various stages of remodelling and rebuilding until 1900, and has remained largely unaltered since then.

04 Cross the **Millennium Bridge** (pictured), then turn left towards the city. After a short distance cross a distinctive blue bridge on your left and continue on along the riverside until you reach the Lowther. Turn right and at the junction keep going straight over into Coppergate (signposted to The Shambles). Keep going in the same direction over two more junctions then, just past M&S, turn left along **The Shambles**. Just before you head up The Shambles, nip around the small church in front of you and you'll reach the delightfully named Whip-Ma-Whop-Ma-Gate. At just 24m long it is the shortest street in York and the name is thought to mean 'neither-one-thing-nor-the-other street'. During the busier months The Shambles can be very busy, with queues for some shops filling the narrow walkway.

05 At the top of The Shambles bear right, then left, through King's Square and along Low Petergate to reach York Minster again.

 York Minster

The first record of a church on this site is in 627 when it was called a 'minster' to denote that it was a place used for teaching. The stained-glass windows are immense and the 24m-high *Last Judgement* in the Great East Window is the UK's largest medieval stained-glass window. It is made of 311 panels that depict the story of the Bible from the Creation to the Last Judgement. The minster has seen five major fires in its lifetime, including one in 1984 when the south transept was destroyed following a lightning strike.

 Take a Break

The city is awash with wonderful independent places to eat and drink, including **Crumbs Cupcakery** (crumbs-cupcakery.co.uk), just behind the Minster, and the **Two Hoots Ice Cream Boat** (@twohoots icecream) – an ice-cream van welded to a tug boat! – near Millennium Bridge. The **Lowther** (thelowther.co.uk) is right on the river and offers a good range of filling dishes to round off a hike. If you've packed sandwiches, there are plenty of benches along the river and city walls where you can rest and refuel.

BEST DAY WALKS: ENGLAND 155

Also Try...

Holy Island

Remote, windswept Holy Island (also known as Lindisfarne) is one of the cradles of Christianity in Britain (St Aidan founded a monastery here in 635).

Walk a clockwise circuit of the island from the main car park, taking in the north coast's bird-haunted sand dunes (look for seals on the offshore rocks), the restored 16th-century castle perched picturesquely atop a prominent crag, and the red and grey ruins of the priory (pictured), where the illuminated manuscripts known as the Lindisfarne Gospels were created in the 8th century. The island is only accessible at low tide – pay close attention to crossing-time information, posted at tourist offices and on noticeboards throughout the area and at holy-island.info. If you're after something very different, then the Pilgrim's Way across the mudflats is a wonderful way to approach the island, but only if you are 100% certain of tide times.

DURATION 2hr
DIFFICULTY Easy
DISTANCE 4 miles/6.4km

Three Pubs Walk

The most picturesque pub crawl in England, this route heads north from Buckden in the heart of the Yorkshire Dales to Cray, where the White Lion makes a great lunch stop.

The route traverses high above the valley floor, with grand views down the length of Wharfedale, to Scar House (George Fox, founder of the Quakers, preached here in 1652 and there are still a number of temperance bars in the area). It then descends to the village of Hubberholme and the George Inn. The ashes of the writer JB Priestley, who loved the Yorkshire Dales, and Hubberholme in particular, are buried in the churchyard. Then it's back along the riverside to your starting point, where a pint awaits at the Buck Inn.

DURATION 3hr
DIFFICULTY Moderate
DISTANCE 5 miles/8km

Brimham Rocks

Set on a hilltop 14.5km northwest of Harrogate is the otherwordly landscape of Brimham Rocks (pictured), where the weather has carved the sandstone outcrops into weird and wonderful shapes, offering a fun-filled family outing.

The rocks are over 340 million years old and were laid down in the beds of fast-flowing rivers. The Ice Age and several millennia of wind and water erosion have created the intriguing shapes we see today. Easy paths meander through the rock formations – pick up a 'Spot the Rocks' leaflet at the information office and see if you can find the imaginatively named formations, or maybe name some new ones of your own!

DURATION 1hr
DIFFICULTY Easy
DISTANCE 1.5 miles/2.4km

Stanhope Burn

The valley of Weardale is spectacular and much underexplored. It forms part of the North Pennines Area of Outstanding Natural Beauty (AONB; north pennines.org.uk/visit-explore) and is a UNESCO Geopark.

There's a pretty steam railway running along the valley and numerous walks that take in the local geology, wildlife and history, with a great selection to choose from. This particular walk heads out along the river valley to Stanhope Mine – this now-tranquil area was once at the heart of the mining industry, and you'll pass lead mines and various quarries along the way. Watch for waterfalls too, and cross the river at the mine then head back along the higher path to take in beautiful views of the surrounding hills.

DURATION 2hr
DIFFICULTY Easy
DISTANCE 3.5 miles/5.6km

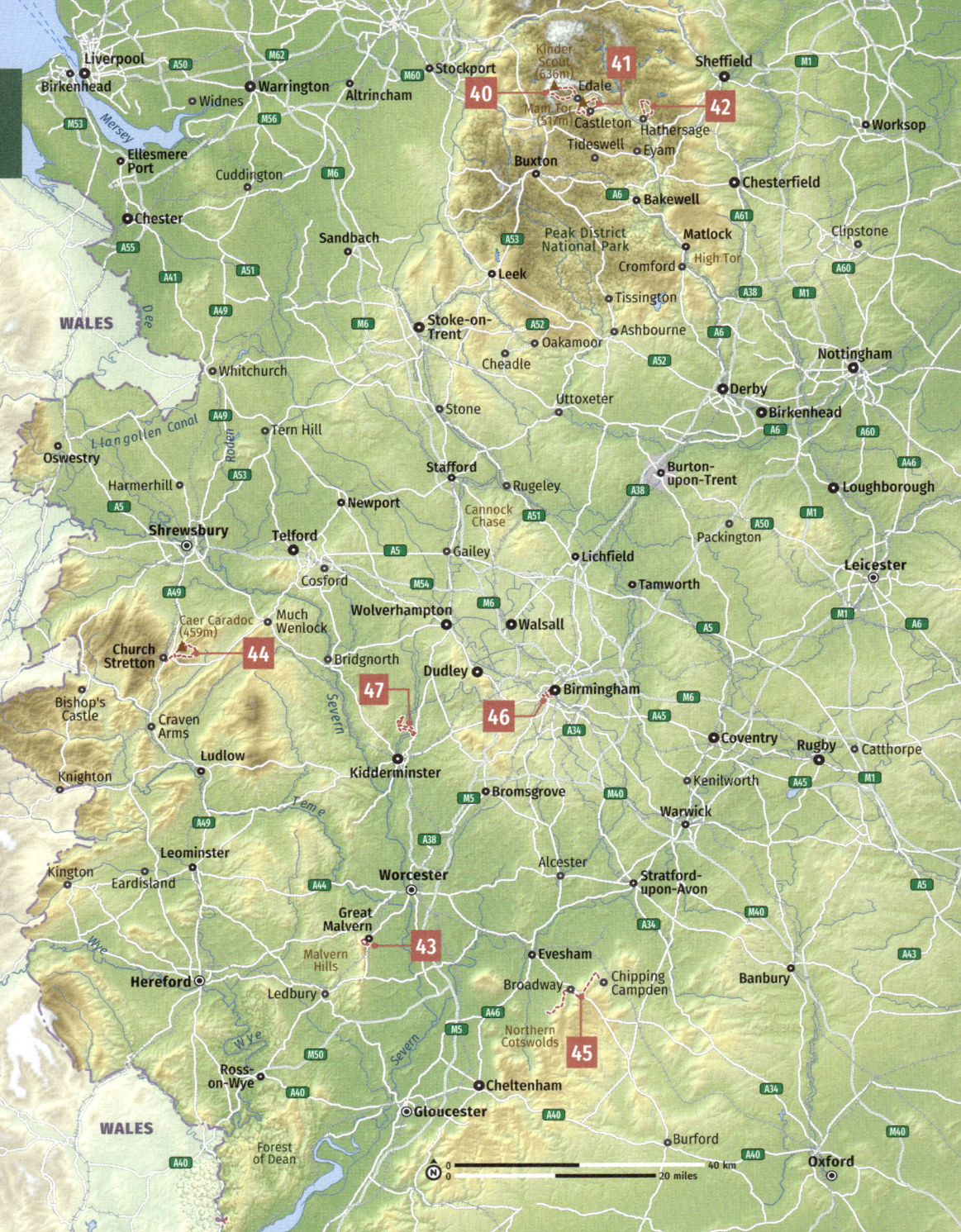

The Cotswold Way (p174), and St Michael and All Angels church (p175)

Central England

40 Kinder Scout
Take a hike up the gritstone slopes of this high plateau. **p162**

41 Mam Tor
This venerable 'mother hill' is topped by a Bronze Age fort. **p166**

42 Stanage Edge
A high escarpment with climbing opportunities as well as wild walking. **p168**

43 The Malvern Hills
Green hills with hidden springs and ancient rock formations. **p170**

44 Caer Caradoc
A fort-topped hill above the attractive market town of Church Stretton. **p172**

45 The Cotswold Way
Walk a section of this long-distance path, linking the prettiest villages imaginable. **p174**

46 Birmingham City & Canals
Explore the restored canal network that surrounds this freshly refurbished city. **p176**

47 Kinver Edge
Ancient rock dwellings, far-reaching views, canal-side paths and a perfect lunch. **p180**

BEST DAY WALKS: ENGLAND   159

Explore
Central England

The landlocked terrain of central England has plenty to explore, with the gentle Shropshire hills to the west, the groundbreaking Peak District to the north and, right at the heart of it all, Birmingham, a city with a new lease of life following the Commonwealth Games of 2022. Further south lie the Cotswold Hills, where walks lead from one picture-postcard village to the next and the layers of history pile up, one on top of another. This is the region that inspired everyone from JRR Tolkien to Ozzy Osbourne, so who knows what it holds in store for you?

Coventry

If cities are your thing, then take the time to visit Coventry with its two cathedrals, one ancient, one modern. If you're feeling brave you can climb the spire of the old cathedral for unique views across the city. Keep the cathedral theme going with a trip to Lichfield, just to the north of Coventry, where the soaring spires of the elegant cathedral define the city skyline.

Telford

For a more industrial diversion head over to Telford and nearby Ironbridge Gorge where you'll find the Iron Bridge, the first major bridge in the world made entirely from cast iron. It has no nuts and bolts, and every junction is joined using mortise and tenon woodworking techniques.

Liverpool

We couldn't mention cities without talking about Liverpool. A great way to explore this most musical of cities is by following the Liverpool Heartbeat Sculpture Trail (liverpoolheartbeat.co.uk) that takes in many of the statues commemorating the great musicians to emerge from the city.

Stratford-upon-Avon

If you're in need of a cultural interlude then where better than Stratford-upon-Avon, birthplace of William Shakespeare? There are plenty of riverside strolls to enjoy as well as the theatre and a generous assortment of glorious Tudor buildings to admire.

Cheltenham

The endlessly elegant town of Cheltenham is a worthy addition to any itinerary, with its jazz, science and literature festivals, plus it's a great base for exploring the Malvern and Cotswold Hills.

When to Go

Many of the cities in the region have winter markets that brighten long winter nights. Spring and autumn are ideal times to visit the Cotswold, Malvern and Shropshire Hills, and the longer walks in the

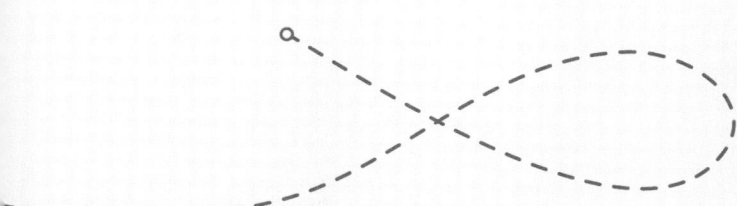

Peak District are best tackled on long summer days when there's plenty of daylight and less need to rush.

 **Transport**

Birmingham is at the hub of the UK rail network and all the cities and major towns are well served by buses and trains. There are bus networks in the rural areas but check locally as there will be seasonal variations. All walks are easily accessible by car but look for park-and-ride schemes around cities.

 **Where to Stay**

The Mailbox (mailboxlife.com) in central Birmingham is a local landmark with accommodation, food and shopping. In the Cotswolds there are plenty of quaint hotels and B&Bs to choose from: cotswolds.com/accommodation is a local guide that will help you find the perfect spot. Hartington Hall Youth Hostel (yha.org.uk/hostel/yha-hartington-hall) in Buxton offers an affordable place to stay and the chance to sleep in a 17th-century manor house.

For those with a caravan or campervan there's a campsite in the middle of Cheltenham racecourse (caravanclub.co.uk/club-sites/england/cotswolds/gloucestershire/cheltenham-racecourse-caravan-club-site) that's basic, but quiet and convenient for the town (it's not open during race events).

What's On

Cheltenham Festivals (cheltenhamfestivals.org) A variety of festivals throughout the year, including jazz, science and literature.

YNot Festival (ynotfestival.com; Aug) Held in Pikehall, Derbyshire, the perfect Peak District setting for a carnival of music, comedy and cinema.

Resources

Visit Birmingham (visitbirmingham.com) Full of different ways to explore the city.

Mountain Weather Information Service (mwis.org.uk/forecasts/english-and-welsh/peak-district) To keep you safe on the Peak District hills.

Peak District National Park (peakdistrict.gov.uk) All you need to know about staying, eating, drinking and hiking in the national park.

Explore the Cotswolds (explorethecotswolds.com) The place to look for itineraries and travel tips.

Visit the Malverns (visitthemalverns.org) The website has a whole section on Malvern Hill walks, plus listings of places to stay and eat in the town and around.

The Big Feastival (thebigfeastival.com; Aug) Hosted by Alex James of Blur fame on his farm, this Costwolds festival is all about good food and great music.

Ludlow Food Festival (ludlowfoodfestival.co.uk; Sep) Take time off from your hiking for this three-day celebration of good food, held in the fine medieval market town of Ludlow.

Matlock Bath Illuminations (derbyshiredales.gov.uk/leisure/matlock-bath-illuminations; Sep/Oct) The Matlock Bath Venetian Boat Builders' Association place lighted models onto boats and float them along the River Derwent.

40

Kinder Scout

Best for

WILD VIEWS

DURATION	DIFFICULTY	DISTANCE	START/END
4-5hr	Hard	8 miles/ 13km	Edale

TERRAIN	Rocky ascent, some boggy ground

The highest peak in the Peak District, Kinder Scout is a brooding moorland plateau that offers some of the area's most challenging walks. The place is famous not least because of the role it played in securing the right to roam: it was the site of the 1932 Kinder Mass Trespass, often cited as one of the most successful examples of direct action in British history. This route from Edale is popular for its scramble up Grindsbrook Clough and the peculiar rock formations along the southern edge, before it loops back down Jacob's Ladder – the first section of the Pennine Way.

Getting Here
Edale railway station is served by Manchester and Sheffield. There's pay-and-display parking at Edale Village Hall Car Park.

Starting Point
Whether you park or take the train, the walk starts at the bottom of the road heading through Edale village, a popular destination for ramblers.

01 Walk north up the road through Edale from the car park or station, passing the Moorland visitor centre to your right, to the Old Nags Head – the official start/end of the Pennine Way. Carry on along the road behind the pub to where it becomes a gravel track. Follow this track until you see the footpath to your right, marked 'Grindsbrook'. Follow this path down into the woods to cross Grinds Brook and bear left, sticking to the paved path which leads through the valley into **Grindsbrook Clough**, the original route of the Pennine Way.

02 As the valley narrows, the paved path begins to deteriorate and the route now becomes more interesting as you clamber over rocks and boulders to follow the stream uphill. As you climb higher, some hand work may be necessary, but this is classed as an easy Grade 1 scramble that can be managed by most with a decent level of stamina. As you near the top of the clough (gorge), the route forks. Stick to the left path for the steeper but more direct route, or if you choose to take the slightly easier option up the stream to your right, head left at the top to follow the rim and rejoin our route.

03 At the top of **Grindsbrook Clough** you're greeted by a cairn. From here you can savour the views back down the valley, and for the first time appreciate the isolated wilderness of Kinder's vast and featureless plateau. In poor visibility Kinder can be confusing, so knowledge of how to use a map and compass is strongly recommended. Head west leaving Grindsbrook Clough – the path here can be a little difficult to locate but after the first section you'll essentially keep to the path along the southerly rim, enjoying the weird and wonderful rock formations (pictured) along the way until you reach Crowden Clough. Cross the clough and head left to ascend to the rocky outcrop of Crowden Tower.

04 Carry on to reach **the Woolpacks**, a scattering of large, weather-sculpted rocks, so-called because of their likeness to old-fashioned wool bales. The path winds through this remarkable site and continues along to two other notable rock formations: **Pym Chair** and the anvil-shaped **Noe Stool**.

📔 Mass Trespass

On 24 April 1932, more than 400 men and women marched upon the moorland – then used exclusively by gentry for grouse shooting – to demand access for all. At the fore was 20-year-old Benny Rothman, who argued that all peaks and uncultivated moorland should be accessible to everyone, especially workers in polluted industrial towns and cities. The protest resulted in Rothman and four others being jailed, but paved the way for the establishment of Britain's national parks (the first of which, fittingly, was the Peak District), and ultimately led to today's Countryside and Rights of Way (CRoW) Act.

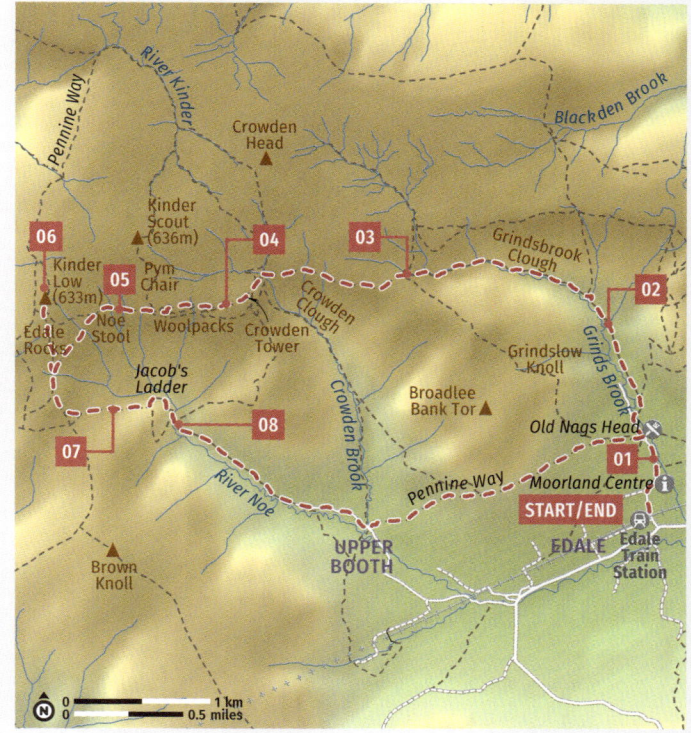

05 From Noe Stool continue along the path until you meet the Pennine Way. Although you'll eventually head left here to return to Edale, on a clear day it's worth making the 400m detour right to reach **Kinder Low** – as close to a summit as you'll find on Kinder Scout. Although 3m lower than the actual highest point (which lies unmarked to the northeast of Kinder Low, and is rather underwhelming), it's somewhat easier to find, being marked by a trig point, and has become a pilgrimage destination for ardent hikers. It was along here that hundreds of brave trespassers took on the gamekeepers to fight for access to the countryside: be sure to say a silent thank you to the protesters to whom we owe the sense of freedom that can be felt up in places like Kinder Scout. You'll find the trig just to the east of the Pennine Way, but it can be disorientating in poor visibility. It gazes down towards Hayfield where the mass trespass began, another popular starting point for a Kinder Scout hike.

06 Retrace your steps heading south from the trig point, passing Edale Rocks to the cairn marking the top of the Pennine Way. Bear right slightly and continue down to where the path forks. Take the left along the broad, eroded path and then left again to pick up the more established path of the Pennine Way and former packhorse route leading from east to west.

Kinder Scout Wrecks

This area of the Dark Peak – notably Kinder Scout and neighbouring Bleaklow, the region's second highest peak – is littered with aircraft wreckages. More than 150 aircraft are believed to have crashed in the Peak District in the last century and there are as many as 11 crash sites on Kinder alone. The weather here can be very changeable, and in low rain or thick fog (known by local hillwalkers as 'clag') it's easy to imagine how a pilot could become disorientated and the endless moorland slopes could pose a danger to low-flying aircraft. Due to the vast and featureless nature of the high moorland, it's recommended that you enlist a local guide to visit these wreckages unless you are an experienced navigator. Alternatively, Peak District rangers often run organised walks to these remarkable and eerie sites.

07 Descend along this track until you reach the top of **Jacob's Ladder**. Turn left for a steep but more direct route along Jacob's Ladder – named after Jacob Marshall who occupied Edale Head Farm and kept a small enclosure for packhorses, the ruins of which are close to the packhorse bridge at the bottom. He is credited with constructing the steep path to give the packhorsemen respite while their horses took the zigzagging route to the right (a longer but gentler option). Both routes emerge at the packhorse bridge across the River Noe (pictured).

08 From here follow the Pennine Way through Upper Booth and up the lower slopes of **Broadlee-Bank Tor** – the last slog before a well-earned beverage. After this you'll head through several gates and stiles before emerging back at the Old Nags Head.

 **Take a Break**

The obvious choice for walkers descending from Kinder Scout is the **Old Nags Head** (☏ 01433 670291; the-old-nags-head.co.uk; Grindsbrook Booth, Edale; jacket potato £10, steak & ale pie £17; ⏱ noon-9pm Mon-Sat, to 8pm Sun), a packhorse inn (and former smithy) with tankards hanging from the beams and rugged flagstone floors. This is a proper walkers' pub with good food and log fires; it even serves its own ale, the 'Nags Head 1577'.

BEST DAY WALKS: ENGLAND 165

41

Mam Tor

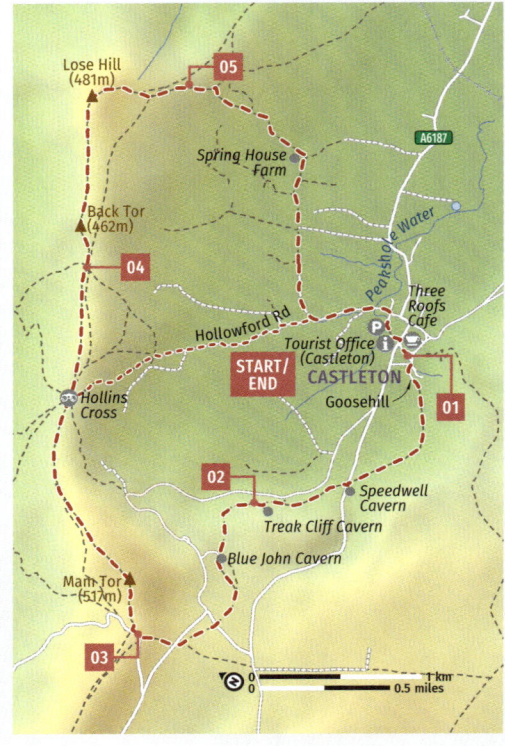

DURATION	DIFFICULTY	DISTANCE	START/END
4hr	Hard	6.5 miles/ 10.4km	Castleton visitor centre
TERRAIN	Steep inclines, rocky trails, steps		

Mam Tor, meaning 'Mother Hill' – also known as the 'Shivering Mountain' for its frequent shale landslides – is consistently voted one of Britain's best walks for its vast panoramic views. This route takes you from the enticing town of Castleton up to Mam Tor and along the Great Ridge.

Getting Here
Buses run here from Sheffield; alternatively, there's a pay-and-display car park at Castleton Visitor Centre.

Starting Point
The walk starts and ends at the visitor centre in Castleton town centre.

01 Cross the main road in front of the visitor centre and walk behind the jewellers to follow the footpath running beside Peakshole Water. Cross the bridge and walk up Goosehill, until it turns into a stony path with the wall on your right. Follow this path until it meets the road, with Speedwell Cavern to your left, and cross over to take the path to **Treak Cliff Cavern**.

02 Take the steps up to the cavern and follow the path right behind the building and up the hillside to **Blue John Cavern**. Cross the car park in front of the cafe-shop and go through a gate to take the path uphill. Veer right to head through a gate in the corner of the field. Continue straight along this path all the way up to the foot of Mam Tor, crossing two roads along the way.

03 Take the stepped path up to the summit of **Mam Tor** and hold on to your hat as you do – the winds can be strong up on top. On a fine day, you're likely to spot gliders taking off from the edge.

Mam Tor in History

As well as being a great place for a hike, Mam Tor (pictured) is an important archaeological site; evidence of prehistoric use (two round barrows near the hilltop) dates from the Bronze Age, and even earlier finds include flint tools and a Neolithic polished stone axe. During the late Bronze and early Iron Ages it was occupied as a hill fort, one of the largest and highest in Britain. Look out for the iron plaques set into the steps up to Mam Tor, whose designs conjure these early settlers and are a good motivator for children to make it to the top. Among the images are a round house, a dagger, a neck torc (an item of jewellery), a plough, an urn and the face of the sun god Lugh.

Continue along the ridge to **Hollins Cross** – if you look to your right you can see the old Mam Tor road beneath you, closed in 1979 due to repeated landslips. At Hollins Cross you have the option to cut the route short by heading down to the right, back into Castleton.

04 Otherwise continue along the ridge, taking the stile left to climb the steep section up to the rocky outcrop of Back Tor and along to the final summit at **Lose Hill Pike** (if you don't fancy the steep ascent, take the lower path which misses out these two summits). On a clear day you can see right along the ridge, back towards Mam Tor. From Lose Hill, bear right down the stone path and cross two stiles before following the path down to your left, alongside the field boundary.

05 Continue on this path down the hill, passing a line of trees on your right. Shortly after, as the path veers left towards Hope, fork off right and continue down the hill (which is quite steep in places) until you emerge on a farm track. Turn right and head down the hill to Spring House Farm, after which you'll turn right into Castleton. Then keep going straight ahead, through a series of gates while ignoring any turnoffs, until you reach the training and conference centre. Turn left on to Hollowford Rd leading back into Castleton – a shortcut right before the Ramblers Rest takes you straight back to the car park.

 **Take a Break**

The **Three Roofs Cafe** (threeroofs cafe.com; The Island; dishes £9-15; 9.30am-4pm Mon-Fri, to 5pm Sat & Sun;), opposite the Visitor Centre, is Castleton's most popular purveyor of cream teas, and dishes up filling sandwiches, pies, fish and chips, burgers and jacket potatoes plus teas, coffees and a selection of alcoholic drinks.

42

Stanage Edge

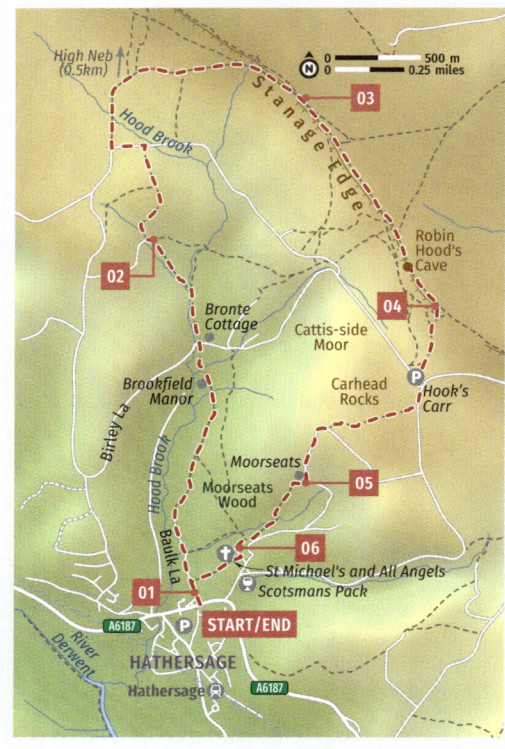

DURATION	DIFFICULTY	DISTANCE	START/END
3-4hr	Moderate	5.6 miles/ 9.1km	Hathersage

TERRAIN	Footpaths, tracks, some rocky terrain

Loved by walkers and climbers alike, Stanage is one of the Peak District's best-known gritstone edges. This varied, circular route from the village of Hathersage offers some of the best views over Hope Valley as well as of the edge itself.

Getting Here
Hathersage station is served by Manchester and Sheffield. There's a pay-and-display car park on Oddfellows Rd.

Starting Point
Baulk Lane, just off the main road (A6187) in Hathersage. You'll spot the public footpath sign immediately to the right of outdoor shop Alpkit.

01 Follow Baulk Lane for almost a mile to where it passes **Brookfield Manor** and reaches Birley Lane. Cross the road, with **Bronte cottage** to your right, and take the footpath through the field opposite and into woodland. Where the path forks, take the footbridge left and head uphill into open fields, the second of which has a small boardwalk over boggy ground. Cross a stile in the wall, then go up the narrow path.

02 Where the path reaches a T-junction, turn left (signposted Stanage). Just after the wide gate, follow the footpath sign right up the hill. As this path tapers right, go through the gap in the wall so it's now on your left. Stick to this path until you reach the lane, where you turn left to a car park. Then turn right along the track leading up to **Stanage Edge**.

03 At the top, turn right to follow the edge. If you want to summit the highest point, first head left to the trig at **High Neb** (458m) before

Best for

WILD VIEWS

Stanage Edge in Literature

You may recognise Stanage Edge (pictured) from the 2005 film version of *Pride & Prejudice*. In an iconic shot, Elizabeth Bennet – played by Keira Knightley – stands on a rocky outcrop with her coat blowing behind her, feeling the full force of her freedom. It's become a local sport to emulate Knightly's pose, one to be undertaken with a bit of care given the dramatic drop. And, as mentioned in the route description, Moorseats is where Jane Eyre flees to 'the grey small antique structure, with its low roof, its latticed casements, its mouldering walls, its avenue of aged firs all grown aslant under the stress of mountain wind.'

retracing your steps. You'll pass above a cave where Robin Hood is rumoured to have sheltered.

04 Take the path diagonally down to Hook's Carr car park. Turn left out of the car park and immediately right along the road (The Dale). Shortly after, take the gate in the wall on your right leading uphill towards Carhead Rocks. At the top, you're treated to great views of Stanage Edge. Follow the path down the other side to a farm track. Turn right and continue down into the grounds of **Moorseats**, which inspired Moor House in Charlotte Brontë's *Jane Eyre*.

05 Walk through the grounds and immediately upon exiting go right through a wooden gate between two pillars. Follow this path down through **Moorseats Wood**, where you'll pass through a freestanding stone gateway. Upon emerging from the woods, continue straight where the path forks, ignoring the left turn to the metal kissing gate, until you reach a gate and stile with the church ahead.

06 Turn left onto Church Bank. Either follow the road down to the Scotsman's Pack Inn and the village, or pass through the second gate on your right into St Michael's and All Angels churchyard, where Robin Hood's right-hand man Little John is reputedly buried. Exit through the gate opposite where you entered and walk down to rejoin Baulk Lane into the village.

☕ Take a Break

The **Scotsman's Pack** (📞 01433 650253; scotsmanspackcountryinn.co.uk; School Lane, Hathersage; mains from £15; ⏰ 11am-midnight Mon-Sat, from noon Sun) is a traditional inn that's ideal for a post-walk pint: it serves hearty food and real ale. The place is named for the Scottish packmen who stopped here to sell tweeds.

BEST DAY WALKS: ENGLAND

43

The Malvern Hills

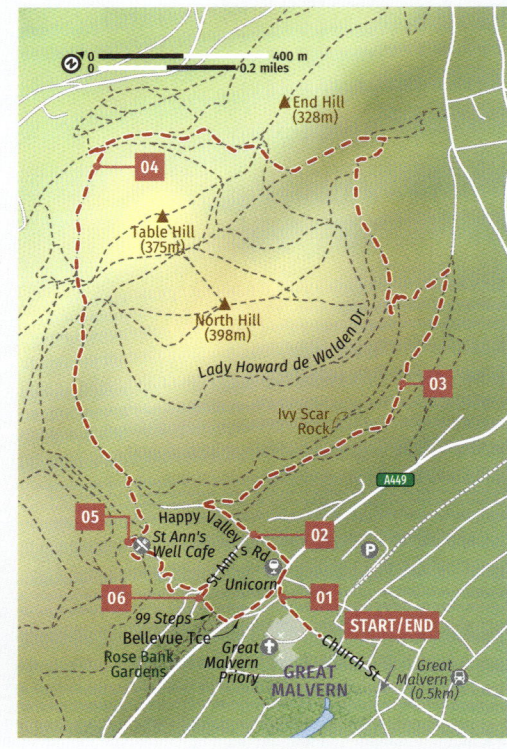

DURATION	DIFFICULTY	DISTANCE	START/END
1½hr	Moderate	2.5 miles/ 4km	Great Malvern

TERRAIN	Steep grassed paths

The green spine of the Malvern Hills rises to unexpected heights out of the gentle contours of three counties: Worcestershire, Herefordshire and Gloucestershire. The rocks from which the hills are formed are the most ancient in the country, something which perhaps adds to the mystical feel of the area, with its mineral springs, prehistoric earthworks and caverns. All this beauty has provided plenty of inspiration, from the 14th-century *Visions of Piers Plowman* by William Langland, to the works of JRR Tolkien and CS Lewis and the music of Elgar.

Getting Here
Great Malvern is best reached by train; a 2½-hour journey northwest of London's Paddington Station.

Starting Point
The walk starts in the heart of picturesque Great Malvern, close to the ancient Great Malvern Priory, which is a 10-minute walk west of the town's beautifully preserved Victorian train station.

01 Starting at the top of Church Street just north of Great Malvern Priory, turn right onto the main road and then, at the **Unicorn** pub, almost immediately left onto St Ann's Rd.

02 Where St Ann's Road bears left, go straight ahead away from the houses and onto Happy Valley Rd. Continue along the path, which eventually joins a gravel track, looking down to the clustered houses of Great Malvern.

03 Continuing past the outcrop of Ivy Scar Rock, take the left-hand path rather than following the North Hill sign. From here the path

Spring Water

Sixty litres of collected rainwater per minute shoot out of the tough limestone and granite rock of the Malvern Hills, in the past providing hoped-for relief for those suffering everything from poor eyesight to gout. The water-cure fad reached its height in the Victorian period: Charles Darwin brought his daughter Anne here for the cure, though sadly she died at the age of 10 and is buried in the priory graveyard. Spring water spurts from 70 locations around the town and the hills, famously at St Ann's Well. Malvern water has been commercially bottled since the 1920s, though a more eco-friendly way to sample it is from one of the town's wonderfully artistic water fountains.

rises steeply for a stretch. Continue straight ahead, then follow the sharp left turn, then zig zag to the right on Lady Howard de Walden Dr and continue to ascend the curve of North Hill.

04 The track begins to descend and then splits – turn left and head uphill past the little quarry. Head up and over the hill, from where you can detour up **Sugarloaf Hill** (pictured). Otherwise, start to head downwards. You cross a path and walk down an avenue of sycamores, turning right at the paved driveway.

05 Continue on the path as it bears left to St Ann's Well Cafe, a worthy refreshment stop, then take the zig-zagging path back to St Ann's Rd.

06 Turn right on St Ann's Road, and then left down the staircase known as **99 Steps**, with the spacious Rose Bank Gardens to your right. The steps deposit you back in Great Malvern; at their foot there's a plaque which credits the local gas lamps with inspiring *The Lion, the Witch and the Wardrobe*. Turn left on wide Bellevue Tce to arrive back at the top of Church St where the walk started.

Take a Break

Quaint **St Ann's Well Cafe** (01684-560285; stannswell.co.uk; St Ann's Rd; mains £8, cakes £4; 10am-4pm;) is set in an early-19th-century villa, with mountain-fresh spring water bubbling into a Sicilian marble basin by the door. All-vegetarian food (including vegan options) spans warming soups and gut-busting burgers to spicy snacks, filled baguettes, cakes, pastries and puddings. Drinks include homemade elderflower cordial and dandelion latte. The well here is said to have been used by the monks who built the priory back in 1085.

44

Caer Caradoc

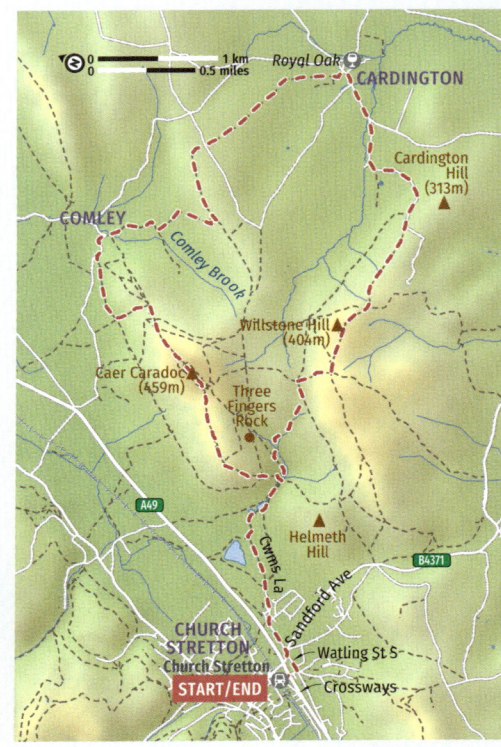

DURATION	DIFFICULTY	DISTANCE	START/END
4hr	Moderate	8 miles/ 13km	Church Stretton station

TERRAIN	Grassed paths

Caer Caradoc is ancient Britain at its most ruggedly appealing: this prehistoric hill fort was the last stand of the Celtic Catuvellauni against the Romans, and swirls with Arthurian legends. The walk starts in the attractive market town of Church Stretton, leading via the fort to a fine village pub.

Go straight ahead out of the station, crossing Crossways, then turning left onto Watling St. Carry on, crossing over Sandford Ave, then branch right onto Cwyms Lane. Ascend the lane, with a lake to your left, and turn right at the T-junction, clipping the woodland of Helmeth Hill.

From here it's a stiff climb of 459m (1500ft) to the volcanic summit of **Caer Caradoc** (pictured) passing outcrops known as Three Fingers Rock. At the top you'll see the circular outlines of prehistoric defensive ditches; there are also superb views of Long Mynd and the Breacon Beacons.

Cross Caer Caradoc and descend it, passing the small amphitheatre-like **quarry** at Comley: since the 1880s it has been revealing fossils of trilobites, which went extinct before the dinosaurs appeared.

At Comley the path veers right, and continues in an easterly direction, bringing you to the village of Cardington, where the 15th-century **Royal Oak** pub serves locally renowned Fidget Pie.

Take the lane south out of the village, then follow the paths which run west up Cardington Hill, then along the ridge of Willstone Hill.

Here you rejoin the path in the woodland at Helmeth Hill. Take the route you took earlier in the day, back to Church Stretton station.

Best for
ANCIENT HISTORY

45

The Cotswold Way

DURATION	DIFFICULTY	DISTANCE	START/END
4hr	Moderate	9 miles/ 16km	Chipping Campden/ Stanton

TERRAIN	Paths, steep ascents

This long-distance walk runs in all its glorious entirety for 164km (102 miles), along the Cotswolds escarpment from the lovely little wool town of Chipping Campden to the Georgian splendour of Bath. We've focused on the first day of the walk, which breaks in Broadway, a wonderfully attractive village with strong Arts and Crafts connections, and ends at idyllic Stanton. It's well worth factoring in time to explore the start, middle and end points of this lovely route.

Getting Here

The nearest train station to Chipping Campden is Moreton-in-Marsh, 9km to the south. Buses run here from all the major nearby towns.

Starting Point

The walk starts in the heart of town at a limestone disc marker, poetically inscribed with a quotation from TS Eliot and place names from along the Cotswold Way. It sits near the arcaded market hall on the High St.

01 From the Cotswold Way marker, turn right on Lower High St and then take a right on Hoo Lane. Heading up the lane, a **cottage** on the left has a blue plaque recording that Graham Greene lived here in the early 1930s.

02 At the T-junction cross Kingcombe Lane, turn left briefly and then go straight ahead to ascend steep **Dover's Hill** (pictured), an exhilarating high point with views of the Worcestershire Plains. This is the site of the archaic spring Olimpick Games, which started in 1612 and continue to this day with tugs of war, shin kicking and other capers.

Broadway & the Arts

Part of the beauty of Broadway stems from the Arts and Crafts influence on its architecture; the movement found its spiritual home in the village, with William Morris setting up his studio in Broadway Tower. Writers and artists flocked here, including John Singer Sargent, who painted the luminous *Carnation, Lily, Lily Rose* here in 1886. Turner sketched the village, Alma Tadema and Evelyn Waugh drank in Tudor coaching inn the Lygon Arms, and JM Barrie, creator of *Peter Pan*, played cricket on the green. The **June Broadway Arts Festival** (broadwayartsfestival.com) pays homage to the village's creative past, as well as nurturing current talent with workshops, talks and concerts.

03 The Cotswold Way runs west for a short stretch to a National Park car park, where you turn left down the lane. At the crossroads turn right, continuing on the Cotswold Way. After 500m take the track which leads off to the left. Having climbed the escarpment, the route eventually crosses Fish Hill road and reaches **Broadway Tower**, a 1794 folly conceived in the style of a Saxon turret by Capability Brown.

04 The path takes a sharp right turn at Broadway Tower, running to the beautiful village of **Broadway**. Go through the village and turn left on Church St, where you'll see the Crown & Trumpet pub on the left. Just beyond is **St Michael and All Angels church**, built in 1839 but incorporating elements such as an ornate 17th-century pulpit from an earlier chapel.

05 Beyond the church, turn right to pick up the Cotswold Way once more. From here the path meanders for 4km to **Shenberrow Camp** with its Iron Age hill fort, before taking a sharp right to lead to lovely Stanton where the walk ends.

Take a Break

Much the nicest of Broadway's pubs, its cosy bar and front garden filled at the weekend with lively locals, the 17th-century **Crown & Trumpet** (01386-853202; crownandtrumpet.co.uk; 14 Church St; soup £6.50, sandwiches £8, mains £12; 11am-11pm;) has been honoured by CAMRA (the Campaign for Real Ale) for its carefully kept, seasonally varying array of fine beers. It also offers a tempting bunch of ciders. There's good pub grub on offer, including classics such as ploughman's lunches, steak and kidney pie and breaded scampi, and frequent live music.

46

Birmingham City & Canals

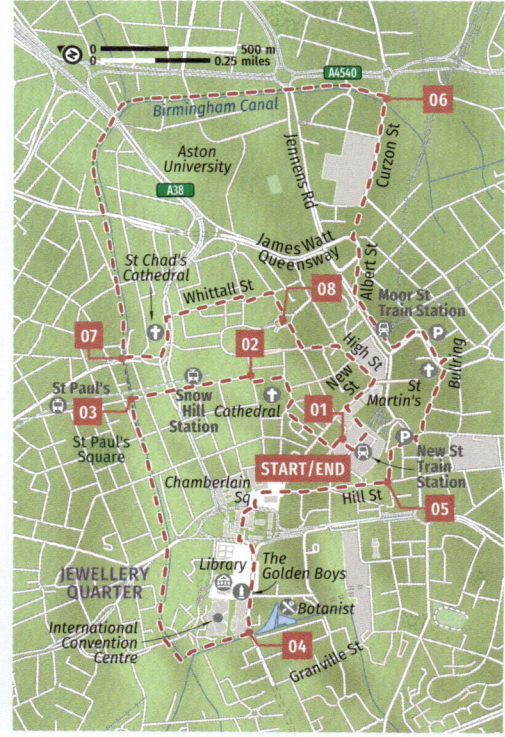

DURATION	DIFFICULTY	DISTANCE	START/END
2½-3hr	Moderate	5.5 miles/ 8.8km	Ozzy the Bull, Grand Central

TERRAIN	Tarmac, canal towpath

No series of walks around central England would be complete without Birmingham, a city that has done much to shake off its dirty, industrial past and has regrouped into a modern, colourful metropolis with much to explore and enjoy. This walk combines the ancient and modern using parts of the aquatic 'ring road' of canals that encircle the city.

Getting Here
Grand Central/New Street Station is a hub for trains from across the country, and there are tram and bus stops nearby. Parking is available across the city.

Starting Point
The 2022 Commonwealth Games truly showed off the city at its very best, so where else could we begin this walk than with the star of those games, Ozzy the Bull, who now resides in Grand Central.

01 Like the Eiffel Tower, Ozzy the Bull was only ever meant to be a temporary construction, but he proved such a hit at the Commonwealth Games that he has now been given a permanent home in Grand Central. With your back to Ozzy, bear right to exit the station via Stephenson St and the tram stop, then take Lower Temple St leading away from the station. Keep going straight on, over New St, until you reach **Birmingham Cathedral** (pictured). Enter the grounds and take the path that forks right, around the cathedral, and keep going to the road beyond.

02 Cross the road and walk down Livery St. Use the underpass to cross the dual carriageway and exit right towards 'Snow Hill', then continue following the road down to reach a white arch on

The Golden Boys

The *Golden Boys* is a striking statue commemorating three of the men who literally built the foundations of the city. Matthew Boulton manufactured metalware and joined forces with Scottish engineer James Watt. Between them they built an innovative new steam engine that played a central role in the Industrial Revolution. William Murdoch was so keen to join them that he walked 300 miles from his Ayrshire home and went on to improve the engines. They were members of the Lunar Society, a group of scientists and intellectuals who met during the full moon with the aim of making the world a better place.

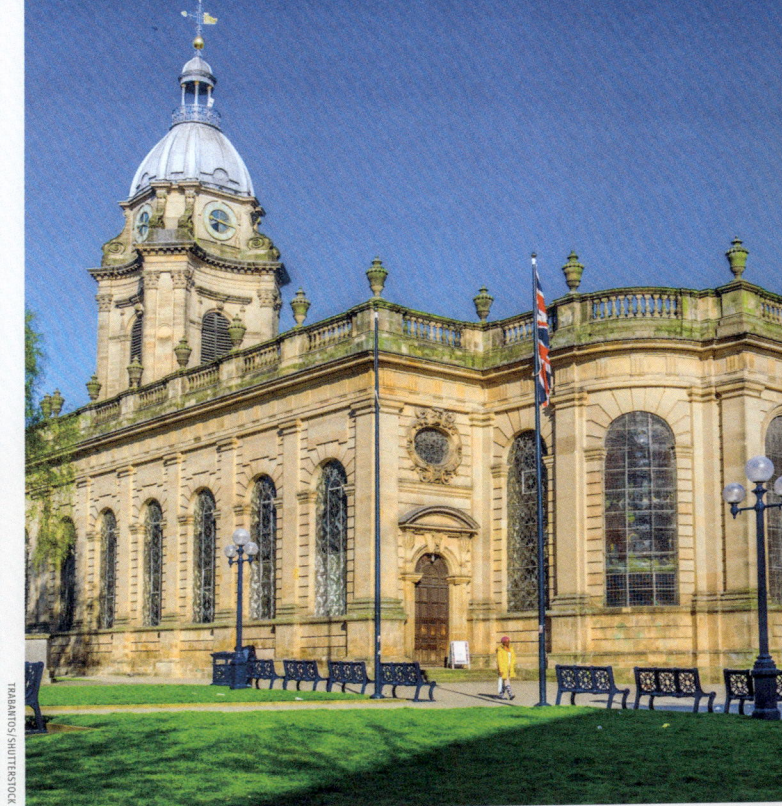

the right. Go through the arch and down the steps to the **canal**. Most of Birmingham's canals were built in the 18th and 19th centuries and would have provided vital transport for goods around the city and beyond. The last commercial traffic ceased in 1980 and much of the network fell into disrepair before being rescued and revitalised with shops, housing and walkways.

03 On the towpath turn right to pass under the road you just walked along and keep going, passing a flight of locks, until you reach a distinctive black-and-white bridge at the major canal junction. Cross the bridge and follow signs to the **International Convention Centre (ICC)** until you reach Black Sabbath Bridge (Broad Street Tunnel). Exit the canal here and turn left. The ICC was opened in 1981 by Queen Elizabeth II and is built on the site of Bingley Hall, the world's first purpose-built exhibition hall, which opened in 1850.

04 Continue on (checking out local stars in the pavement) to reach the **statue of the Golden Boys** and **Birmingham Library**. After passing the tram stop take the distinctive red paved path leading slightly left, then remain on this until you emerge onto the square in front of the town hall. Turn right to locate the **Iron Man sculpture**, then follow the road beyond it (Hill St) down and around the back of New Street Station.

05 Immediately after the station turn left into Station St, passing the **Electric Cinema**. Continue around and under a large bridge, then bear left toward a pedestrian area and Birmingham Markets. After passing **St Martin's Church** on your left, turn left and remain on this road as it leads around and up to Moor Street station. Cross to pass in front of the station entrance then turn right

BEST DAY WALKS: ENGLAND

in front of the major hotel to follow a pedestrian area, passing the university.

06 When you reach the canal, cross it and turn left, rejoining the towpath after 50m. Remain on the towpath, taking the stone footbridges that sweep around to the left at the canal junction. Continue until you reach **Snow Hill Bridge**.

07 Exit the canal using the ramp, then turn left to cross Shadwell St to **St Chad's Cathedral**. St Chad was the Apostle of the Midlands and the church was built in the mid-19th century to cater for the expanding Catholic population of the city. Head to the pedestrian crossing in front of the cathedral entrance and cross to the far side, then turn right along Whittall St. At the end take a right then left into Newton St, turning right at the end.

08 Stop at the **Tony Hancock statue**, a monument to the hugely popular comedian of the 1950s and '60s who was born in Birmingham. From the statue continue across the road, then take the first left down to Dalton Walk, then turn right and continue until you reach the Bull. Turn right along New St, then turn left up the ramp back into **Grand Central** (pictured). Once inside, bear right to locate the escalators back down to Ozzy.

 Ingenious Railways

The railways played a pivotal role in the history of the city and Moor Street station is a beautifully preserved example. The building is a combination of the original 1909 station, which was a terminus, and modern additions to allow through trains. Its role as a terminus led to the ingenious addition of a pair of 'traversers' – 60ft sections of track that allowed locomotives to be moved to an adjacent track and repositioned at the other end of the train. Thanks to the efforts of volunteers in the 1980s and '90s the station was preserved, and it is now a Grade II–listed building.

 Take a Break

There are an abundance of places to pause for a break along this route, with plenty of shops and cafes to choose from. If you've brought a packed lunch, then the seating around the Town Hall square or library are lovely places to pause and enjoy the city. If you'd prefer a cafe, explore around the canal junction in stage 03 of our walk, where you'll discover an excellent assortment of eateries, including the **Botanist** (thebotanist.uk.com/locations/gas-street-basin-birmingham), which offers a range of food and drink with canal-side views.

47

Kinver Edge

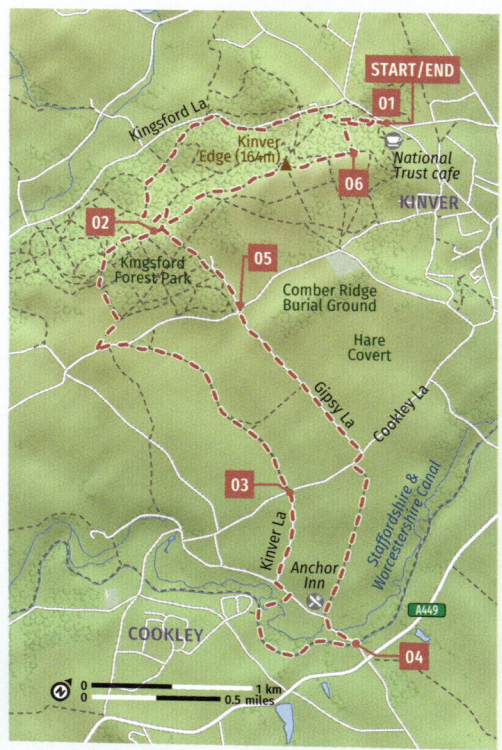

DURATION	DIFFICULTY	DISTANCE	START/END
3½-4hr	Moderate	7.3 miles/ 11.7km	Rock Houses car park
TERRAIN	Hard track, tarmac, woodland trail		

Tucked away between the hustle and bustle of the West Midlands and the peace and tranquillity of the Shropshire Hills, Kinver Edge is missed by many, but always delights those who stumble across it. This beautiful sandstone escarpment and the nearby Rock Houses are owned by the National Trust, and during the summer months the shaded woodland offers refreshing shade on even the hottest of days. In winter the views from the summit stretch for miles in all directions, making the modest climb to the trig point well worth the effort. In the 'hike to view' ratio, the view definitely wins.

Starting Point

There's free parking in the car park on Compton Rd adjacent to the Rock Houses. Kinver is well served by local buses and the start point is a short walk from the village.

01 From the car park at the **Rock Houses**, cross through to the grassy area and turn right to follow a path leading gently uphill. Before you reach the road at the top, turn left along the Permissive Bridleway. Remain on this until you reach a T-junction with a large track. Turn left here to reach a crossroad with a distinctive large tree trunk. The woods we see today once formed part of the ancient Mercian forest that covered much of central England, and the site was so popular with Edwardians that trams used to run all the way from Birmingham to Kinver so they could enjoy a day out.

02 Turn right and follow the broad track gently downhill towards the woodland edge. Turn left to walk along the edge of the woods and remain

Remarkable Rock Houses

There are several rock houses dotted around Kinver Edge. Look for Nanny's Rock and Vale's Rock near the route, though the ones at Holy Austin Rock have been restored and preserved and are now open to visitors. There is a 1777 record of a Joseph Heely – local author and landowner – sheltering here from a storm and being looked after by a family who lived in the house. Additional rooms could be dug out as required and the 1811 census shows there were 11 families living here. The homes were cool in summer, easy to heat in winter and offered plenty of fresh air and fantastic views.

Best for

WILD VIEWS

on the track as it turns right past houses. Before you reach the road, fork left then turn left onto the small road. After 25m take the waymarked bridleway on the right. After a short distance turn left then right and follow the **North Worcestershire Path** down to the road.

Much of the woodland is made up of broadleaf trees such as birch, sweet chestnut and oak, and creatures you may spot along the way include buzzards and jays high above, lizards sunning themselves on a path in summer, and maybe even a red fox if you're lucky.

03 Cross the road and continue down Kinver Rd to Caunsall. Turn left, passing the **Anchor Inn** pub, then take the track on the right leading down to the canal. After a distinctive black-and-white bridge over the River Stour you will emerge onto the canal towpath. Turn left and follow the canal to Bridge 26.

The canal connects the River Severn in the south to the Trent and Mersey Canal in the north. In total it is 46 miles long and has 43 locks to navigate along the way. Along this stretch there are plenty of beautiful sandstone cliffs to admire and, if time and legs allow, it's definitely worth exploring more of the towpath.

04 Exit the canal here and turn left along the road. After crossing a small bridge turn right to take the public footpath up a paved driveway. Continue straight on, following the path through kissing gates until you reach a large field. Keep to the right-hand field edge and continue on up through the field, then through the next field to a track. Turn left here to reach a road. Turn right along the road then take the first left to follow **Gipsy Lane** back towards the woods.

BEST DAY WALKS: ENGLAND

The area is criss-crossed with an assortment of tracks and lanes, and this entire region was once part of a major transport hub. Before the canal and trams there was the Great Irish Road that ran from Bristol to Chester and passed through Kinver. Over the centuries the town has traded iron ore mined from the rocks, and it was home to a thriving woollen industry that made use of the nearby River Stour.

05 At the end of Gipsy Lane continue on and take a very slight right to follow a paved bridleway alongside the woods. This path will switch to the other side of the fence, but continue in the same direction until you reach the crossroad with the tree trunk from stage 01 of the walk. Turn right and remain on the path, passing the trig point until you reach the viewpoint at the end.

With the far-reaching views across the local landscape, it's no surprise to find a **hillfort** here, but there is also another, less visited one, at the southern end of the edge at Drakelow Hill.

06 Retrace your steps back from the viewpoint to take a path on the right leading sharply downhill through the woods. At the junction turn right to follow the signed path to the Rock Houses (pictured) and the starting point.

🔭 A Strategic Viewpoint

The hillfort near the viewpoint was built during the Iron Age around 3000 years ago and would have been a busy community full of traders, animals and families. All that remains visible now are the large ramparts that would have surrounded this community. Although the site has never been excavated, markings of what are believed to be round homes and roadways have been spotted. The fort is close to the boundary of two ancient tribes – now the county boundary between Staffordshire and Worcestershire – so, as well as offering an excellent vantage point, it would also have had significant strategic importance.

☕ Take a Break

Throughout the Kinver Edge woods there are plenty of benches and tree stumps on which you can perch and enjoy a packed lunch. There are no benches alongside the canal stretch but the dog-friendly **Anchor Inn** (theanchorinncaunsall.co.uk; 11am-11pm) in Caunsall is well known locally for making a 'proper cob' (filled bread roll) and has plenty of indoor and outdoor seating. The Rock Houses' **National Trust cafe** (nationaltrust.org.uk/visit/shropshire-staffordshire/kinver-edge-and-the-rock-houses/eating-and-shopping-at-kinver-edge) offers a traditional range of cakes, coffees and sandwiches, plus there's a secondhand bookshop.

Also Try...

STEVE HORSLEY/SHUTTERSTOCK ©

Padley Gorge

Padley Gorge (pictured) is a favourite among Peak District photographers. This stunning, woodland-shrouded chasm has an entirely mystical feel to it at any time of year, but especially in autumn when orange leaves burn bright against green mossy boulders and dappled sunlight.

From Grindleford Station, walk up through Yarncliff Wood, initially with Burbage Brook to your left but crossing over midway to follow it up on your right, enjoying the small waterfalls and cascades. The top of the gorge, where grassy banks border shallow pools, is a popular spot for picnics and paddling. From here head west to the road, passing Surprise View car park, before taking the path down through Bolehill Quarry – a former industrial site now covered by silver birch trees – and back to Grindleford.

DURATION 1½hr
DIFFICULTY Easy
DISTANCE 2.3 miles/3.7km

Malvern, End to End

Earlier in the chapter we described a short Malvern Hill hike. But hardy hikers might want to tramp the full roller-coaster ridge. It includes North Hill, traversed in the route we covered previously, as well as Perseverance and Raggedstone Hills. It's not an especially long walk, but steep ascents make it a challenging option.

The first ascent is of North Hill, then Sugarloaf Hill and, beyond this, the imposing Worcestershire Beacon. Summer Hill is next, followed swiftly by Perseverance, Jubilee, Pinnacle and Black Hills. Next up are the ancient fortifications of the Herefordshire Beacon. The next crest is Swinyard Hill, then Midsummer. Those who are flagging will need to brace themselves for steep Raggedstone Hill; smaller Chase End Hill comes last…and then a well-earned rest!

DURATION 4½hr
DIFFICULTY Hard
DISTANCE 10 miles/16km

Ilam to Dovedale

This walk is a great choice for families. Starting in Ilam (east of Stoke-on-Trent), with its atmospheric church and alpine-style houses, head east out of the village.

After the last house, cross the road and go through a gate that descends to the footpath. Turn right and walk along the bottom of Bunster Hill, continuing along through fields and over stiles until you reach Dovedale car park, from where a track leads to the popular stepping stones (pictured). Add to the adventure by ascending Thorpe Cloud from the stepping stones, or continue further into the limestone valley. If you fancy a grand place to stay, try Ilam Hall Youth Hostel, located in the ancient manor house.

DURATION 1hr
DIFFICULTY Easy
DISTANCE 1.5 miles/2.4km

Cannock Chase

Cannock Chase is 26 sq miles of woodland and open heath sitting right on the edge of the West Midlands. A glance at an OS map will reveal numerous routes crossing the Chase (as it's known locally), and this route it simply one suggestion.

From the Beggar's Hill car park take the furthest right fork until you reach the ford at Devil's Dumble, and from here turn left along Haywood Slade and down Marquis Drive to the trig point at the end. Turn left here then left again along Abraham's Valley and back to the start point. Although the area is hugely popular it's quite easy to lose yourself in a quiet hike, disturbed only by the birds and occasional passing horse.

DURATION 2hr
DIFFICULTY Easy
DISTANCE 4.4 miles/7km

Lifeboat House (p195), Blakeney Point

Southeast & East England

48 **The Seven Sisters**
Adventure along high chalk cliffs. **p190**

49 **Blakeney Point**
Explore shingle, sand and marshes. **p194**

50 **The Backs**
Stroll riverside lawns in Cambridge. **p196**

51 **Leith Hill**
Ascend the wooded Greensand Ridge. **p198**

52 **Rye to Winchelsea**
Take in two lovely seaside towns. **p200**

53 **St Albans**
A market town and Roman remains. **p204**

54 **The Viking Trail**
See where the Scandinavian raiders first landed in Britain. **p206**

55 **Devil's Dyke**
Follow the South Downs Way to reach Britain's longest and driest valley. **p210**

56 **Mersea Island**
This quirky island is all about oysters, wildlife and old-fashioned fun. **p214**

Explore
Southeast & East England

The southeast corner of the country may look like it's dominated by London on the map, but take a train trip out of the capital and you'll find an amazing richness and diversity of landscapes, from the open spaces of the South Downs with their white cliffs to the densely forested ridges of the home counties. This chapter takes you on a trip to downland, woodland, sandy strands and lush meadows, as well as to the sea marshes of East Anglia, the back streets and riverbanks of lovely Cambridge and the mysterious delights of the Devil's Dyke.

Alfriston

If you're planning to walk the Seven Sisters and the South Downs, or explore the curlicues of the Cuckmere River, the village of Alfriston is a lovely place to site yourself. The seaside towns of Brighton and Eastbourne are bigger and buzzier, but Alfriston offers country seclusion as well as some excellent eating and pub options, including superb afternoon teas. The village church is known as the Cathedral of the South Downs for its grandeur, and there are a couple of ancient half-timbered hotels to stay in, as well as cottage and farmhouse B&Bs.

Brighton

Brighton deserves its crown as the UK's most vibrant seaside city, and is a captivating blend of bohemian charm, creative energy and slightly faded coastal grandeur. Explore the iconic Brighton Palace Pier and the Royal Pavilion's exotic architecture and shop independent in the quirky Lanes, a quarter of narrow alleys filled with independent boutiques. On the coast, the lively Brighton and Hove promenade is where locals come to walk, cycle or just take in the sea air by the pebbled beaches. At night the city is buzzing, and there's an eclectic food scene and rich cultural calendar. When you're ready to escape back to nature, the South Downs is on your doorstep.

Cambridge

The university city of Cambridge is a lovely spot if you're exploring The Backs walk in this chapter, and is a couple of hours' drive south of the north Norfolk coast. Founded in 1209, the University of Cambridge comprises marvellous Gothic and medieval architecture. The place is well used to accommodating and feeding students, university staff and tourists, and there are plenty of great places to stay, eat and drink, perhaps the best of them being the riverside pubs. Cutting through town, the River Cam provides sylvan walking routes

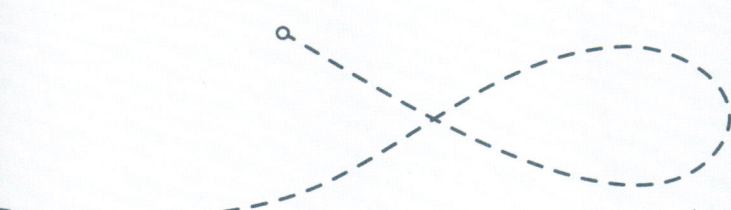

that guide you away from the tourist crowds and is also fabled for its punts: shallow gondola-like vessels pushed through the water with a long pole.

St Albans

Sitting comfortably in the county of Hertfordshire northwest of London, St Albans is a small and handsome city with a very long history: it was known in Roman times as Verulamium, and has substantial Roman walls and the remains of an amphitheatre as well as a magnificent cathedral. You'll find excellent places to eat and drink, including medieval inns, and boutique hotels and B&Bs provide cosy accommodation. The sedate farmland surrounding the city is undramatic but quietly attractive.

 When to Go

The south of England has a mild climate and while the weather can be wet and grey, it's not often you have conditions so severe that walking is impossible. Spring is a lovely time to walk and summer days can be gloriously warm. Autumn brings seasonal bounty in the hedgerows, as well as the sight of the leaves changing colour.

 Transport

This is a well-connected region: nearly all towns have a railway station, and some villages, too. Train prices are annoyingly unpredictable, and peak times should be avoided as you pay more at commuting time. Country buses are an option, though services tend to be infrequent. Some routes may be easiest to access by car.

 Where to Stay

You'll find some great youth hostels here – the South Downs, for example, has a delightful new hostel in a converted farmhouse. Camping and glamping are good summer options. Otherwise, it's the land of the B&B, with many comfortable and welcoming places where a large breakfast will fuel you up for a day's walking. Harry's Campsites are three charming wild spaces in the New Forest where you can sleep under the stars, or you can stay in quirky Skoolie, an old American yellow school bus parked in the Sussex South Downs, or Ditchling Cabin, a wooden retreat with its own swimming lake near the South Downs Way.

What's On

The Great Escape (greatescapefestival.com; May) Held on Brighton Beach, Great Escape is a festival of new music, along with gigs, debates and speeches.

Into the Wild Festival (intothewildgathering.com; Aug) Featuring woodland crafts and bushcraft classes as well as world music.

Kent Green Hop Beer Fortnight (kentgreenhopbeer.com; late Sep) This boozy event held across Kent gives you the chance to sample 30 newly released brews.

Resources

Ramblers (ramblers.org.uk) Walking inspiration, with a list of favourite Southeast England walks, as well as plenty of general hiking advice.

Visit Britain (visitbritain.com) The tourist board website has a round-up of best walks in the southeast.

Visit Southeast England (visitsoutheastengland.com) Get ideas for places to stay and visit in Kent, East Sussex, West Sussex, Hampshire, Surrey, Berkshire, Buckinghamshire and Oxfordshire.

48

The Seven Sisters

DURATION	DIFFICULTY	DISTANCE	START/END
5hr	Hard	12.5 miles / 20km	Eastbourne / Alfriston

TERRAIN	Grassed paths and woodlands

Brace yourselves for a big bold walk, which leads from Eastbourne, with its long stone beaches and grand Edwardian seafront, up onto the high chalk cliffs whose most famous landmark is the red-and-white-striped Beachy Head lighthouse. You're then on the ups and downs of the famous Seven Sisters, which will give your legs a great workout and your eyes some gorgeous English Channel vistas. The route drops down to the Friston Forest, winds past lovely Westdean village, then follows the bends of the Cuckmere River to the beautiful downland settlement of Alfriston.

Getting Here

Eastbourne, which sits southeast of London on the Sussex coast, is easily reached from London's Victoria Station – trains take around 1½ hours.

Starting Point

The route starts at Eastbourne station, from where it's a 1.5km walk through the streets and along the fabled seafront to the base of the cliffs.

01 From the station, head south down Gildredge Rd, which leads into College Rd. At the T-junction where College Rd meets Carlisle Rd you'll see the **Towner Eastbourne Art Gallery** (free entry). It's well worth making a stop here: the purpose-built structure has temporary shows of contemporary work on the ground and 2nd floors, while the 1st floor is given over to rotating themed shows created from the gallery's 5000-piece collection. From the Towner, go left briefly onto Carlisle Rd, then take a right onto Wilmington Gardens and then head straight down to the **Wish Tower**, a blunt structure built in the early 1800s as a defence against feared Napoleonic attack.

02 Beyond the Wish Tower slopes garden and before you reach the sea, the South Downs route commences. Turn right onto the route, heading towards the high cliffs. This is a lovely stretch before the walk proper begins – to the right are Eastbourne's grand hotels, and to the left are shingle pleasure beaches, divided by distinctive wooden sea defences known as **groynes**.

03 A narrow wooded path takes you for a vertiginous walk up the hillside, skirting Beachy Head Rd and landing you at the famous beauty spot of **Beachy Head**, the candy-striped lighthouse (pictured) sitting below. This has a much sadder reputation too, as there have been a high number of suicides here. On a sunny day though it's a wonderfully uplifting place: it's the highest sea cliff in Britain, rising 162m above the crashing English Channel below. You'll notice the lack of a beach here – it's said that the name Beachy Head instead derives from the French for 'beautiful headland': *beau chef*. From here you begin the roller-coaster ride part of the walk, plunging up and down the undulations of the cliff top. The open landscape is a perfect habitat for skylarks, radiant songbirds who nest on the ground and feed their chicks on spiders and other insects. Look to the skies when you hear their trickling song, and you may see a skylark high above.

04 After 3km you reach **Birling Gap**; it's a tiny settlement that comprises little more than a collection of windswept 19th-century coastguard

Adonis Blue

Striding across the Seven Sisters (pictured following page) with just a few sheep for company, you may feel you're in an almost empty landscape. But the Downs, cleared of forest by our Neolithic forebears thousands of years ago, shelter some 30 or 40 species per square metre. The most famous is the Adonis blue butterfly, which feeds on the nectar of the horseshoe vetch; males are a brilliant cobalt blue, while the females are chocolate brown. Their pupae produce a honey-like goo which feeds ants, and the ants in turn protect the pupae, sometimes even burying them in the ground for safekeeping. This delicate symbiotic relationship is just one of the wildlife marvels of the Downs.

BEST DAY WALKS: ENGLAND

cottages. A detour may not be the first thing on your mind on this long walk, but if you leave the cliffs here on Birling Gap Rd and head inland, in around 15 minutes you'll arrive at **East Dean** village, where the Tiger Inn is renowned for its pub food and bucolic village green setting. If you make the detour, return the same way to continue the route or, to save your legs, you have the option of walking the high ridge road leading west to Westdean village.

05 Back on the sea cliffs, more undulations lead along to the point where the Cuckmere River joins the sea. It's a steep descent to **Cuckmere Haven**, as the scenic estuary with its oxbow lakes is known. Once infamous for smuggling, the estuary is an important site for overwintering wildfowl, and you might also see aquatic birds such as oystercatchers.

06 The route runs downhill, crossing the East Dean Rd, and entering the woodland of the **Westdean Forest**, which shelters the medieval village of Westdean. You might see 13th-century Charleston Manor through the trees (not to be confused with Charleston Farmhouse, the spiritual home of the Bloomsbury Group).

07 Exiting the woodland, the path leads on through farmland to Litlington, where a bridge takes you over the Cuckmere.

Alternative Route

There's another way to tackle the South Downs Way, which takes sea views out of the equation, but gives you instead the Long Man of Wilmington, an ancient chalk figure cut into the hillside depicting a man carrying two staffs. This route (10km) cuts inland from Eastbourne along a high downland ridge, and goes via the historic smugglers' village of Jevington and the 300-year-old Eight Bells pub. The Long Man sits between Jevington and Alfriston. A great way to get the best of both worlds would be to start at Eastbourne, take this route to lovely Alfriston for an overnight stay, and return the next day via the cliff walk to Eastbourne.

DAVID C TOMLINSON/GETTY IMAGES ©

08 The next stretch of the walk is particularly lovely, as you follow the gentle meanders of the Cuckmere, lined by rushes and surrounded by lush meadows. In around 30 minutes, the river walk deposits you in beautiful Alfriston.

09 The village of **Alfriston** is well worth a few hours of anyone's time, and if you haven't factored in an overnight stay here you may wish you had. The Tudor Star and George Inns are equally historic spots for a pub meal and a bed for the night. Fourteenth-century **St Andrews** is surprisingly grand for a village church, and is known as the cathedral of the Downs. Another compelling sight is the thatched **Clergy House**, now a National Trust property. You'll find other enticements in the form of tearooms and an excellent independent bookshop, Much Ado Books. Leaving Alfriston, the nearest station is at Berwick; take a bus or taxi from the village to reach it.

Take a Break

Located inland from Birling Gap in the village of East Dean, the 15th-century **Tiger Inn** (01323-423209; The Green; mains £13-18; noon-10pm;) is one of Sussex' best taverns, serving a gastropub menu to walkers and day trippers alike. In summer the action spills out onto the village green.

49

Blakeney Point

DURATION	DIFFICULTY	DISTANCE	START/END
4hr	Easy	12 miles/ 20km	Blakeney

TERRAIN	Paths, soft shingle

This is a walk of two halves, through extraordinary north Norfolk terrain. The first part describes a loop round the Blakeney Freshes, a freshwater grazing marsh that's a fantastic spot for birders. The route then takes you to Cley next the Sea, from where you can head out to the elongated shingle strand of Blakeney Point, which is famous for its seal colony. From the end of October until the middle of January seal pups are born, adding extra magic to this unearthly landscape.

Getting Here

Blakeney is frustratingly hard to reach by public transport. Take the Coastliner bus to Wells Next the Sea, then the CH1 Coasthopper bus to Blakeney. As Blakeney has a fairly remote location, we've suggested a pub stop that's an overnight stay as well as a great place for a post-walk pint. Otherwise, there are several car parks in Blakeney.

Starting Point

The route starts in the heart of Blakeney village, on the main coastal road.

01 From the main junction with the coastal road through Blakeney, head north on Westgate St, passing the **Kings Arms** which will either set you off with a pub lunch or provide a good incentive at the end. The road curves round to become The Quay as it follows the east bank of the River Glaven. Where Mariners Hill leads off to the right, turn left to follow the North Norfolk Coast Path.

02 Follow the path along the bank, with the Freshes down to your right, and continue as the path curves round the often waterlogged marshes, passing **Stiffkey Freshes** to the left. Keep to

Seals & Sea Kale

The ground beneath your feet on this route is vegetated shingle, a precious habitat that nurtures some rare plants. Crinkly sea kale and shrubby sea blight grow in thick clusters, sea lavender turns patches of shingle purple in summer, scurvygrass produces delicate white flowers and scarlet pimpernel may be spotted in the grasses. These and other low-growing beauties help to create the unique ambience of this ragged coastline. And the spit is home to Britain's largest seal colony, with 3000 pups being born in winter. Adorable to look at, the seals (pictured) can be aggressive, especially when pups are around. Stick to the fenced paths, and keep a wide berth round the creatures.

the footpath on the bank until you reach New Rd, between Blakeney and Cley next the Sea.

03 Turn left onto New Road, then left again, following the High St as it heads into **Cley** (pronounced Cly). Unbelievably, this small place was a thriving medieval port, till it was hit by plague and a silted-up harbour. Just after the point where the road curves right, turn left on The Quay, which leads to the village's 19th-century windmill. From here you join the Norfolk Coast Path, which runs north, crossing the River Glaven and heading north to the Beach Car Park.

04 From the car park, walk north to the sea and turn left, to begin the long walk up the shingle spit. Pass the Watch House building, and continue along the water. Eventually you ascend a ridge and turn left, towards the blue wooden **Lifeboat House**; from here a boardwalk leads through the dunes to the beach, and gives a wonderful view of the seals.

05 This is the end point of the route; retrace your steps along the spit, and from the car park head south, returning to Cley. Once back at the coastal road on the edge of Cley, it'll take around 20 minutes to walk back to Blakeney, where the Kings Arms awaits.

Take a Break

Situated at the north end of the village en route to the shingle spit, the **Kings Arms** (01263-740341; kingsarmsblakeney.co.uk; Westgate St; d £130; P) offers sweet, simple, old-style rooms (expect bright colours and pine) in a pub that's so welcoming you might not want to leave. Order some substantial pub grub (its fish and chips are famous; mains from £10 to £25; meals served noon to 8.30pm), then, for great theatre gossip, ask landlady Marjorie about her career on the stage.

50

The Backs

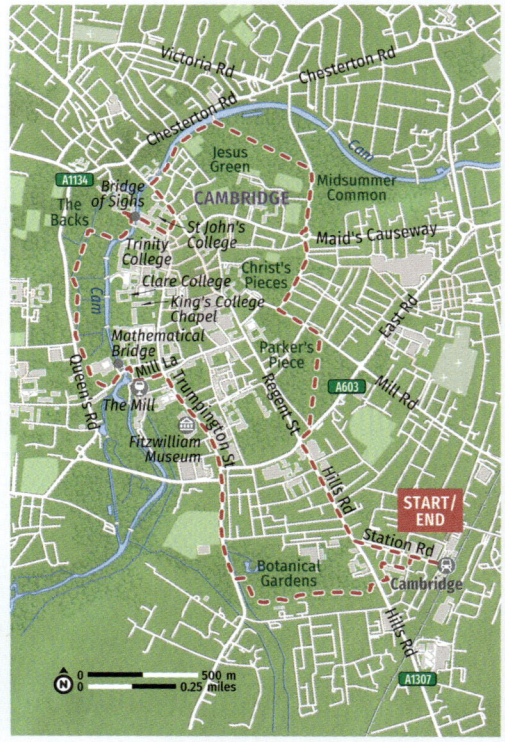

DURATION	DIFFICULTY	DISTANCE	START/END
2hr	Easy	4 miles/ 7.5km	Cambridge station

TERRAIN	Streets and paved paths

Cambridge University was founded way back in 1209, and the town is dotted with ancient colleges, whose Gothic vaults and pinnacles create a townscape like no other. All this is best viewed from the lush Backs, the spacious lawns along the River Cam which are the green lungs of the city. Watch the punters drift by, and round off your walk with a riverside pint.

Leaving the station, head up Station Rd, then turn right on Hills Rd. Cut across the open parkland of Parker's and Christ's Pieces. Head along Midsummer Common, cross Jesus Green and turn left to walk along the River Cam.

Follow the river heading south, crossing it by entering ancient St John's College (a fee of £12 applies but the college is the only was to access the bridge),

and heading over the the famous covered **Bridge of Sighs**, built in 1831 and named for its counterpart in Venice. Here the path leads through The Backs, providing sublime views of King's College Chapel and Trinity and Clare Colleges.

Cross the river again: look out for the wooden **Mathematical Bridge**, ingeniously built from straight pieces of timber which appear to curve. The 19th-century **Mill** is an excellent pub stop on the river. For a longer rural walk, head south down the Cam for 3km to **Granchester**, associated with the war poet Rupert Brooke, where you can take a break in the orchard tearoom.

To get back to the station, walk up Mill Lane and then turn right onto Trumpington St, passing the treasure-house Fitzwilliam Museum. Head south, then cut through the beautiful **Botanic Gardens** (pictured) back to the station.

BEST DAY WALKS: ENGLAND

Best for

A POST-HIKE PINT

51
Leith Hill

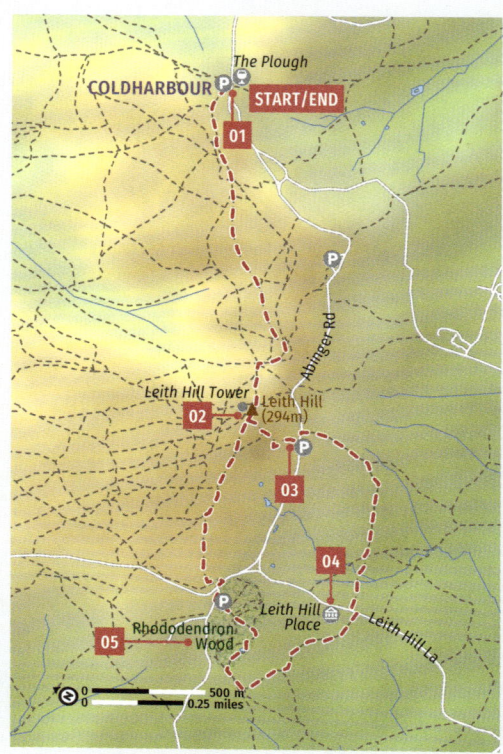

DURATION	DIFFICULTY	DISTANCE	START/END
2hr	Moderate	4 miles/ 7km	Coldharbour

TERRAIN	Paths and tracks, some steep

Leith Hill, like Box Hill, is a fabled Surrey beauty spot, with elevations that seem almost exotic in the south of England. This route takes you from the scenic village of Coldharbour, and then leads in a loop through wooded hills. It takes in the Gothic folly of Leith Hill Tower, and Leith Hill Place, the former home of Ralph Vaughan Williams, who composed the ecstatic tribute to the 'Lark Ascending'. You're likely to see plenty of birds on this bracing and sometimes steep route, including red kites and hovering goshawks.

Getting Here
Coldharbour is a little tricky to reach by public transport. There's an intermittent bus service between here and Dorking, but a more realistic option is to take the train to Holmwood (45 minutes from Clapham Junction), and then take a taxi for the 10-minute journey to the village. Otherwise, you can drive to Coldharbour and park up there.

Starting Point
The walk starts at the Surrey Hills village of Coldharbour, in an area of almost Alpine beauty. There's an excellent pub-shop where you can buy a picnic for the walk.

01 Cross the road from the Plough pub in Coldharbour, and take the paved path that leads gently uphill, keeping the red post box to your right. The path climbs the ridge into woodland, then crosses the ground of the Coldharbour Cricket Club. From there it's back into the woodland, until you emerge at Leith Hill Tower.

02 Lofty **Leith Hill Tower** is a decidedly quirky construction, built in the 1760s by Richard

The Battle for Leith Hill

Bizarre as it seems, until 2018 leafy Leith Hill was the centre of a battle over oil. Despite its status as an Area of Outstanding Natural Beauty, Europa Oil & Gas wanted to sink a borehole for oil and gas explorations under Leith Hill, with a horizontal rig passing under Coldharbour village. The locals were horrified, and launched a campaign vigorously opposing the drilling work, fundraising a legal defence. The debate went on for almost 10 years, and the oil company's lease on the land expired before the work could begin. The lease was not renewed, and to the relief of locals this unspoiled spot looks to stay that way.

Hill, the then owner of Leith Hill Place, in order that it should be the highest point in southeast England. The tower was restored by the National Trust in the 1980s; you can stand at the top (entry costs £3) and see as far as the London Eye through the telescope.

03 From the tower the track leads downhill through dense and lovely woodland, crossing Abinger Rd. Further on you come to a junction, which you cross over to pass Leith Hill Place.

04 **Leith Hill Place** dates from 1600, but was entirely refaced by the energetic Richard Hill in 1760. The composer Ralph Vaughan Williams was brought up here; inside, a soundscape pays homage to the composer, and you can see his piano. With the house on your right, go through the kissing gate and cross the field, going through the gate below a pond to head uphill through some woodland.

05 You emerge at a **rhododendron wood** (pictured), where you pass through a car park. Just beyond this point, cross the road, and follow the path along a wall to head up through more woodland and get back to Leith Hill Tower. This last section of path follows the Greensand Way (see p218).

Take a Break

The **Plough** (01306-711793; ploughinn.com; soup £7.50, mains from £17; noon-10.30pm Mon-Fri, 8am-11pm Sat, to 9pm Sun) is a warmhearted community-owned pub in the high Surrey Hills village of Coldharbour. Pick up a packed lunch for the walk in the form of a fresh pasty or a bacon butty at the wonderfully old-fashioned Shop at The Plough. And after the hike, return to sample one of their own ales, made using traditional methods and all natural ingredients.

BEST DAY WALKS: ENGLAND

52
Rye to Winchelsea

DURATION	DIFFICULTY	DISTANCE	START/END
4hr	Moderate	9 miles/ 15km	Rye

TERRAIN	Path, track, shingle

This walk takes in two of the Cinq Ports, seaside towns which formed a defensive cluster in Anglo-Saxon times; the beautiful little settlements of Rye and Winchelsea were latecomers to the federation in the 12th century. Along the way you'll explore the unique watery marshland and reedbeds of the Rye Harbour Nature Reserve. There's even a shingle beach en route, so bring a swimming costume in good weather. And there's a pub stop at the ancient Mermaid Inn in Rye, where you might want to stop over for a night.

Getting Here
Trains to Rye from London's St Pancras station take 70 minutes, with a change at Ashford International.

Starting Point
The route starts and ends at Rye station, leaving town to the west initially, but circling back to Rye's enchanting town centre at the end of the walk.

01 Exit the arcaded red-brick train station and turn right, with the railway line to your right. Where the road splits, turn left, crossing the railway line. Head down Ferry Rd (the B2089), passing whitewashed cottages and brick terraces. Follow the curve of the road left; it turns into Udimore Rd. Where you see the Udimore Rd street sign on the red-brick house on the left and the blue cycling sign on the lamppost, turn left up the lane named West Undercliff. The houses soon peter out and the lane turns into a rough track. Where the track veers left, go straight ahead up the path.

02 You're now cutting across the farmland of Rye Marsh on a short stretch of the **1066**

200   BEST DAY WALKS: ENGLAND

Country Walk, which, in its entirety, follows the route the Norman conquerors took from Pevensey to Battle. Follow this path for 1.5km till it joins the weirdly named Dumb Woman's Lane. There are two stories behind this: one says that a woman witnessed contraband goods being smuggled here, and had her tongue cut out so she couldn't tell the tale, another that a mute woman dispensed herbal remedies here. Follow the lane for a few metres, then turn left down hedgerow-lined Winchelsea Lane. You pass Winchelsea Station off to the right, then walk down the lane (now Station Rd) which follows the undulations of the River Brede as it leads south, crossing a bridge towards the beautiful little town itself.

03 Station Road emerges at a tight curve in the A259. Cross over onto the pavement, then follow the right-hand part of the road, which climbs gently up Ferry Hill. The entrance to Winchelsea is unmissable: a **medieval stone gate** on the left. Go through the gate, and head down North St. There are all sorts of ways of exploring the town's little grid, but we suggest taking a right onto School Hill.

04 The hill follows a gentle rise, lined by tile-hung and timbered houses with lush gardens. Where the lane emerges you'll see the 18th-century New Inn ahead of you. Turn left here onto the High St, passing an ancient lattice windowed building on your left – to the right is the grand **Church of St Thomas** (pictured), much damaged but containing some lovely 14th-century effigies. Walk down a couple of blocks, then follow the road (now Strand Hill) straight ahead; it curves left, departing Winchelsea via another ancient stone gate and running gently uphill to a T-junction.

05 Turn right at the T-junction, crossing over to follow the pavement for a short

Cinq Ports

Before Britain ever had a navy, its southern towns allied to provide a fleet for the monarchy, initially for Edward the Confessor and then for the Norman kings. The original five ports in the alliance were Dover, Hastings, Hythe, New Romney and Sandwich, with Rye and Winchelsea joining in the 12th century. The power of the Cinq Ports – still pronounced, in Norman French, as *sink* rather than *sank* – was at its greatest in the 13th and 14th centuries. Ultimately the greatest enemy of the proud ports was silting, which reduced Winchelsea, for example, to a shade of its former self. Only Dover now remains as a major port.

stretch on the A259. Where the road curves left at an unlikely log cabin store, turn right onto Sea Rd. This is a pleasant and leafy suburban stretch, with verdant grazing opening up to your right. On your left you'll see Sutton's Fish Shop.

06 Follow the road, and take the sharp right as it runs south; to your right you'll see Dimsdale Sewer (which is actually a water channel) and some flower-dotted meadows. Eventually, opposite the Co-op store turn left, then immediately go left again down Smeatons Lane. Follow this lane for 600m, then take the first left, onto The Ridge. Or, if you fancy a swim, go straight ahead onto the shingle strand of Winchelsea Beach.

07 The Ridge, which turns into Nook Road, takes you on a ramble through the **Rye Harbour Nature Reserve**, with its atmospheric mix of saltmarsh, lagoons, reedbeds, gravel pits and grazing marshes. Nook Rd emerges at some semi-industrial sprawl, where you should turn left, up Harbour Rd. After a short stretch you'll see the Church of the Holy Spirit to your left. Continue up the road past more sprawl, and then back into open countryside. Eventually the road makes a sharp right, joining New Winchelsea Rd at a T-junction. Immediately across the road is a circular **Martello Tower**, one of many low defensive structures build to resist a feared Napoleonic attack.

08 Turn right onto New Winchelsea Road (the A259), which after 500m curves right and crosses a roundabout to join Wish St. Take the first right onto Wish Ward at the Pipemakers Arms to enter the lovely heart of Rye.

09 Walk down Wish Ward, passing Rye Pottery, established in the 1700s, on your right. Take the first left up **Mermaid St**, which soon narrows to become cobbled. It's one of the prettiest streets in this enchanting town, bristling with 15th-century timber-framed houses with quirky names such as 'The House with Two Front Doors' and 'The House Opposite'. Towards the end of the street on the left is the ramblingly characterful Mermaid Inn, a great stop for a pint. At the end of the street take a right, and follow the lane as it curves round Church Sq, stopping to look at medieval **Church of St Mary the Virgin**, which has a Burne-Jones window. At the top northeast edge of the square turn right onto Market St, and then left onto East St, passing the Rye Castle Museum on the left. At the T-junction turn left onto the High St and then right onto Market Rd. Go straight ahead to reach the station.

Rye Harbour Birds

The waterlogged harbour is a haven for birds, including many winter visitors; the Sussex Wildlife Trust estimates you can spot more than 40 species at any given time of year. Year-round, look out for grey heron feeding at the water's edge or egret using their yellow feet to disturb fish and shrimp from their hiding places. Oystercatchers (pictured) plunge their orange bills into the ground to root out worms, and lapwing nest in the wet grassland. Come the colder months, Brent geese winter on the saltmarshes after breeding in the Arctic, and linnets form large undulating flocks, while stonechats sit in pairs on posts. There are five hides dotted around the harbour, where birders train their binoculars on the open skies.

Take a Break

Few inns can claim to be as atmospheric as the ancient **Mermaid Inn** (☎01797-223065; mermaidinn.com; Mermaid St; s/d from £120/190; P 🛜), dating from 1420. Each of the 31 rooms is different, but all are thick with dark beams and lit by leaded windows, and some are graced by secret passageways that now act as fire escapes. The inn also has one of Rye's best restaurants, where you can dine on Rye Bay cod and Romney Marsh lamb.

Best for

COASTAL SCENERY

53
St Albans

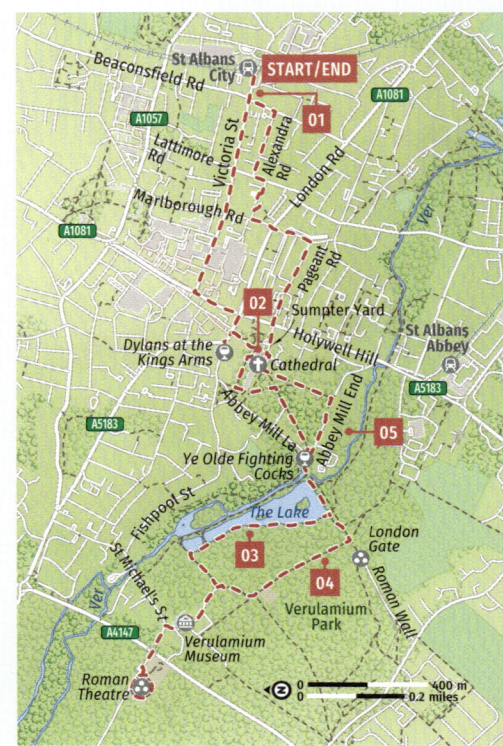

DURATION	DIFFICULTY	DISTANCE	START/END
2hr	Easy	5 miles/ 8km	St Albans City station

TERRAIN	Streets, paved paths

The medieval market town of St Albans is one of the most attractive places within easy striking distance of London. For a small place it has a mighty impressive cathedral, as well as dramatic Roman remains and some exceptional pubs. This walk explores all three aspects of the town, leading you round the spacious ruins of the former Roman settlement of Verulamium, which was sacked by Boudica way back in 61 CE.

Getting Here
Despite its cosy county town feel, St Albans is just a 25-minute train journey north of London's St Pancras station.

Starting Point
The route starts at St Albans City station, which sits just east of the cathedral and historic centre.

01 From the station, turn right up Victoria St, heading into the historic heart of St Albans. At the T-junction, turn left on Chequer St and right on the High St. If you'd like lunch before you set off, go straight ahead for 350m to Dylans Kings Arms on the left. Otherwise, an alley on the left by the Raindrops on Roses charity gift shop leads into the cathedral precinct.

02 It's well worth pausing to explore the mighty Norman brick and flint **cathedral** (pictured), with its tomb to St Alban, the first Christian martyr in Britain. The onward path leads round the north side of the cathedral, then cuts horizontally across the lawns to the extraordinary **Ye Olde Fighting Cocks**, which makes a strong claim to be the oldest

Verulamium

The impressive walls and amphitheatre you see in St Albans still convey the power of Verulamium, as the town was called in Roman times: this was once the third largest city in Roman Britain. It had a forum, a basilica and a theatre, and was powerful enough to be raided by Boudica, the warrior queen of the Celtic Iceni, back in 61 CE: a layer of black ash has been excavated at the site dating back to her attack. Later, stone from the settlement was plundered to help built the cathedral. It's a tantalising thought that much of the ancient town remains unexcavated, lying under the green parkland that you traverse on the walk.

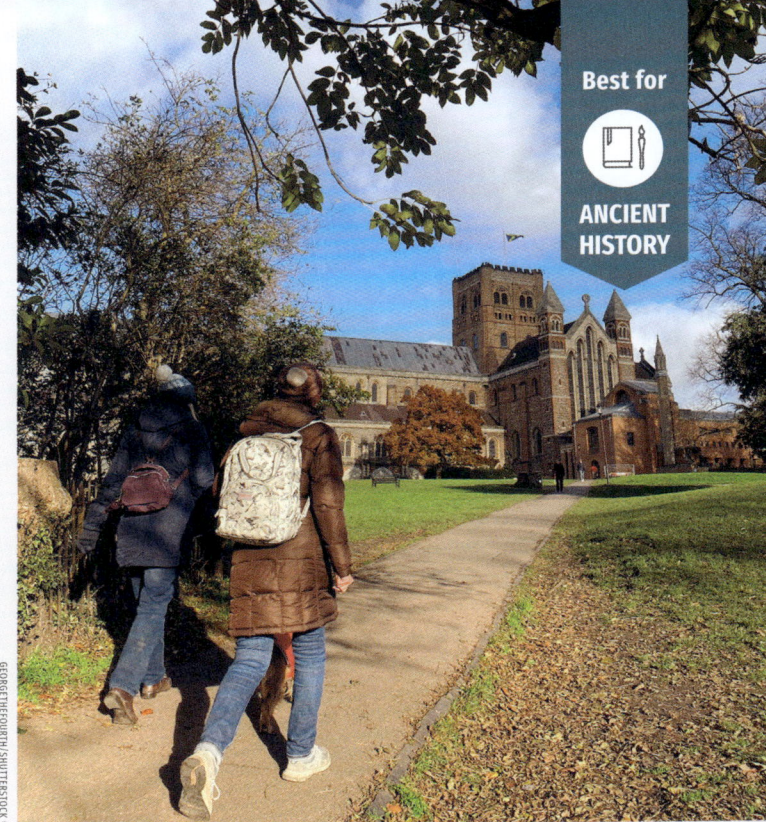

Best for ANCIENT HISTORY

pub in England. The octagonal pub is thought to be 11th century, but built on 8th-century remains with – allegedly – secret tunnels running to the cathedral.

03 From the Fighting Cocks, continue past the lake and then turn right and walk up along it. The path leads to the absorbing **Verulamium Museum**, which displays five floor mosaics from around 200 CE. From the museum, continue up St Michael's St, cross the road and carry on up to the Roman Theatre, with tiers of seating still visible. Retrace your steps via the museum.

04 Turn right to cross Verulamium Park, then left to follow the course of the impressive **Roman city walls**. You pass the remnants of the London Gate, then pass the southern end of the lake and Ye Olde Fighting Cocks.

05 Turn right onto Abbey Mill End, then left to skirt the edge of the parkland. At the cathedral turn right onto Sumpter Yard, then carry on down Pageant Rd, turning left at Keyfield Tce. Carry on – the terrace turns into Marlborough Rd, and then turn right on Victoria St to return to the station.

Take a Break

Dylans at the Kings Arms (01727-530332; dylanskingsarms.com; 7 George St; bar snacks £10, mains £30; bar 5-11pm Tue (bar only), noon-11pm Wed-Sun;) took a long-closed Tudor pub and turned it into an eating and drinking destination. Mains – dished up in the back room of the pub – might include potato Dauphinoise with mushroom Wellington or ox cheek slow-cooked in port, while classy bar snacks such as sole goujons are way out of the ordinary. Craft beers, ales and good wines are served. The timbered exterior is spectacular, the modernised interior stylish but unostentatious.

54

The Viking Trail

DURATION	DIFFICULTY	DISTANCE	START/END
3hr	Easy	6 miles/ 9.7km	Margate/ Broadstairs
TERRAIN	Level coast path shared with cyclists		

Here be Vikings – well, kind of. Kent's Viking Trail is a 32-mile circular route around the Isle of Thanet peninsula, where the Scandinavian marauders first landed in Britain in 449. The paved route is shared by cyclists and walkers, and one of the most interesting sections is the part stretching between the seaside towns of Margate and Broadstairs. While this walk is mostly urban when facing inland, it also follows the wild coastline, passing beaches where smugglers once plotted and where surfers now catch waves. In summer the chalk grasslands are bright with wildflowers and in winter this route is a bracing treat.

Getting Here

Margate and Broadstairs are easily reached by rail from London St Pancras in around 90 minutes and 87 Southeastern trains run from Broadstairs back to Margate daily.

Starting Point

Start your Viking trail at the Margate train station.

01 From Margate train station walk towards the coast, skirting around the A28 roundabout to reach **Margate Beach**, where rides, arcades and a tidal swimming pool make this stretch of gold sand popular with holidaymakers. Walk right past the clocktower and along Canterbury Rd (the A28) and follow the route to the left onto Marine Dr when the road forks. The imposing building shaped like a modernist clutch of sugar cubes is the art gallery **Turner Contemporary** (free), named for the Romantic painter and watercolourist JMW Turner.

Before you reach it, take a detour to the left to stroll up and down the **Margate Harbour Arm**, a

Dickens by the Sea

Charles Dickens had a deep connection to Kent and found inspiration for works including *Great Expectations* and *The Pickwick Papers* in the county. He first visited the area as a child and returned frequently, eventually purchasing Gad's Hill Place near Rochester in 1856. The writer holidayed in Broadstairs, staying at a clifftop house called Fort House (later renamed Bleak House) and wrote parts of *David Copperfield*, which he called his 'favourite child', while gazing out at the coast. Dickens' connection to Broadstairs is still celebrated today, with an annual Dickens Festival taking place each June.

Best for

ANCIENT HISTORY

DARRYL SCOTT/SHUTTERSTOCK ©

breakwater stretching protectively around the bay. The Arm is crammed with little eateries and food vendors, and at the tip is the sculpture by local artist Ann Carrington of Turner's landlady and lover Sophia Booth, with whom he lived in the town between 1827 and 1847. On a summer's day this is a nice spot for coffee, while in rough winter weather waves crash and boom against the stone sides of the Arm. Head back down the Arm and join the coast path (follow Viking Trail signposts) to reach **Walpole Bay**, a sandy beach home to another tempting tidal pool (it's one of the largest in the UK).

02 Continue along the coast past and around Foreness Point to reach **Botany Bay** (pictured), a beautiful beach where huge chalk stacks stand like sentinels looking out to the North Sea. Walk between them to feel dwarfed by the power of millennia of erosion. At low tide, the seaweed-strewn rock shelves here hide all manner of sea anemones, crabs and shellfish as well as fossils. Despite this prolific wildlife, the beach wasn't named Botany Bay until the 18th century, when smugglers were caught using it to bring in contraband and were deported to Botany Bay in Sydney, Australia.

03 Pass Kingsgate Bay (Kingsgate Castle, perched on top of the grassy cliffs, was built in 1763 for Henry Fox, the 1st Baron Holland) to reach **Joss Bay** (pictured following page). The beach is named after another infamous smuggler, Joss Snelling, who operated in the area during the 18th century and was even presented to Queen Victoria as the 'famous Broadstairs smuggler'. It's now a popular spot to catch a wave – the best conditions are in the winter months – and there's a beachside surf school.

04 The path continues along East Cliff – turn

BEST DAY WALKS: ENGLAND 207

right along Crescent Rd to visit **North Foreland Lighthouse**, which has shone a light out to sailors for hundreds of years. A fire burned here as early as 1499, but the lighthouse still working today was built in 1636. Reach **Viking Bay**, where there's a row of pastel-coloured beach huts and another human-made tidal pool. Originally called Main Bay, its name was changed in 1949 when the Danish government commemorated the 449 Viking invasion of Britain by constructing an authentic Gokstad Viking ship, *Hugin,* and sailing it from Denmark to Broadstairs.

To the left of the beach, Bleak House watches over proceedings – this was once novelist Charles Dickens' summer residence, and he wrote *David Copperfield* here. Broadstairs loves to play its literary trump card – Charles Dickens lived here on and off from 1839–59 and now you can visit the Dickens House Museum, grab a coffee at the Old Curiosity Shop or eat at the Charles Dickens pub. In some ways, not much has changed since Dickens wrote about his holidays on this stretch of coast – 'the sun was shining brightly; the sea, dancing to its own music, rolled merrily in; crowds of people promenaded to and fro'.

05 Turn right up the high street to walk into the genteel town of **Broadstairs**. Stop off at Morelli's for its famous ice cream or grab fish and chips on the way to the train station to catch the train back to Margate, further along the high street.

Turner's Top Town

JMW Turner (1775–1851), one of Britain's most celebrated Romantic painters, found endless inspiration in Margate – he called the skies over this coastline 'the loveliest in all Europe'. He was drawn by Margate's dramatic coastal vistas and changing colours, and it became a muse for many of his works, particularly those that depicted the power of nature, such as *The Storm* and *Margate from the Sea*. Today, the Turner Contemporary gallery in town celebrates his legacy by showcasing modern pieces such as Antony Gormley's eerie *Another Time* figures, although if you're a fan, the Tate London actually has the largest collection of Turner's work.

Take a Break

The first **Morelli's Gelato** (morellis gelato.com; 8am-6pm Mon-Fri, 8am-8pm Sat & Sun) opened in 1932, overlooking Viking Bay. The Morelli family still serve iced treats from this delightfully old-fashioned ice-cream parlour, which feels like it's straight out of the film *Grease* thanks to a soda fountain, jukebox, Formica-topped tables and pink leatherette booths. The most requested artisanal gelato flavours, apparently, are mint choc chip and pistachio, but sundaes, coffee and desserts are also on the menu. Expect happy crowds of holidaymakers in the summer.

BEST DAY WALKS: ENGLAND

55

Devil's Dyke

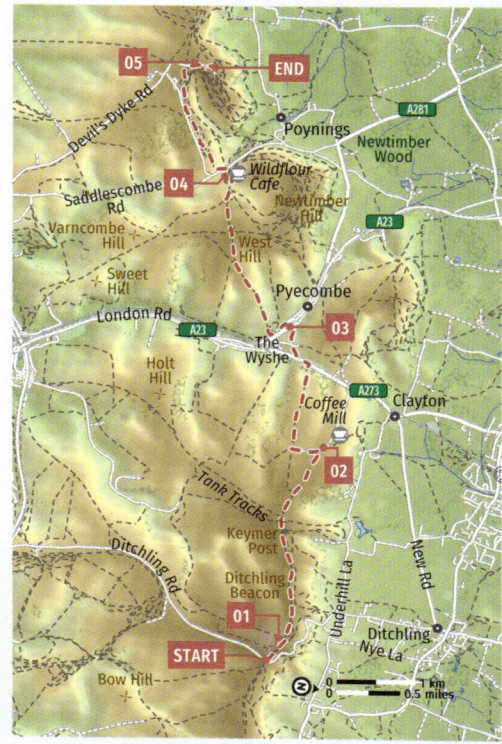

DURATION	DIFFICULTY	DISTANCE	START/END
3hr	Moderate	6.5 miles/ 10.5km	Ditchling Beacon/ Devil's Dyke

TERRAIN	Grassy path, pavement

This is a heavenly walk, despite the name. If you're itching for a bit of space, the 100-mile South Downs Way is the answer, following a winding ridge of chalky grassland that looks out over Sussex. We've covered another section of this long-distance trail (p190), but this slice is another must-hike, beginning at Ditchling Beacon, the highest point in East Sussex, and going in search of Devil's Dyke, Britain's longest, deepest and driest valley. This grassy expanse with far-reaching views to Brighton and the English Channel is where the Devil himself is said to be buried.

Getting Here
The start of the walk is easily reached from Brighton on the hourly Breeze 79 bus. Get back to town on the Breeze 77 from Devil's Dyke. Both buses run hourly.

Starting Point
Start at Ditchling Beacon, just south of the village of Ditchling.

01 At 248m above sea level, **Ditchling Beacon**, now managed by the National Trust, is the highest point in East Sussex and offers panoramic views of the coast, downs and the Weald on clear days. Take the chalk and flint path leading out of the car park to the west and head along the chalk ridge, passing a trig point.

02 Continue west along the (signposted) South Downs Way, passing two dew ponds (artificial pools for watering livestock). Keep going west until you reach a junction signposted left for Devil's

📓 Devilish Legend

The name 'Devil's Dyke' comes from an old Sussex legend. According to the tale, the Devil dug the valley in an attempt to flood the surrounding villages but was thwarted when an old woman lit a candle, making the Devil believe the sun was rising. Frightened by the light, he fled, leaving the valley unfinished. The truth of the matter is that the area around Devil's Dyke has been settled for thousands of years, and archaeological evidence suggests that the site was used by neolithic people and later by the Celts, who may have constructed defensive earthworks here.

Best for

WILD VIEWS

Dyke and right for Clayton windmills. Turn off the South West Coast Path to visit the windmills – just before you reach them you'll pass the ancient ash and beech trees of Clayton Holt, a woodland estimated to be 10,000 years old. The postcard-worthy **Clayton windmills**, affectionately known as Jack and Jill after the traditional English nursery rhyme, were built in the 1820s to mill corn. Jack is not open to the public, but **Jill** (jillwindmill.org.uk; entry by donation) has been restored to working order by volunteers and is open some Saturdays and most Sundays between May and September.

You can even buy Jill's stone-ground wholegrain flour. Even if the windmill is closed, she's lovely to admire as you walk past.

03 Continue on the South Downs Way (pictured) passing New Barn Farm, now a riding stables. Just past the farm turn right, following signs for the South Downs Way and passing alongside Pycombe golf course on your left. As you drop down the hill and into the village of **Pyecombe** take care crossing a busy road (the A273), then walk along School La and Church Hill through the village.

04 Go past the church and at the end of the road turn left and cross the A23. Turn right, following signs for the South Downs Way, and head up the hill. You'll reach the crest of West Hill, where there's a wooden gate and your first glimpse of Devil's Dyke. To the left you can also see down to Brighton and the sea. Walk down the hill towards **Saddle-scombe Farm**, snug at the bottom of the valley, passing through a metal gate in a copse of trees to enter the farmyard. There has been a working farm here since prehistoric times, and in the 14th century the Knights

BEST DAY WALKS: ENGLAND

Templar built a windmill, chapel and garden on the site.

You can still visit the farm's old donkey wheel, where drinking water was raised from a 50m-deep well via a huge wooden wheel powered by a donkey. Walk through the farmyard and stop off at the Wildflour Cafe, an old caravan that now serves coffee and lunches in a pretty walled garden.

05 Cross Saddlescombe Rd and walk through a small car park and up the hill along the South Downs Way. The Way skirts along the top of Devil's Dyke but is enclosed by trees, so once the trail levels out drop down to the right to a lower path that hugs the side of the Dyke to fully appreciate this natural wonder. **Devil's Dyke** (pictured) is the longest, widest and deepest dry chalk valley in the country, and legend has it that the Devil dug the valley to drown the parishioners of the Weald. Scientists believe it was actually formed in the last Ice Age, and it has welcomed hikers and day-trippers since Victorian times, when there was a fairground, a funicular railway, and a cable car that crossed the valley – all hard to picture now when you stand looking out at the peaceful grassy sides of the Dyke, given back to nature. Turn right at the head of the valley and continue uphill until you reach the car park, where you'll also find the bus stop.

Tilting at Windmills

Are you in the Netherlands or the nether regions of England? Sussex is dotted with charming windmills, first built for milling grain, with the first record of a windmill built at Amberley in 1185. While some famous windmills, such as Shipley, made famous in TV's *Jonathan Creek*, or Hog Hill Mill, which Paul McCartney uses as a recording studio and where The Beatles wrote their final song, are sadly closed to the public, others can still be visited. As well as charming Jack and Jill from this walk, you can pop into Windmill Hill, a beautifully restored post mill in Herstmonceux, on summer Sundays.

Take a Break

Tucked away in a tiny field behind the Jill windmill is the **Coffee Mill** (10am-4pm year-round, but sometimes closed in bad weather), a dinky horsebox serving hot coffee and homemade cakes (the banana bread is a stunner) to hungry hikers passing by on the South Downs Way. Make sure you're peckish again when you arrive at Saddlescombe Farm – the **Wildflour Cafe** (9.30am-4pm Tue-Sun) serves veggie-based lunches, coffee and more baked treats, with wooden tables outside among the flowers.

BEST DAY WALKS: ENGLAND

56

Mersea Island

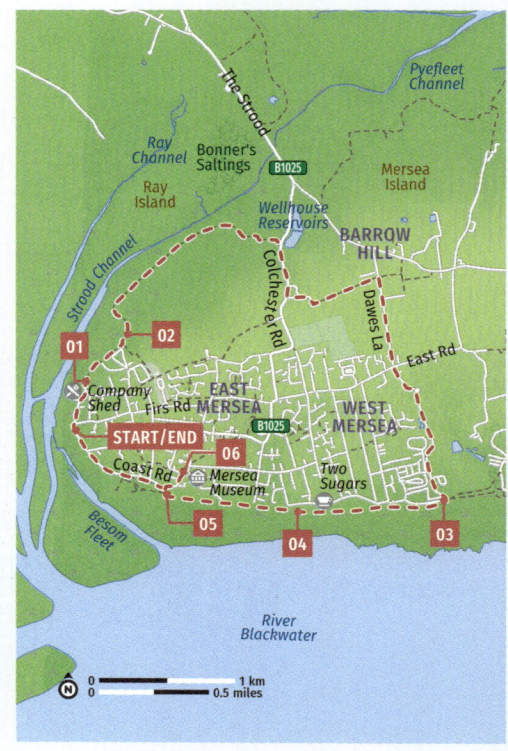

DURATION	DIFFICULTY	DISTANCE	START/END
2hr	Moderate	6 miles/ 9.7km	Coast Road

TERRAIN	Coast path, steep steps

Escape to a slower pace of life on Mersea Island. Sometimes called the 'best-kept secret in Essex', the island deserves to be better known for its centuries of oyster farming as well as sandy beaches, sailing and birdlife-rich nature reserves. Inhabited since pre-Roman times, Mersea was used as a holiday destination in Roman Britain for occupants of Camulodunum (Colchester). This 6-mile loop encircles West Mersea's harbour and sandy stretches of coast, but you can easily add on another circuit around East Mersea to explore nature reserves and quieter beaches.

Getting Here

Reach Mersea from the mainland along a causeway called the Strood, which is occasionally submerged during high tide.

Starting Point

This circular route begins at the western tip of West Mersea on the Coast Road. Parking is available at the Coast Road car park.

01 From the Coast Road car park pass a floating pontoon where boats bob up and down on the tranquil estuary waters – in summer you'll spot locals fishing for crabs while hungry gulls circle overhead. Turn left past the **Company Shed** (the-company-shed.com), a cosy fish restaurant that serves the island's famous oysters as well as the catch of the day.

Mersea at War

During WWII, Mersea Island played a significant role in Britain's coastal defences. The island's strategic position in the North Sea led to the construction of various military fortifications, including pillboxes (gun emplacements) and anti-aircraft batteries, and their crumbling remnants can still be seen today. The waters around Mersea were also mined to prevent enemy ships from approaching, and the island served as a base for the Royal Navy. For a few weeks in 1940 the island was considered to be the front line and bombs fell on Mersea. Residents were involved in war efforts, hosting evacuees and contributing to defence work.

02 Continue straight to **Carriers Close**, passing a row of fishermen's cottages. Turn left along the Strood channel. With tidal waters to your left, take the well-worn track along the embankment northwards towards the Strood causeway. The causeway was built in Roman times and is one of a handful of periodically flooded roads in the world – it's impassable when tides are high enough. At low tide, you'll pass samphire-strewn marshlands and waders on the flats – most of the area surrounding the island consists of saltmarsh and mudflats and is an important sanctuary for wading and migratory birds. At high tide, the channel bed and groynes disappear beneath the rising sea.

03 Continue along the track to reach and cross the Colchester Rd (B1025). This is a busy road, so take care when crossing it. Turn right along the grassed verge. Keep an eye out for the bridleway near the Paeony Chase junction, which provides a safe route as the verge gives over to the roadway, leading to farmed fields before reaching Dawes La. Cross and head right until you reach a residential area. At the East Rd junction, head straight over to Cross La and join a tree-lined footpath that brings you back out onto the estuary. Turn right and take the path running past colourful beach huts. There are almost 400 of these charming huts on the island, almost all beautifully looked after, and some can even be hired for the day via the **Little Beach Hut Company** (thelittlebeachhutcompany.co.uk). During WWII the island beaches were festooned with barbed wire, and all beach huts were removed; most were stored in back gardens and replaced in peacetime.

04 The entrance to **West Mersea Beach** by Seaview Ave provides a great vantage point for watching kitesurfers do battle with the wind on blustery days, and the sandy beach here is perfect for beachcombing – look out for iridescent oyster shells as you make your way past yet more pretty beach huts.

05 Reach **Monkey Beach** (the name is believed to come from a coastguard lookout post that locals thought resembled a monkey in a cage). A short stretch of path leading up to this area can be temporarily cut off during high tides. Take the Monkey Steps up to the Coast Road or continue along the beach and follow the boardwalk over the wetlands back towards the road. Halfway up the Monkey Steps you can also detour along a boarded path to seek out St Peter's Well, a sacred spring that sustained the island's residents for 1000 years.

06 At the top of the steps head right towards West Mersea town centre's high street to find shops, cafes and the attractive St Peter and St Paul Church. It's also worth stopping for a nose around the local **Mersea Museum** (merseamuseum.org.uk, 2-5pm, £2), which catalogues the island's fascinating history and its key defensive role in WWII. Head back along the Coast Road, passing barges and houseboats before coming to the quay and yacht club (this area is also prone to occasional flooding), and arriving back at the car park.

Don't forget to check tide times before leaving the island by car – visitors are regularly caught out by rising waters on the causeway and have to be bailed out – literally – by the island's emergency services. A regular bus service links West Mersea to Colchester. Or stay on the island to walk another loop exploring East Mersea, where there's a nature reserve and a vineyard.

Mersea's Oysters

Mersea is renowned for its oyster fishing, particularly for its native Colchester oysters. Oyster farming on the island dates to Roman times, with the shallow waters providing ideal conditions for growing these pearlescent beauties – it's said that the invading Romans loved them so much that they would tow oysters in nets behind their boats all the way back to Rome. The island's estuaries and mudflats still offer a rich environment for oysters to thrive, and local fishermen continue using traditional harvesting methods. Try a few in local restaurants such as the Company Shed and the Dukes Seafood.

Take a Break

A former WWII pillbox on Victoria Esplanade in West Mersea, **Two Sugars** (10am-5pm Tue-Sun) is now a pocket-sized cafe serving proper cups of tea, locally baked bread and full English breakfasts. Outdoor seating has a view of the sea and you're steps away from a line of bright beach huts (pictured). Two Sugars also stocks buckets, spades and other seaside-ready items. The cafe is cash only and has no airs and graces but is as close as you'll get to a proper greasy spoon on the island.

Also Try...

Pilgrims' Way

Stretching all the way from Winchester, and joined by pilgrim routes from London, the Pilgrims' Way has been taking the faithful to Canterbury for centuries. This final stretch runs from the Kentish village of Chilham, via apple orchards and woodlands, to Canterbury and its fabled cathedral.

It's well worth having a wander round the timbered houses and flint church of Chilham before you set off. The route runs via the oddly named village of Old Wives Lees, through a lime-tree avenue and across hopfields to Chartham Hatch. From here you enter No Man's Orchard and head uphill to Harbledown, before entering the medieval West Gate at Canterbury, and walking through town to the cathedral.

DURATION 3hr
DIFFICULTY Moderate
DISTANCE 7.5 miles/12km

Greensand Way

This long-distance walk takes you on a bucolic route through Surrey and Kent, leading from Haslemere to Hamstreet via a high sandstone ridge. The entire route runs for 175km, but we've selected the section that links Sevenoaks with Shipbourne, via some extraordinary country houses.

You leave the town of Sevenoaks via farmland and parkland (pictured), heading to vast 15th-century Knole, built by an Archbishop of Canterbury, enlarged by Henry VIII and once the home of Vita Sackville-West. From here you walk through the ancient woodland of One Tree Hill, and then enter the Ightham Mote estate. With its moat and 13th-century great hall, this is old England at its most magnetic. The route then runs cross-country to Shipbourne.

DURATION 2½hr
DIFFICULTY Moderate
DISTANCE 6 miles/9.7km

BEST DAY WALKS: ENGLAND

HELEN OGBOURN/GETTY IMAGES ©

Box Hill

Anyone who thinks there's no drama in the landscapes of southeast England should try Box Hill (pictured), a much-loved green escape for Londoners. This fabled beauty spot, immortalised by Jane Austen in an eventful outing in the novel *Emma*, rises to nearly 200m, its chalky folds dotted with evergreen box trees.

Box Hill & Westhumble Station is the starting point for the route, which first runs to the downland village of Mickleham. From here you can ascend Mickleham Downs or stop at the foot of the hill, where there are famous stepping stones crossing the River Mole, before tackling the steep slopes of Box Hill itself to reach the remnants of a 19th-century fort, where there's a handy National Trust tea room.

DURATION 3hr
DIFFICULTY Moderate
DISTANCE 5.5 miles/9km

South Downs Way

The Seven Sisters and the Devil's Dyke walks described earlier in this chapter are two outstanding stages of this 100-mile trail, which starts in Winchester and ends at Eastbourne and follows old routes and droveways along the chalk escarpment and ridges of the South Downs.

Most people take nine or 10 days to traverse the entire route and it's a surprisingly wild and peaceful escape for a walk so close to London and Brighton. Other highlights include the Bignor Roman Villa, Queen Elizabeth Country Park's 2000 acres of woodland, the far-reaching views from Old Winchester Hill and the stretch between Pyecombe and Lewes via two windmills.

DURATION 10 days
DIFFICULTY Hard
DISTANCE 100 miles/160km

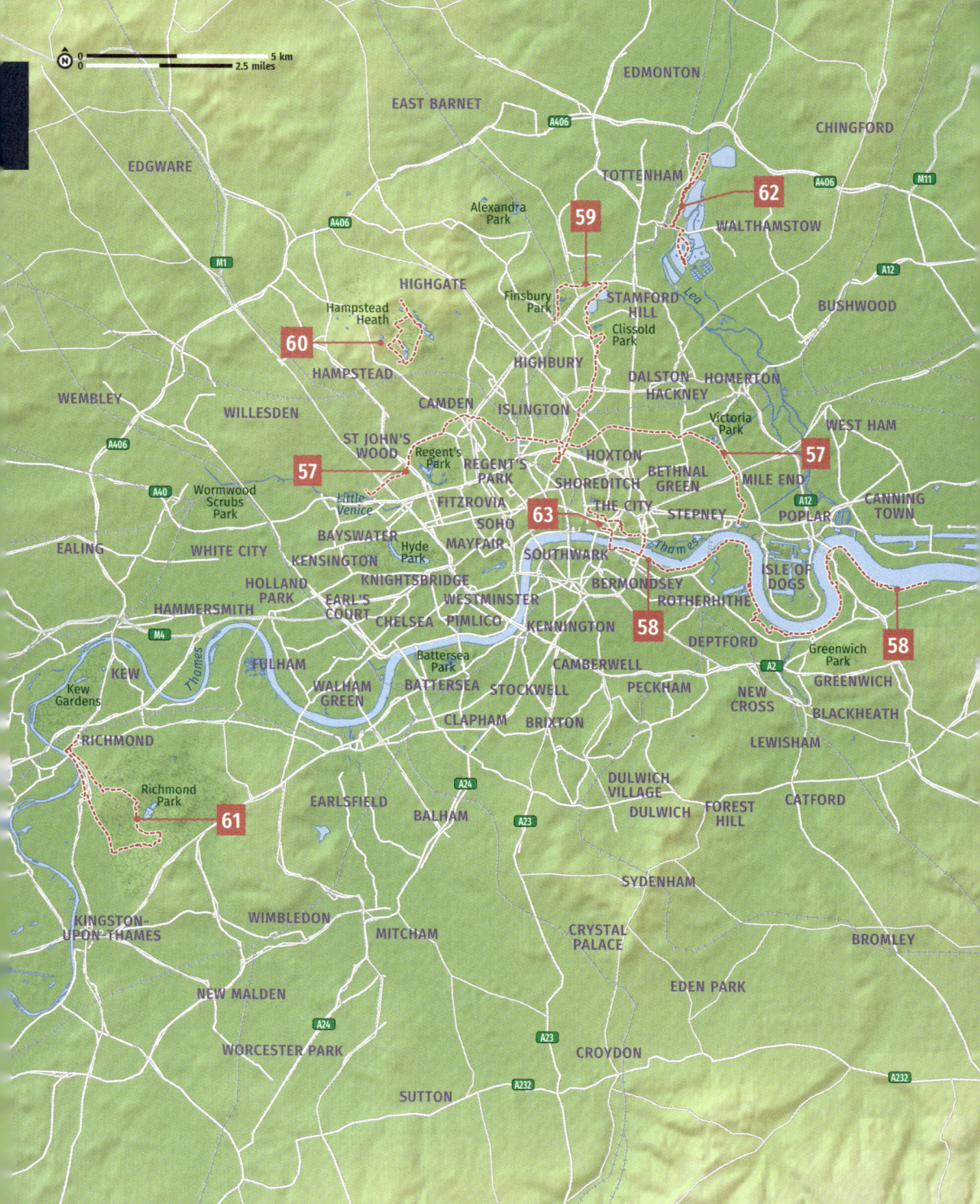

Deer, Richmond Park (p233)

London

57 Regent's Canal
This watery route cuts across London from west to east. **p224**

58 Thames Path
The south bank of the Thames is packed with cultural and historic treasures. **p228**

59 New River
Follow the traces of the 17th-century canal that once provided London with water. **p230**

60 Hampstead Heath
Wild and rolling heathland with panoramic views and an excellent gallery. **p232**

61 Richmond Park
Great herds of deer roam the capital's largest park. **p233**

62 Tottenham Marshes
Leave behind the urban sprawl for a walk through wetlands to spot wildlife and savour views along the River Lea. **p234**

63 Roman London
A vast world of secret Roman history is hidden throughout central London – this city walk explores the vestiges of ancient Londinium. **p238**

Explore London

London needs no introduction – buzzing with energy and a hub for art, business, culture and architecture, England's capital draws in 30 million visitors a year. London is also a remarkably and refreshingly green city – 47% of the capital is made up of parkland and gardens as well as 'blue' space (canals, reservoirs and rivers), all making for some lovely walking. The Royal Parks in the city's centre are manicured idylls with artful planning, while Hampstead Heath and Richmond Park in particular offer a wilder feel among ancient trees. The New River route takes you from the northeast into the heart of town, via an ingenious 17th-century canal.

London

London may be a huge metropolis but the capital becomes manageable if you treat it as the locals do – as a series of villages, each of which harbours diverse communities and has its own personality.

The proper name for London's administrative areas is boroughs, but most people place their loyalty in smaller and more distinct areas. In terms of green spaces, North London has some wonderfully wild places: Hampstead Heath, where meadows, woodland and swimming ponds may trick you into thinking you're in the countryside; Queen's Wood and Highgate Woods with their remnants of old English forest; and more open and spacious Finsbury Park. Tottenham, best known for its multicultural sprawl, also has secret green lungs in Tottenham Marshes and Walthamstow Wetlands, rich in birdlife. In East London, the expansive Victoria Park, with its lakes, gardens and cafes, provides a welcome contrast to the busy streets.

Way out west, genteel Richmond boasts the largest park in the city, with a huge deer population, miles of shady trails and some inspiring river walking. You can follow the gentle curves of the wide Thames from here down to Hampton Court Palace and beyond.

Stay central to explore the three connected Royal Parks at the geographical heart of the city, or take a hike down the fascinating Thames Path as it runs east to Greenwich. Even the City of London has ancient oddities to discover – go searching for Roman London (Londinium) and find slices of the 2200-year-old wall that once guarded the city when a fort stood on the banks of the Thames.

East London, parts of which are gritty and built up, also has a surprising amount of greenery, and a network of canals whose towpaths make for refreshing strolls. Don't miss the Olympic Park in Stratford, where you can wander through impressively landscaped gardens or enjoy a peaceful moment by the river.

Wherever you go in London, you're never too far from a great pub or cafe, and while accommodation can be expensive, it is possible to find

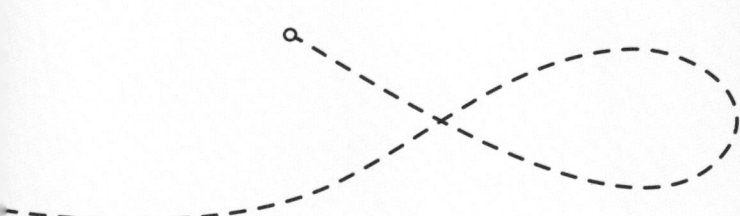

Resources

Time Out (timeout.com) A weekly listings map sold citywide, giving the most comprehensive lowdown on what's new in the capital.

Transport for London (tfl.gov.uk) This website helps you navigate London via public transport.

Visit London (visitlondon.com) The official tourist board site features a comprehensive section on the city's parks. There's also plenty of information on outdoor London more widely, including outdoor events and markets, peaceful green spots, picnic places, riverside pubs and open-air swimming pools.

bargains, as well as affordable eats from all around the world on practically every local high street and at markets such as Borough Market, Leadenhall, Seven Dials Market and Maltby Street.

 ## When to Go

There's no bad time to see London, though the winter months can feel rather drab, with low temperatures, grey skies and short days that may curtail your walking. The city sees lots of tourists year-round, particularly in July and August, but the routes we've suggested have space for everyone. In autumn the Royal Parks are a riot of rich colour as the leaves turn.

 ## Transport

Most of the city's transport is relatively pricey, but also very quick and efficient. The Underground (Tube) system connects major spots and is an affordable option, and a network of red double-decker buses and nippy overground trains fill in gaps to connect the metropolis. London has become a decent city to cycle in, with a network of cycle superhighways and an affordable bike-hire scheme.

 ## Where to Stay

Centrally located accommodation in London doesn't come cheap, though there are a few decent hostels, and some chain hotels have fabulous locations. B&Bs and Airbnb options give you the experience of London with a local: an insider view is a big plus in the big city. The further out you go, the better the bargains are and, given the connectedness of the transport system and the hip appeal of some of the outer boroughs, staying away from the centre can be a plus. For something quirky, try the Good Hotel, a modern hotel on a floating barge on Royal Victoria Dock.

 ## What's On

Kenwood House Concerts (english-heritage.org.uk/visit/places/kenwood/events) This grand villa holds concerts, festivals and theatre performances in its grounds.

Notting Hill Carnival (nhcarnival.org; Aug) Held on the August bank holiday, this is a massive street party where the city comes together to sing, dance and celebrate Caribbean culture.

Thames Festival (totallythames.org; Sep) Celebrating mudlarking and the river's wildlife, with local bands plus kayaking and heritage walks.

57
Regent's Canal

DURATION	DIFFICULTY	DISTANCE	START/END
3½hr	Moderate	9 miles/ 14.5km	Warwick Ave/ Limehouse

TERRAIN	Paved towpaths

Those who are fed up with the busy streets of London should take to this towpath, a meandering watery route which leads all the way across London, from Little Venice in the west to Camden, Kingston and Hackney. The path then curves round past Victoria Park, heading south to spacious Limehouse Basin before joining the mighty River Thames.

Getting Here
The starting point for the walk is Warwick Ave tube station on the Bakerloo underground line.

Starting Point
From the tube station, head down Warwick Ave to the canal, following signs for Little Venice.

01 **Little Venice** (pictured), where the walk starts, is one of the prettiest spots in the city. The canal basin was once known as Browning's Pool – the poet lived in a house overlooking the basin. The area still has a slightly bohemian and colourful feel, and is surrounded by handsome white regency buildings.

02 The first stretch of the towpath hugs the north bank of the canal along beautiful **Bloomfield Rd**, with bright flower-bedecked houseboats sitting in private moorings.

03 The path joins Aberdeen Place at the point where the canal disappears for a stretch into the narrow 250m **Maida Hill Tunnel**, built in 1812. It was the first of the city's canal tunnels, built because the Portman estate refused to allow permission for an open canal. Beyond this, steep steps lead back to the towpath.

04 From here the path leads past the minarets and bulbous golden dome of London Central Mosque, then skirts the northern boundary of **London Zoo**, the most visible element of which is the soaring Lord Snowdon–designed aviary. Recently restored and revamped, the aviary is now home to a raucous troop of colobus monkeys.

05 Beyond the zoo to the north are the slopes of attractive and village-like **Primrose Hill**, part of a chase (hunting reserve) which was owned by Henry VIII. Despite its historic antecedents Primrose Hill is mostly made up of graceful lines of Victorian terraced houses.

06 Leaving the green embrace of Regent's Park and Primrose Hill, the path then curves round towards Camden. At Oval Rd, where a bridge crosses the canal, there's a diversion in the form of a typically provocative **artwork** by street artist Banksy: it depicts a small girl with a lollipop in one hand, and a missile in a cart in another.

07 Past Kentish Town Lock, the canal continues around to **Camden**, a still slightly scruffy and raffish area with a famous **market** which is well worth a stop – it's also a good point to grab some affordable street food or a coffee. Located in former stable buildings, the market features 200 stalls, and is most famous for selling funky vintage clothes.

08 Under a series of bridges and locks, you continue on the northern bank of the towpath to St Pancras Lock, with its cosy Victorian lock cottage. On the south bank you'll see an old Victorian water tower, and then **Camley Street Natural Park**, a sylvan community space that provides a rich habitat for birds, butterflies and amphibians. Also to either side are the modern developments around King's Cross Station, including a vast Google building on

Canal Museum

The little **London Canal Museum** (canalmuseum.org.uk) explores what life was like for families living and working on Britain's impressively long and historic canal system. The exhibits in the stables upstairs are dedicated to the history of canal transport in Britain, including recent developments such as the clean up of the Lea River for the 2012 Olympic Games. The museum is housed in a warehouse dating from 1858, where ice was once stored in two deep wells. The ice trade was huge in Victorian London, with 35,000 tonnes imported from Norway in 1899 alone, arriving in the city at Regent's Canal Dock before being transported along the canal.

BEST DAY WALKS: ENGLAND

the south bank, and the swish campus of Saint Martin's College to the north. Canal aficionados might want to cross the canal at Maiden Lane Bridge to detour to the London Canal Museum (p225), which sits on the basin here.

09 Where the canal disappears into the Islington tunnel, the route leaves the water for a stretch, and takes to the quiet streets of **Islington**. You head down Duncan St to the north of Angel station, and rejoin the canal just beyond the Duncan Terrace Gardens. This incidentally is where the New River intersects with the Regent's Canal – for more on this other fabled waterway, see p230.

10 From here the towpath takes you on into Hackney – it's a sociable stretch with plenty of walkers and cyclists, and a mix of new developments and characterful warehouses. Immediately beyond the point where the De Beauvoir Rd crosses the canal, the booth-like **Towpath** cafe is an idyllic spot for lunch or cake. You can sit outside, or shelter in a brick alcove.

11 From here you'll see moored boats on the enclave of the Kingsland Basin to the left. The surrounding swish modern apartments belie the fact that the basin was created back in 1822. The next notable stop is the Cat & Mutton Bridge, where you might want to detour from the canal (pictured) left onto **Broadway Market**. It features a mix of hip and neighbourhood shops, and on Saturday is taken over by an outstanding food market.

12 Beyond the point where trafficky Mare Street crosses the canal, you curve round to walk past the southern edge of spacious **Victoria Park**. It was opened back in 1845, and became a crucial amenity and leisure space for East Enders in the later 19th century. Beyond the park, the Hertford Union Canal leads off to the left, but you should carry on straight ahead, heading south.

13 To your left is long **Mile End Park**, a new green space with an indoor climbing centre that sits on the spot where WWII bombing ravaged the area. At the southern edge of the park the fascinating Ragged School Museum is testimony to the work of Dr Thomas Barnardo in the East End – he worked to relieve the plight of the destitute, particularly children.

14 From here it's a short stretch south to **Limehouse Basin**, whose rather anodyne modern appearance is at odds with its amazing salty history. Named for lime kilns that sat by the river here in the 14th century, it became an important port from Tudor times. But actually it was the building of the Regent's Canal that made the basin come alive, as goods from ships docked here could be easily transported inland. It has an important part in the history of immigration in the capital too – African and Chinese sailors disembarked here, and made the area their home. The growth of the railways eventually heralded a decline in canal transport, and the basin was shattered by bombing during the war, leading to the exodus of the Chinese community to Soho. At one point you could apparently cross the basin by stepping from ship to ship. Today, it's a quiet and somewhat bland residential spot, though the crowded yachts add a little life to the scene. You can circle round either side of the basin to emerge at the River Thames, startlingly wide at this point. The nearest transport onwards is the Limehouse DLR station, immediately northwest of the basin.

Take a Break

Occupying four small units facing Regent's Canal towpath, the simple **Towpath** (☏020-7254 7606; rear 42-44 De Beauvoir Cres, N1; mains £8-11; ⓧ9am-5pm Wed & Sun, to 9.30pm Thu-Sat; Ⓤ Haggerston) cafe is a super place to sit in the sun and watch the ducks and narrow boats glide by. The coffee and food are excellent, with delicious cookies and brownies on the counter and cooked dishes chalked up on the blackboard daily.

58

Thames Path

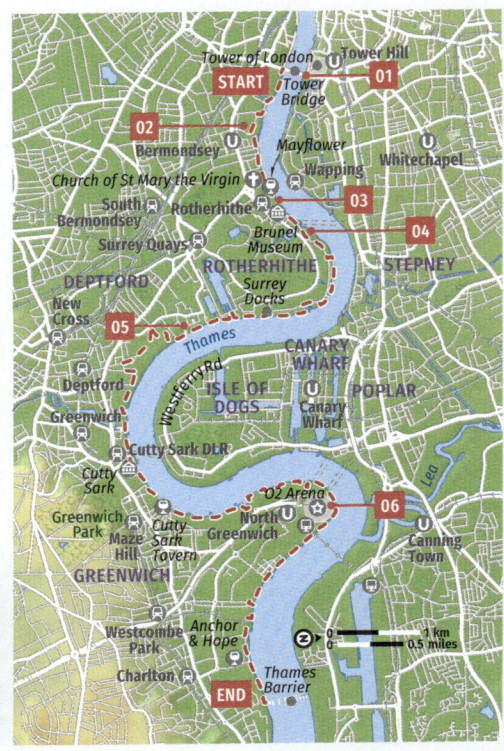

DURATION	DIFFICULTY	DISTANCE	START/END
4½hr	Moderate	11 miles/ 17.5km	Tower Bridge/ Thames Barrier
TERRAIN	Paved paths and roads		

The Thames Path starts way outside of London, 180 miles away in Kemble in Gloucestershire at the Thames Head. Its end point is the Thames Barrier, the shiny construction that prevents the Thames from flooding. Here we focus on the south bank of the river and the last stage of the walk, starting at Tower Bridge and ending at the barrier.

Getting Here
Leave London Bridge station from the Tooley St exit and cross over to Hay's Galleria, once a docking point for 19th-century tea clippers. Once through the gallery, turn right onto the Thames Path, passing HMS Belfast and City Hall to reach the tall pillars of the bridge.

Starting Point
This walk starts at Tower Bridge, the late-19th-century suspension bridge that connects the Tower of London with the south bank of the river.

01 From Tower Bridge, the route runs eastwards along the river, leading along Shad Thames, crisscrossed with high iron bridges. You then cross a muddy inlet at **St Saviour's Dock Footbridge**, the site of Bill Sykes' grisly death in Charles Dickens' *Oliver Twist*.

02 Passing the revitalised wharf buildings of Bermondsey, the path briefly leaves the river, joining it again at the touching memorial to the Salters, a Quaker couple who worked to improve living conditions here in the early 20th century. Beyond you come to Rotherhithe, and the 1716 **Church of St Mary the Virgin**, outside of which sits a memorial honouring the Pilgrim Fathers who left for America from here. Nearby, the 16th-century riverside Mayflower pub looks onto what was the docking point for the Mayflower ship.

🔍 Mudlarking

The huge daily surge of the tide disrupts the treasures of the Thames, and lays them on the foreshore for eager mudlarkers to collect. Sadly, the original Victorian mudlarkers were children who scoured the banks of the Thames for sellable items. Today, various tour companies lay on guided mudlarking tours, a safe and fun way to rummage in the mud and occasional filth of the river. In fact, unless you have a Port of London Authority licence, you'll be looking only – you're not permitted to dig or use a metal detector. Visit the Museum of London to see some of the rarer items found on the foreshore. And to see inspiring mudlark finds as they happen, follow @london.mudlark.

Best for

A POST-HIKE PINT

03 Just past the pub, the intriguing **Brunel Museum** honours the master engineer's father, who designed the Thames tunnel here at Rotherhithe.

04 Cross the red lift bridge at Surrey Water. The next major landmark is the lovely **Surrey Docks** city farm on the site of an 18th-century shipyard.

05 The river loops south to enter Deptford. You walk through Pepys Park and along some back streets to enter historic Greenwich, where the **Cutty Sark** tea clipper (pictured) is a spectacular and unmissable sight. Continuing along the river, the Cutty Sark Tavern makes a fine lunch and/or pint stop.

06 The next stretch takes you round a sharp loop in the river, and past the tent-like 02 Arena. From here it's another 3km along the river to the mighty **Thames Barrier**. Since 1982, the glittering gates of the barrier have prevented storm surges from flooding the capital. The nearest transport from here is Charlton Station: to reach it, retrace your steps on the Thames Path, turning left at the Anchor & Hope pub onto Anchor and Hope Lane.

 Take a Break

Housed in a delightful bow-windowed, wood-beamed Georgian building directly on the Thames, the 200-year-old **Cutty Sark Tavern** (☎020-8858 3146; cuttysarkse10.co.uk; 4-6 Ballast Quay, SE10; ⊙11.30am-11pm Mon-Sat, noon-10.30pm Sun; 🛜; Ⓤ Cutty Sark) is one of the few independent pubs left in Greenwich. Half a dozen cask-conditioned ales on tap line the bar, there's an inviting riverside seating area opposite and the upstairs dining room looks out on to glorious views.

59
New River

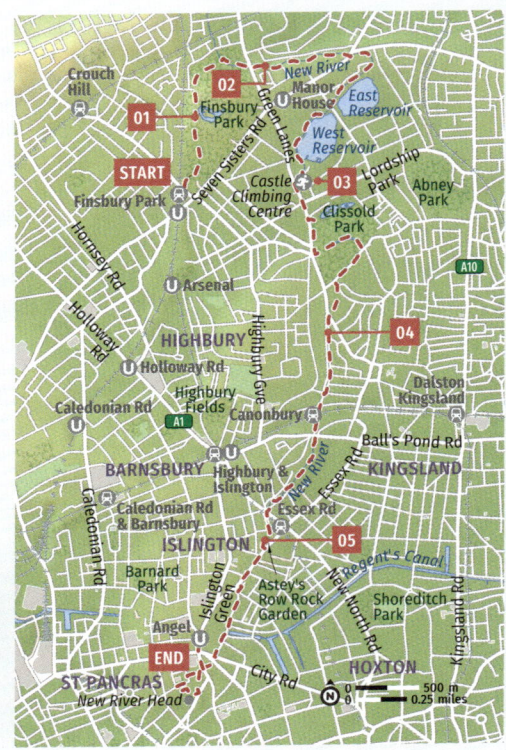

DURATION	DIFFICULTY	DISTANCE	START/END
2hr	Moderate	5.3 miles/ 8.5km	Finsbury Park station/ Angel station
TERRAIN	Tarred paths, some streets		

This north London walk follows a now modest waterway with a fascinating place in the social and health history of the capital. It is not in fact a river at all, but a manmade channel which revolutionised London's contaminated water supply when it opened in 1613. The whole walkable route is 62km, but this section follows the last stage, a green ribbon leading into the centre of the city.

Getting Here
This north London walk is easily accessible on London's tube system: Finsbury Park is on the Victoria Line, Angel on the Northern Line.

Starting Point
Come out of busy Finsbury Park train/tube station, and follow signs for Finsbury Park, entering it through the Stroud Green Gate.

01 Head north through **Finsbury Park**, passing the boating lake to your right, curving to the right, and then taking the little bridge over the water channel. This is your first encounter with the New River. Take the path along the left bank of the channel, cutting through the park and exiting it over Green Lanes road.

02 Go through the green gate to join the scenic raised path along the waterway. Follow the river, leaving it briefly to cross Seven Sisters Rd, until it curves to join the East Reservoir, used for canoeing and boating, and then the wetland of the West Reservoir.

03 The crenellated **Castle Climbing Centre** is an unmissable landmark, and its cafe makes a great spot for lunch or cake. It was built as a water pumping centre, with all the grandeur of the Victorian age. From the centre, turn left onto Green

Creating the New River

The creation of explorer, banker and engineer Sir Hugh Myddelton, the New River (pictured) replaced the dirty old River Thames as London's water source. Running for 62km from Hertfordshire on a gentle incline, it was so well structured back in 1613 that it still carries water for treatment and, over the centuries, saved thousands from death by cholera. You can veer off the route to see a statue of Sir Hugh, in ruff and pantaloons, which stands on Islington Green flanked by urn-clutching cherubs. At the end of the walk at the New River Head, scant traces of a watermill, engine room and pump house are all that remain to show the spot where water was brought to generations of Londoners.

© WEI HUANG/SHUTTERSTOCK ©

Lanes, cross Lordship Park and head into Clissold Park. The waterway is submerged, but you soon pick it up as it leads through and out of Clissold Park, and onto Church St. Clissold Cres and the New River Path lead to spacious Petherton Rd, where a tree-lined central strip conceals the water below. Go straight ahead up Wallace Rd.

04 The route now follows meandering landscaped areas, created in the mid-20th century to follow the turns of the waterway. The conical brick structure was a watchhouse, built in the 18th century to prevent fishermen and bathers from contaminating the water.

05 Continue to Astey's Row Rock Garden, head south on Essex Rd, then follow the now submerged waterway along Colebrooke Row and Duncan Terrace Gardens. Coming out of the gardens, head up Owen St to Myddelton Sq, named for the creator of the New River. Go up Myddelton Passage to the New River Head. To get from here to the tube, walk north up Arlington Way and then turn left and head up busy St John St, which joins Islington High St; the station is on the right-hand side.

Take a Break

An utterly unique London experience, **Castle Café** (020-8211 7000; castle-climbing.co.uk; The Castle Climbing Centre, Green Lanes; soup £4, cakes £3; noon-8.30pm Mon-Fri, 9am-5.30pm Sat & Sun) is a sustainable social enterprise set within a spacious climbing centre, itself set within a wildly eccentric Baronial-style castle around 45 minutes into the walk. Food is vegetarian, homemade and created with care and flair; they produce their own herbal teas, salads, honey and fruit in the picturesque garden. Daily specials include seasonal stews, soups and curries.

BEST DAY WALKS: ENGLAND   231

60

Hampstead Heath

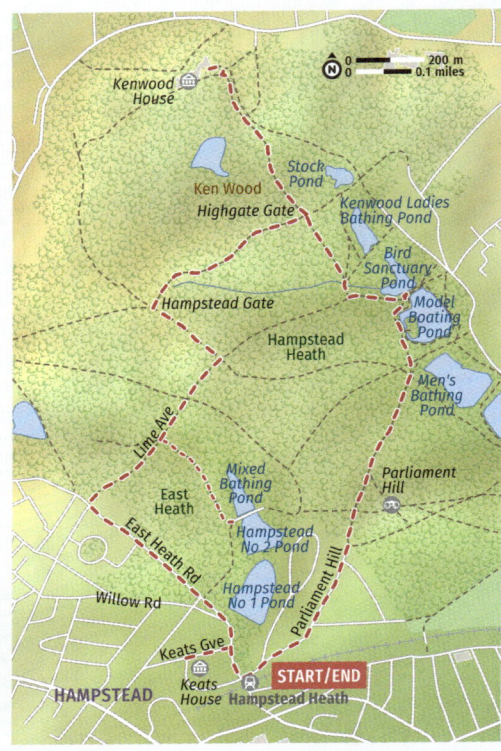

DURATION	DIFFICULTY	DISTANCE	START/END
1½hr	Moderate	3.4 miles/ 5.5km	Hampstead Heath overground

TERRAIN	Some steep paths and woodland

Even hardened Londoners are amazed by the size and wildness of Hampstead Heath. Set on a sandy ridge, it provides sweeping urban views as well as dense ancient and more recent woodland. On a sunny day bring a swimming costume, as the natural ponds provide a gorgeous spot for a dip. Kenwood House is a good stop for art lovers, and Keats House, the poet's home from 1818 to 1820, is a stroll away.

Start from Hampstead Heath station, heading up Parliament Hill towards the Heath. You soon leave the streets behind and ascend the heath itself, climbing uphill for a classic London panorama. Press on and you come to a row of **ponds** with self-explanatory names: the Men's Pond, Model Boating Pond, Bird Sanctuary Pond and Ladies Bathing Pond. (The Mixed Bathing Pond sits close to the end of the route, perfect for a post-walk dip.)

Beyond, you come to Highgate Gate: go through it to plunge into Ken Wood. After a short stretch the views open up again, with parkland and lovely neoclassical **Kenwood House** ahead of you. There's a wonderful art collection here and its **Brew House** cafe is a great lunch or cake stop.

Head back to Highgate Gate, turning right to descend the heath to Hampstead Gate. Follow the wide **Lime Ave** down to the edge of the heath, with a possible detour to the left before you get there to the Mixed Bathing Pond.

Otherwise, you come to busy East Heath Road, where you should turn left. Some 600m down the road on the right you'll see Keats Grove, where the short-lived poet's home **Keats House** is well worth a stop.

61

Richmond Park

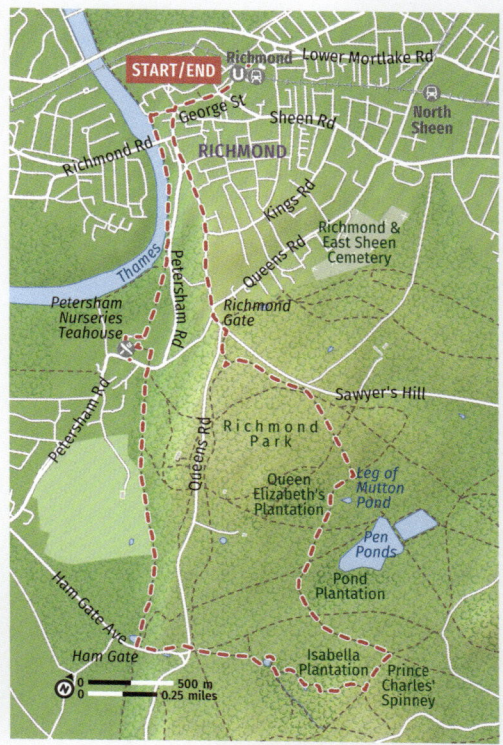

DURATION	DIFFICULTY	DISTANCE	START/END
2¼hr	Easy	6.2 miles/ 10km	Richmond station

TERRAIN	Tarred or grassed paths, some inclines

Richmond Park is London's largest green space, and its wildest. Until you've visited, it's hard to believe that the city limits can encompass such a verdant space, where huge herds of deer roam freely, and where there are more than a thousand 'veteran' trees. From the 13th century this was a royal hunting ground, which was enclosed by a brick wall on the order of Charles I in 1637.

Start from Richmond Station, looking out for River Thames signposts. Turn left at the river, walking past pubs, Georgian villas and houseboats for 1km, and then follow signs across the meadow to **Petersham**. The plant-filled glass houses of Petersham Nurseries Teahouse make a gorgeous food stop.

Retrace your steps from the Nurseries and take the lane towards the church, following a Capital Ring sign. This will bring you into the park, where you'll see Ham Gate down to your right. Take the network of undulating paths towards the **Isabella Plantation**, with its heather garden and rhododendrons, and Pen Ponds.

Follow the paved curving road and approach **Pond Plantation**, where you turn left, up the horse ride. Ascend the gentle hill with Leg of Mutton Pond to the right, and the dense Queen Elizabeth's Plantation to your left. From the plantation you join a broad track with a Capital Ring sign.

Walk towards the large red-brick building, the former Star and Garter care home, and exit the park at Richmond Gate. Out on the street, head down grand Richmond Hill. At Richmond Bridge go straight ahead on Hill St, which curves right to become George St, to arrive back at Richmond Station.

62

Tottenham Marshes

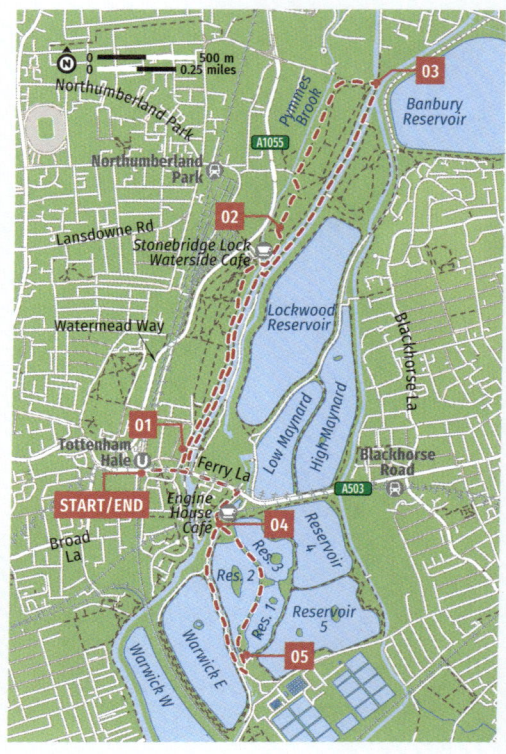

DURATION	DIFFICULTY	DISTANCE	START/END
2½-3hr	Easy	5 miles/ 8km	Tottenham Hale station

TERRAIN	Flat paved paths and dirt paths

Think 'Tottenham', and the footy club and a multicultural urban community are more likely to spring to mind than a green lung home to wetlands, wildlife and wide-open views. But the home of the Hotspurs also has a hidden gem, perfect for escaping the city's buzz. Tottenham Marshes is a patchwork of grasslands, scrublands and waterways in the Lea Valley, which stretches from here all the way out of London. This walking route follows the River Lee Navigation and passes the Lockwood Reservoir before looping around Walthamstow Wetlands (check opening times first). Bring binoculars to spot skylarks, short-eared owls, sedge warblers and many more unlikely city dwellers.

Starting Point

Start and end this walk at Tottenham Hale Underground station. There's also parking by Stonebridge Lock and at Walthamstow Wetlands.

01 Hop off the Tube at Tottenham Hale and you'll still feel very much like you're in London – but not for long. Turn down along Ferry Lane and follow the road along the pavement as it passes over bridges and under the shadow of high-rise flats. At a sign for Lea Valley Walk turn left and follow the left-hand side of the canal path, passing Tottenham Lock and following along the **River Lee Navigation** (a navigation is a canal running parallel to a river).

02 Follow the canal path, passing brightly painted canal boats. When you reach Stonebridge Lock, where there's a friendly cafe to take a

Wild North London

London isn't somewhere that wildlife spotters would usually pack their binoculars for, but the Tottenham Marshes are a secret sanctuary with abundant wildlife. Look out for kestrels hunting for field voles in the grasses or perched above you on electricity pylons, as well as Painted Lady butterflies and bright purple bee orchids dotting the marshes in the summer months. In winter, large flocks of linnet can be seen feeding on the seed heads of teasel, dock and thistle along the walk. The river channels are also good places to look for the blue flash of a darting kingfisher hunting in the reeds.

break at, take the footpath to the left to leave the canal path and walk through **Tottenham Marshes** along a paved trail through grasslands and wooded areas. The marshes are made up of three main areas: Clendish Marsh, Wild Marsh West and Wild Marsh East, and footpath junctions have handy maps and distances displayed on them.

Continue onwards into Wild Marsh West, where the path becomes turf. From some parts of the marshes you can just about see the buildings of Canary Wharf in Docklands and the far-off Gherkin in the City of London. The marsh was the first home ground of Tottenham Hotspur Football Club in 1882, which feels rather unbelievable when you're gazing at tall grasses and listening to the twittering of birds. The marshes have actually existed for thousands of years, formed by small waterways scything through wetlands to join the River Lea. As humans began to develop the land, the marshes and forest gave way to agriculture and meadows, and in medieval times the marshes would have produced reeds and grass for thatching and hay. Despite this rich history, this is now one of the last natural wetlands remaining in all of London.

03 At the T-junction at the top of Wild Marsh West turn right and then follow the path as it crosses the navigation on **Chalk Bridge**. Follow the canal path down the other side of the River Lea Navigation back down to Ferry La, with the canal and its line of bobbing boats on your right and bushes and trees lining the path on your left. As you approach Tottenham Lock you'll also pass the **Paddock Community Nature Park**.

04 When you reach Ferry La, turn left, away from the Tube station, and walk along the pavement until you reach a large metal sign that reads

BEST DAY WALKS: ENGLAND 235

'Wetlands' on the right. Turn right through the gate to explore a loop of **Walthamstow Wetlands London Wildlife Trust** (wildlondon.org.uk; 9.30am-4pm Oct-Mar, to 5pm Apr-Sep). This internationally important reserve sprawls over an astonishing 160 hectares, supplies drinking water to millions of Londoners and is teeming with life, from tufted ducks to peregrine falcons.

For centuries, the River Lea provided transport and powered mills that were vital for local industries. But from the mid-19th century this rural landscape of rivers, marshes and farmland was dramatically transformed by the creation of the reservoirs, as London's rapidly growing population urgently required a supply of clean water. The local authorities opened the areas around the Walthamstow reservoirs to the public in 2017 and today there are over 13 miles of trails to explore, many of which are accessible for wheelchairs and buggies.

05 From the gate, pass the car park and the Engine House cafe. The reservoirs are numbered and walking a loop around Reservoir 1 or around Reservoirs 2 and 3 brings you to the **Richard Woolley bird hide** and the **Coppermill Tower**, an old copper mill crowned by an Italianate spire. Turn back up a path passing Coppermill Stream on your right and East Warwick Reservoir on your left to reach Ferry La again. Turn left and follow the road back to Tottenham Hale station.

236 BEST DAY WALKS: ENGLAND

 ### Football Fanatics

Tottenham is, of course, better known for soccer aces than for secret wildlife havens. Premier League club Tottenham Hotspur, often called Spurs, was founded here in 1882. Their home ground, the state-of-the-art Tottenham Hotspur Stadium, seats over 62,000, with fans flocking to watch their heroes win two English league titles, eight FA Cups and the UEFA Cup twice. Renowned players like Jimmy Greaves, Gareth Bale and Harry Kane have graced the ranks of the club, whose motto is 'To Dare Is to Do'. The stadium is a 30-minute walk from Tottenham Hale station if you're ending your walk with some live footy.

 ### Take a Break

Stroll along the Navigation until you reach **Stonebridge Lock Waterside Cafe** (10am-5pm), a peaceful spot to savour coffee, fresh cakes and sandwiches (including moreish bacon butties) by the water, and a favourite with locals on bikes or walking their dogs. Over the road in the Walthamstow Wetlands, the **Engine House Café** (wildlondon.org.uk; 9.30am-4pm) serves coffee and baked treats within the exposed brick walls of the original engine house building, as well as on an outside terrace with views over the reserve and across to the skyscrapers of London.

63

Roman London

DURATION	DIFFICULTY	DISTANCE	START/END
2hr	Easy	3.5 miles/ 5.6km	Tower Hill Station

TERRAIN	Pavement

Before London, there was Londinium, a Roman fort by the Thames. Today most of the old city is 7m below your feet, built upon over two millennia. But there are still fascinating signs of the Romans hidden in plain sight, and uncovering them on foot is a great way to explore the City. The 'Square Mile', as the City is known, dates to 50 CE, when Roman invaders bridged the River Thames and built a flourishing city of 18,000, ensconced by a huge perimeter wall. This walk goes in search of the wall and daily Roman life among the skyscrapers and is a fascinating snapshot of London's layered history.

Getting Here

All of this walk is easily accessed via public transport with Mansion House, Canon Street and Fenchurch Street stations also nearby.

Starting Point

The route starts and ends at Tower Hill Underground station.

01 Tower Hill Underground station may feel like the heart of modern London but it's also surrounded by thousands of years of history, including a slice of the remnants of the **Roman wall**, which stands just outside the station next to a **statue of Emperor Trajan**. The Roman section of the wall has horizontal bands of red tiles, which were used to strengthen it. When first built, the Roman wall would have stood at around 6m high and represented the boundaries of ancient Londinium. Cross Tower Hill Rd to reach the Tower of London.

BEST DAY WALKS: ENGLAND

Queen Boudicca

Boudicca, queen of the ancient British Iceni tribe, has become a bit of a national heroine. She led a failed uprising against the conquering forces of the Roman Empire, massing an army of 120,000 in 60 CE. Marching on Colchester, her troops destroyed the then-capital of Roman England and moved on to Londinium, burning it to the ground before she was finally quashed by the Roman forces during a major battle in the Midlands. The first Roman town of Londinium had lasted a mere 13 years. You can still meet Boudicca today – the rampant statue *Boadicea and Her Daughters* stands near Westminster Pier.

Best for

ANCIENT HISTORY

02 The **Tower of London** may be best known as a royal palace, a prison and the home of the Crown Jewels, but it also sits atop Roman foundations, and one of the most impressive sections of the Roman Wall stands directly in front of you. Cross back to the station to head west along Coopers Row and past the ruins of a Roman fort that formed part of the city's defences – it's now part of the Grange City Hotel but is open to the public.

03 Follow Lloyd's Ave and then Fenchurch St before turning right onto Cullum St to reach **Leadenhall Market** (pictured). Beneath the arches and cobblestones of this ornate Victorian market lie the remains of Londinium's basilica (courts) and forum (market), the heart of Roman administration and trade, first built in 70 CE. It's an evocative place to grab a coffee, a site that is still a working market almost 2000 years later. In 1803, excavations in the Leadenhall St area found a stunning example of Roman mosaic artwork 2.75m below street level, depicting Bacchus, god of wine, agriculture and fertility, riding on a tiger and surrounded by drinking cups, cornucopia, serpents and other symbolic objects. What remains of it now resides in the British Museum.

04 Turn right onto Gracechurch St and then left on Threadneedle St, then take Bartholomew La and Lothbury to reach **Guildhall Yard**, where a Roman amphitheatre once stood. The amphitheatre's remains are preserved underground and can be visited in the **Guildhall Art Gallery** (free). Follow London Wall towards the Barbican to see a significant stretch of the Roman wall in St Alphage Gardens – it's a peaceful spot for a breather, with trees and benches arranged below the wall.

05 Walk down Wood St and turn left into Cheapside and then right onto Walbrook to seek out the **Mithraeum** (free; booking is advised). This restored Roman temple dedicated to the god Mithras is one of the most evocative Roman sites in the city. The temple was built in the 3rd century CE, nearly 200 years after the founding of London. Discovered in 1954 during post-WWII excavations, and now located beneath Bloomberg's European headquarters, the site lies over the course of one of London's 'lost rivers', the Walbrook. Explore the temple's ruins and learn about the cult of Mithras, a mysterious religion popular among Roman soldiers.

06 Continue along Walbrook to reach Cannon St. At Cannon Street station look across to the opposite pavement – a grille on the wall houses the mysterious **London Stone**. This lump of rock could be Roman, medieval or once used for occult purposes – it's a mystery, but the name 'London Stone' was first recorded around the year 1100.

07 Reach **London Bridge** and cross the Thames. The first London Bridge was built from wood by the Romans in 43 as part of their road-building programme, to help consolidate their conquest of Britain. The river was central to Roman trade and transport, and Roman baths once stood near Southwark Cathedral on the opposite bank. Turn left and follow the pedestrian path along the river to reach **Tower Bridge**, a more modern icon of London – cross the bridge to end up back at Tower Hill Underground station.

TRAVERS LEWIS/SHUTTERSTOCK ©

St Dunstan-in-the-East

It may not be Roman, but the ruins of St Dunstan-in-the-East (pictured) are well worth seeking out along this walk. This 12th-century church was damaged in the 1666 Great Fire of London and was partially rebuilt by acclaimed architect Sir Christopher Wren. The church was heavily bombed during the Blitz of WWII, leaving only the tower and walls intact. Instead of rebuilding, the site was transformed into a public garden in 1971. Lush greenery now entwines the Gothic ruins, creating a serene oasis right in the heart of the bustling city, and is cherished both by visitors and frazzled businesspeople popping out for a lunch break.

Take a Break

Leadenhall Market (leadenhallmarket.co.uk) is a buzzy, airy market in the heart of the City of London. Built by the Victorians above the centre of Roman Londinium as a poultry and game market, it's now a hodgepodge of outdoor and covered boutiques, shops, restaurants and bars in the heart of the Square Mile. Italian favourite **Osteria del Mercato** might be as close as you can come to Roman fare these days, but the **Lamb Tavern** pulls a good pint and French bakery **Aux Merveilleux de Fred** makes delicious specialist pastries.

Also Try...

RON ELLIS/SHUTTERSTOCK ©

Parkland Way

This route covers the course of the dismantled Great Northern Railway, which cuts a deep green swathe from Finsbury Park, across Crouch End and into the ancient woodland of Highgate and Queen's Wood, with the option to continue to the parkland that surrounds Alexandra Palace.

Keep your eyes peeled, and you just might see tiny muntjac deer along the route and also, come evening time, foxes and hedgehogs. Other pleasures along the way include the evocative remains of Crouch End station, a green man sculpture in the old railway arches, magical Queen's Wood cafe hidden among the trees, and the High Victorian grandeur of Alexandra Palace (pictured).

DURATION 3hr
DIFFICULTY Moderate
DISTANCE 7.5 miles/12km

Thames Path West

Affluent Richmond is the starting point for one of London's loveliest walks, a riverside ramble that eventually brings you to mighty Hampton Court Palace.

From Richmond station, head riverward and then begin to follow the curves of the wide River Thames southeast, passing handsome 17th-century Ham House – both it and its orangery tea room are well worth a stop. Eel Pie Island, accessed via an eccentric river ferry, is also worth exploring. Back on the east bank of the river, the walk continues via the reclaimed Ham Lands to Kingston. Here you cross the river, and continue around Hampton Court Park to access the magnificent palace, built for Cardinal Wolsey in 1516 and subsequently nabbed by Henry VIII.

DURATION 4½hr
DIFFICULTY Moderate
DISTANCE 11 miles/17.7km

Epping Forest

Epping Forest (pictured) is a wonderful survivor, stretching for around 20km into Essex and featuring ancient deciduous woodland that is some of the oldest in Britain.

From Chingford station, the route runs to a fantastic Tudor hunting lodge built for Henry VIII in 1543; close by is one of the last surviving 'forest retreats', refreshment rooms built for late-19th-century day-trippers. From here, a network of paths and 'rides' (wide leafy avenues) takes you across meadows and into dense forest that's home to over 50,000 species of plants, fungi and animals. Visit the conservation centre, where you can learn more about the forest's biodiversity, and the Iron Age Loughton Camp, dating back to around 500 BCE.

DURATION 2½hr
DIFFICULTY Easy
DISTANCE 6 miles/9.7km

Capital Ring

Often described as the M25 for walkers, the Capital Ring sketches a green circuit around the capital. It covers 126km, and takes in attractions such as Eltham Palace, the Thames Barrier and the Walthamstow Marshes.

The Ring can be broken down into 15 manageable sections. For example, Crystal Palace to Streatham leads you through Biggin Wood and Rookery Gardens and past Norwood Grove Mansion, while Woolwich to Falconwood has stunning views over London's skyline, and Richmond to Osterley takes you past grand mansions and Richmond Park's deer-filled landscapes. The route is well-served by public transport, with each section starting and ending near an Underground, train or bus station (visit the Transport for London website to find out about other routes).

DURATION 1½hr
DIFFICULTY Easy
DISTANCE 4 miles/6.4km

# Arriving

However you arrive in England, be it by plane, train or boat, there are a few things to be aware of that will make your first few hours run smoothly, and enable you to get to your accommodation to unpack, freshen up and enjoy a well-earned cup of tea.

It's All in the Boots

There's one bit of kit that can really make or break a trekking adventure – your pair of hiking boots. Proper walking boots are a must if you're out in changeable conditions (hello, England), and will keep your feet warm and dry mile after mile. The two main options are leather or fabric hiking boots – leather is great for cold, wet weather, while fabric boots are ideal for hiking from spring through to autumn. A good walking boot should also be waterproof and breathable – good models use a waterproof membrane such as Gore-Tex to stop moisture getting in but allow sweat to wick away. You should also look for boots with thick, bouncy rubber soles with deep lugs to offer a good grip, plus a reinforced toe box to protect your feet. High ankle support is good for uneven terrain, and if you want to wear your boots for mountaineering as well as hiking, make sure they're crampon compatible.

Airport to City Centre

HEATHROW AIRPORT
On the Tube network; fares start from £5.50.
Taxi fares start from £52.

BIRMINGHAM AIRPORT
Catch the free monorail to Birmingham International (two minutes), then a train to the city centre for £5.
Taxi fares start from £40.

MANCHESTER AIRPORT
Has a regular bus (£5), train (£4.50) and tram (Metrolink £4.60).
Taxi fares start from £25.

EUROSTAR TERMINAL
Central London single fare £2.80 (if you pay by contactless entry).
Taxi fares from £24.

CUSTOMS

There are restrictions on bringing meat, dairy, fish, animal products, fruit, vegetables, nuts and seeds into England from abroad.

TRANSFERS

Many of the major airports are well connected to the local city by train, tram or bus, so no need to shell out for an expensive taxi. You can book most tickets in advance.

CASH

There are cash machines and currency exchanges at every international entry point. Be aware that some ATMs will charge per transaction.

BORDER CONTROL

Many UK airports have biometric entry options including fingerprints and ePassports for swift entry. To speed things up in other lines, have your passport ready and keep family groups together.

Getting Around

With a sprawling network of roads and railways, plus trams, tubes and buses, there's always an easy way to find your way around.

TRAVEL COSTS

Car rental
Around £35 per day

Petrol
Approx £1.38 per litre

EV charging
Around £26 for a full charge

Train ticket
London Kings Cross to Newcastle £63

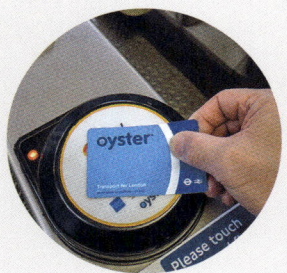

London

For travelling around London, fares are cheaper if you use an Oyster Card or contactless debit/credit card. These can be used on the bus and tube networks. Swipe as you pass through ticket gates and look for swipe points on buses.

On the Rails

There is good rail coverage, but trains don't have a great reputation for being on time. Travel up and down the country can be surprisingly quick (under three hours from Euston to Cumbria), but east to west generally takes longer.

Buses

Buses are a great way to navigate around and get a feel for local life. Different operators work across England but always download the operator's app for real-time tracking and ticketing options. For the best views always sit upstairs.

Car Hire

Car hire is available at all airports. Most offer a good selection of electric/hybrid models. Motorway service areas and major town/city car parks will have recharging points.

NARROW LANES

If you're visiting the more remote areas such as Cornwall, Cumbria or the Peak District, be prepared for narrow, winding roads, often with high hedges. Locals tend to whiz along them at an alarming speed. There are also many single-track roads that have passing places, so you may need to reverse. It's also a good idea to find out how to flatten your wing mirrors when you collect your car as this can help when passing others on narrow lanes.

DRIVING INFO

Drive on the left.

Remember that road speeds are in *miles* per hour.

Some tolls and city charges require payment online.

ABOVE LEFT: CERI BREEZE/SHUTTERSTOCK ©
ABOVE RIGHT: YAU MING LOW/SHUTTERSTOCK ©

Health & Safe Travel

Drinking Water

Tap water is, for the most part, safe to drink and signs will warn you if that is ever not the case. It generally tastes better in more rural areas. There is also a good network of places to refill your water bottles, and the Refill app will direct you to the nearest free filling point.

Wildlife

Unless you suffer from allergies, the local wildlife and insect population is unlikely to cause you much harm. The only venomous snake is the adder, which can give a sharp bite if unwittingly disturbed, but it's likely to flee rather than fight. Also watch for ticks after country walks – they can potentially lead to Lyme disease.

Personal Safety

The violent crime rate is low here and, with some of the strictest firearms licensing laws in the world, gun crime remains low, too. Most public areas are well lit, and CCTV cameras are common throughout towns and cities, as well as on public transport. At major events there is always a strong police presence.

Travel Insurance

Check your insurance policy carefully before your trip – some policies don't cover hiking as the sole purpose of a trip and other policies do cover hiking and trekking, but there may be additional requirements or limitations. The most common is altitude – you may only be covered hiking up to a certain altitude (eg 2000m or 3000m), or if you use specialist equipment on your expedition.

EXTREME EVENTS

England is a country of few extremes with few major natural disasters to worry about. The rain rarely 'stops play' and most activities carry on regardless. If you visit during winter, do be aware that because snow is seldom seen here, the country is poorly equipped to deal with it and roads and rail networks often grind to a halt.

BE PREPARED

For most of the walks in this book, you won't need any special equipment or expertise. But for a few of our harder walks – especially the ones that tackle the Lake District and the more remote parts of Dartmoor and Exmoor – you'll need a bit more gear. Ideally, you should carry a compass, full waterproofs and insulation layers, a head torch, a whistle and perhaps even a bivvy bag.

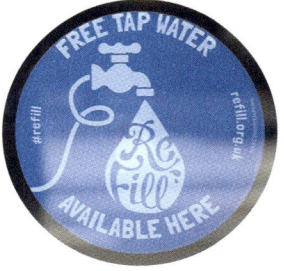

WEATHER CHECKS

The weather in England can change rapidly. Stay safe on any hike by checking the general UK Met Office forecast and, if you're heading up high, check the Met Office Mountain Weather Forecast, too. You can find comprehensive health and safety guidance for year-round hiking around the UK at adventuresmart. uk – it's recommended by all local Mountain Rescue teams.

ABOVE LEFT: TIM GEHLER/SHUTTERSTOCK ©
ABOVE RIGHT: STEPHEN BARNES/SHUTTERSTOCK ©

Responsible Travel

Climate Change & Travel

Lonely Planet urges all travellers to engage with their travel carbon footprint, which will mainly come from air travel. While there often isn't an alternative, travellers can look to minimise the number of flights they take, opt for newer aircrafts and use cleaner ground transport, such as trains.

One proposed solution – purchasing carbon offsets – unfortunately does not cancel out the impact of individual flights. While most destinations will depend on air travel for the foreseeable future, for now, pursuing ground-based travel where possible is the best course of action.

ReFill
refill.org.uk
Discover ways to cut out unnecessary plastic: eat, drink and shop with less waste.

Slow Ways
beta.slowways.org
Collates walking routes connecting England's towns, cities and national parks.

National Rail
nationalrail.co.uk
Official source for train times, fare enquiries and rail-centric inspiration.

RESPONSIBLE DINING

For classy dining with a clear conscience, check out Michelin Green Stars (guide.michelin.com/gb/en) for restaurants, which rewards sustainable practices, including ethical and inclusive behaviour as well as avoiding waste.

KEEPING IT GREEN

Go green in every sense of the word with a trip to the Eden Project in Cornwall (edenproject.com). They keep their carbon footprint low and offer incentives to those arriving by foot/bike/bus.

CAR-FREE IN CUMBRIA

Go Car Free in the Lake District (visitlakedistrict.com/explore/travel/carfree) is an initiative by Visit Lake District to encourage car-free visits by offering a wide range of resources to plan your visit.

Accommodation

VISITING DURING 'LOW SEASON'

In many rural areas the holiday cottage boom has caused issues with locals being priced out of the market, resulting in a drop in local resident numbers. This means that in low season, when visitor numbers drop, local amenities such as cafes and shops may have shortened opening hours and local buses may run on a reduced timetable, so it's always best to check ahead online if there is somewhere specific you want to visit. In tiny villages check if your accommodation comes with parking as it's likely to be scarce.

HOW MUCH FOR A NIGHT IN...

Average 3-bedroom Airbnb
£150/night

YHA youth hostel
from £15 per night

Campsite
£10 to £30 per night

Green Glamping

You'll find eco-pod sites right across England with many fully embracing the concept of sustainability. Places like the Quiet Site in Cumbria (thequietsite.co.uk) have its pods built locally to keep the carbon footprint as low as possible. It's a great way to experience camping but without the hassle of a tent.

Elegant Options

Wolsey Lodges (wolseylodges.com) is a nonprofit organisation that offers an unforgettably English experience. Whether you stay with families in grand stately homes or in a tucked-away 'des rez' (desirable residence) in the suburbs, you'll definitely have something to write home about. This is not a place for anonymity – you will be welcomed as part of the family for the duration of your stay.

English Cottages

If you're looking for 'chocolate box' perfection – think Kate Winslet's house in *The Holiday* – then Stay Cotswold (staycotswold.com) is a great place to start. With properties right across the Cotswolds – and beyond – you can book yourself into the perfect English cottage. Just mind your head on the low beams in the ceiling!

Youth Hostels

There is a large network of hostels in England. Many are privately owned, but there are also the YHA (Youth Hostelling Association) hostels – joining fee £25. It's a great way to keep costs low, stay somewhere quirky and meet lots of interesting people. You don't always need to share a room; many now offer private rooms, too.

CARAVANS & CAMPERS

Instead of a car, consider hiring a camper van. There are plenty of campsites to choose from (check out websites such as pitchup.com), and also plenty of places where it's OK to park for free – the app Park4Night is one way to find the perfect spot. Best tip is to not hire anything longer than 6m for easier parking.

KONMAC/SHUTTERSTOCK ©

Nuts & Bolts

GOOD TO KNOW

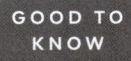

Time Zone
GMT in winter, GMT plus one hour in summer

Country Code
+44

Emergency number
999

Population
56 million

CURRENCY: POUND STERLING (£)

Tipping

In England, tipping is appreciated but not mandatory. In restaurants, a 10–15% tip is customary if service isn't included. For taxis, rounding up to the nearest pound or adding 10% is common. In hotels, tipping porters £1–2 per bag and housekeeping £1–2 per night is acceptable.

Cashless Travel

Most places are fully geared up for cashless payments by card, phone or watch. Some smaller establishments prefer cash as will stallholders at fares, fetes or other small local markets. Most restaurants allow for cashless tipping when settling the bill.

ELECTRICITY 230V/50HZ

Type G
230V/50Hz

Finding ATMs

Since many of England's high-street banks closed local branches, the best place to find a cash machine is in a supermarket, with even small local stores having machines offering free withdrawals. Watch out for ATMs in large venues as they often have fees starting at £2.50 per transaction.

Opening Hours

Large supermarkets are open 24 hours but Sunday trading laws mean that larger stores can only open for six hours on Sundays. Small chain stores will open 8am to 10pm throughout the week.

Internet Access

Most of England enjoys excellent mobile-phone coverage and most chains, coffee shops and hotels offer free internet access, but do be mindful of security.

Weights & Measures

England uses a confusing mix of metric and imperial. Beer is sold in pints, petrol is sold in litres. Road signs will be in miles.

HOW MUCH FOR A...

Coffee
£3.40

Pint in a pub
£4.70

Takeaway sandwich
£2.50

BEST DAY WALKS: ENGLAND 249

By Difficulty

EASY

Avebury & Silbury Hill	100
Backs, the	196
Blakeney Point	194
Castle Crag	34
Catbells	28
Dunstanburgh Castle	132
Glastonbury Tor	98
Richmond Park	233
Rievaulx	142
River Dart Walk	66
Roman London	238
St Albans	204
Tottenham Marshes	234
Viking Trail, the	206

MODERATE

Bath Skyline	96
Berwick-upon-Tweed	144
Birmingham City & Canals	176
Brown Willy & Rough Tor	72
Caer Caradoc	172
Combe Martin	86
Corfe Castle to Langton Matravers	112
Cotswold Way, the	174
Devil's Dyke	210
Hadrian's Wall	134
Hallin Fell	26
Hampstead Heath	232
Haystacks	32
Isles of Scilly	82
Kinver Edge	180
Kynance Cove & Lizard Point	68
Leith Hill	198
Malham Landscape Trail	138
Malvern Hills, the	170
Mersea Island	214
Millom to Silecroft	44
New Forest, the	106
New River	230
Old Man of Coniston	30
Pendle Hill	130
Porthcurno to Land's End	74
Regent's Canal	224
Robin Hood's Bay	140
Rye to Winchelsea	200
Shap & Swindale	48
St Agnes & Chapel Porth	70
Stanage Edge	168
Tarr Steps	104
Teign Gorge	62
Thames Path	228
Tintagel to Boscastle	78
Whitbarrow Scar	52
Wistman's Wood	64
York	152

HARD

Blyth to Tynemouth	148
Helvellyn & Striding Edge	36
Ingleborough	126
Kinder Scout	162
Langdale Pikes	24
Lulworth Cove to Durdle Door	116
Mam Tor	166
Ridgeway, the	108
Scafell Pike	40
Seven Sisters, the	190

Index

1066 Country Walk 200-1

A

accommodation 248, *see also individual regions*
airports 244
Alfriston 188, 193
archaeological sites & ruins
 Alfred's Castle 109
 Avebury 100-3
 Barber Surgeon Stone 102
 Brown Willy Bronze Age cairns 73
 Caer Caradoc 172
 Corfe Castle 112
 Dunstanburgh Castle 132-3
 Fernacre Stone Circle 73
 Fort Hillsborough 86
 Fossil Forest 119
 Garrison 84
 Hadrian's Wall 134-7
 Housesteads 136
 Innisidgen Upper & Lower Burial Chambers 83
 Kenidjack Castle 91
 Lammy Down 108
 Langdale Axe Factory 25
 Lindisfarne Priory 156
 London Stone 240
 Long Meg & Her Daughters 57
 Loughton Camp 243
 Mam Tor 167
 Mithraeum 240
 Rievaulx Abbey 142
 Roman city walls (St Albans) 205
 Roman wall (London) 238
 Rough Tor Bronze Age settlement 72
 Round Tower 87
 Sanctuary, the 103
 Segsbury Camp 110-11
 Shap Abbey 50, 51
 Shenberrow Camp 175
 Silbury Hill 101
 St Dunstan-in-the-East 241
 St Michael's Chapel 98
 Stonehenge 120
 Swindon Stone 103
 Tintagel Castle 78
 Tynemouth Priory & Castle 151
 Uffington Castle 109
 Verulamium 205
 Vindolanda 137
 Wayland's Smithy 109
 West Kennet Avenue 102
 West Kennet Long Barrow 101-2
 White Horse of Uffington 110
art galleries, *see* museums & galleries
ATMs 249
Avebury & Silbury Hill 100-3, **101**
Avon Gorge & Leigh Woods 120

B

Backs, the 196, **196**
Barley 130, 131
Barrow-in-Furness 22
Bass Point 69
Bath 94
Bath Skyline 96-7, **96**
beaches
 Bossiney Haven 79
 Botany Bay 207
 Broadsands 87-8
 Cullercoats Beach 150
 Durdle Door Beach 117
 Embleton Bay 133
 Great Mattiscombe 91
 Joss Bay 207
 Man O'War Beach 117
 Margate Beach 206
 Mill Bay 76
 Monkey Beach 216
 Nanjizal 76
 Pentreath Beach 68
 Porth Chapel 76
 Porthcurno 75
 Porthgwarra 76
 Porthloo Beach 82
 Porthmellon Beach 82
 Treen Cove 75
 Viking Bay 208
 Walpole Bay 207
 Watermill Cove 83-4
 West Mersea Beach 216
 Wild Pear Beach 88
Beachy Head 191
Berwick-upon-Tweed 144-7, **144**
birdwatching 202
 Cuckmere Haven 192
 Hodbarrow Nature Reserve 47
 Long Wood 66-7
 Malham Cove 139
 Robin Hood's Bay 140
 Rye Harbour 202
 Tottenham Marshes 235
 Walthamstow Wetlands London Wildlife Trust 236
Birling Gap 191-2
Birmingham City & Canals 176-9, **176**
Blakeney 194, 195
Blakeney Point 194-5, **194**
Blowingstone Hill 110
Blyth to Tynemouth 148-51, **148**
boat trips 27, 31, 67
Bodmin Moor 73
books 17, 33, 169, 207
border crossings 244
Borrowdale 34-5
Boscastle 80, 81
Botallack & Cape Cornwall 91
Boudicca, Queen 239
Bournemouth 95
Bowness-on-Solway to Drumburgh 57
Box Hill 219
breweries 31, 33, 71, 137

BEST DAY WALKS: ENGLAND 251

bridges
 Berwick Old Bridge 145-6
 Bridge of Sighs 196
 Clifton Suspension Bridge 120
 London Bridge 240
 Mathematical Bridge 196
 Millennium Bridge 154
 Royal Border Bridge 144-5
 Snow Hill Bridge 178
 St Saviour's Dock Footbridge 228
 Tarr Steps 105
 Tower Bridge 240
Brighton 188
Brimham Rocks 157
Bristol 94, 120
Broadstairs 208
Broadway 175
Brockenhurst 107
Brontë, Charlotte 169
Brown Willy & Rough Tor 72-3, **72**
Buckden 156
bus travel 245
business hours 249
butterflies 191
Buttermere 32, 33

C

Caer Caradoc 172, **172**
Cambridge 188-9, 196
Camden 225
Camelford 72
Cannock Chase 185
Canterbury 218
Cape Cornwall 91
Capital Ring 243
car travel 245
Castle Crag 34-5, **34**
castles, palaces & historic buildings, *see also* archaeological sites & ruins
 Alexandra Palace 242
 Bishopthorpe Palace 153-4
 Broadway Tower 175
 Castle Drogo 63
 Clayton windmills 211
 Clergy House 193
 Coleton Fishacre 67

Trails 000
Map Pages 000, **000**

Elizabethan Town Walls 147
Eltham Palace 243
Greenway 67
Ham House 242
Hampton Court Palace 242
Ightham Mote 218
Keats House 232
Kenwood House 232
Kinver Rock Houses 180, 181
Knole 218
Leith Hill Place 199
Leith Hill Tower 198-9
Lendal Tower 152-3
Moorseats 169
Seaton Sluice 149
Sham Castle 96
Tower of London 239
Wish Tower 191
Castleton 166, 167
Catbells 28, **28**
cathedrals, *see* churches & cathedrals
caves 127, 128, 166, 169,
central England 159-85, **158**
 accommodation 161
 festivals & events 161
 internet resources 161
 transport 161
 travel seasons 160-1
Chapel Porth 71
Cheltenham 160
Chilham 218
Chipping Campden 174
Christie, Agatha 67
Church Stretton 172
churches & cathedrals
 Birmingham Cathedral 176
 Church of St Mary the Virgin (London) 228
 Church of St Mary the Virgin (Rye) 202
 Church of St Nicholas 107
 Church of St Thomas 201
 Keld Chapel 49
 St Albans Cathedral 204
 St Andrews Church 193
 St Chad's Cathedral 178
 St Martin's Church 177
 St Michael & All Angels Church 175
 York Minster 155
Cinq Ports 201

Clapham 126, 129
Cley 195
climate 14-15
climate change 247
Cockermouth 22
Coldharbour 198, 199
Combe Martin 86-9, **86**
Coniston 30, 31
Corfe Castle to Langton Matravers 112-15, **112**
Cornwall 15, *see also* Devon & Cornwall
costs 245, 248, 249
Cotswold Way, the 174-5, **174**
cottage rentals 248
Coventry 160
Craster 132
Cray 156
Cuckmere Haven 192
Cumbria & the Lakes 21-57, **20**
 accommodation 23
 festivals & events 23
 internet resources 23
 transport 23
 travel seasons 23
currency 249
customs regulations 244

D

Dalton, Millican 35
dams, *see* lakes, dams & reservoirs
dangers 246
Dartmoor 90
Dartmouth 66
deer 89, 105, 107, 233, 242
Devil's Dyke 210-13, **210**
Devon & Cornwall 59-91, **58**
 accommodation 61
 festivals & events 61
 internet resources 61
 transport 61
 travel seasons 61
Dickens, Charles 207, 208
Ditchling 210
Dittisham 67
Dovedale 185
driving 245
Drumburgh 57
Dulverton 89
Dunstanburgh Castle 132-3, **132**
Durdle Door 117

E

East Dean 192, 193
east England, *see* southeast & east England
Eastbourne 190-1, 219
Edale 162, 165
electricity 249
emergencies 249
Epping Forest 243
events, *see* festivals & events
Exeter 60

F

festivals & events 15, *see also* individual regions
film locations 69, 139, 169
films 16, 169
forests, *see* woods & forests
Foxhill 108

G

galleries, *see* museums & galleries
gardens, *see* parks & gardens
geology 12, 49, 53
Glastonbury Tor 98, **98**
Glenridding 36, 39
Gordale Scar 139
Granchester 196
Grange-in-Borrowdale 34, 35
Great Langdale 24-5
Great Malvern 170, 171
Greensand Way 218
Grindleford 184
Gwennap Head 76

H

Hadrian's Wall 134-7, **135**
Hallin Fell 26-7, **26**
Hallsands 91
Hampstead Heath 232, **232**
Hardy, Thomas 112-13
Hartland Point 90
Hathersage 168, 169
Haverigg 45, 47
Hawsker 140
Haystacks 32-3, **32**
health 246
Helvellyn & Striding Edge 36-9, **37**

High Cup Nick 56
historic buildings, *see* castles, palaces & historic buildings
Holford 121
Holy Island 156
hostels 248
Hound Tor & Haytor 90
Housel Cove 69
Howtown 26, 27
Hubberholme 156
Hugh Town 82

I

Ilam to Dovedale 185
Ilfracombe 86
Ingleborough 126-9, **127**
Ingleton 129
insurance 246
internet access 249
internet resources 247, *see also* individual regions
Isle of Purbeck 112-15
Isles of Scilly 82-5, **82**
Islington 226

J

Jane Eyre 169
Jurassic Coast 117, 121, 141

K

Kendal 22
Kinder Scout 162-5, **163**
King Arthur 79
Kingston 113, 242
Kinver Edge 14
Kinver Edge 180-3, **180**
kippers 133
Kynance Cove & Lizard Point 68-9, **68**

L

Lacy's Caves & Long Meg 57
Lake District, *see* Cumbria & the Lakes
lakes, dams & reservoirs
   Coniston Water 31
   Derwentwater 28
   Innominate Tarn 33
   Lower Ogden Reservoir 130
   Red Tarn 37

   Stickle Tarn 24
   Ullswater 27
   Upper Ogden Reservoir 130-1
   Wastwater 41, 43
Land's End 76-7
Langdale 24, 25
Langdale Pikes 24-5, **24**
Langton Matravers 114
language 17
Leith Hill 198-9, **198**
lighthouses
   Beachy Head Lighthouse 191
   Lizard Lighthouse 69
   Longships Lighthouse 77
   North Foreland Lighthouse 208
   St Mary's Lighthouse 149
   St Nicholas Chapel 86
   Start Point Lighthouse 91
   Wolf Rock Lighthouse 76
Lindisfarne 156
literature 17, 33, 169, 207
Litlington 192
Little Venice 224
Liverpool 160
Lizard Point 68-9
Lizard Village 69
Logan Rock 75
London 221-43, **220**
   accommodation 223
   festivals & events 223
   internet resources 223
   transport 223
   travel seasons 223
Lowry, LS 145
Lulworth Cove to Durdle Door 116-19, **116**
Lymington 106
Lyth Valley 53-4

M

Malham 138, 139
Malham Cove 139
Malham Landscape Trail 138-9, **138**
Malvern, End to End 184
Malvern Hills, the 170-1, **170**
Mam Tor 166-7, **166**
Margate 206-7
markets 225, 226, 239, 241
Maw Wyke 140

measures 249
Mersea Island 214-17, **214**
Mickleham 219
Millom to Silecroft 44-7, **44**
Minack Theatre 75-6
mines & quarries
   Botallack 91
   Caer Caradoc 172
   Castle Crag 35
   Coppermines Valley 31
   Dubs Quarry 33
   Langdale Axe Factory 25
   Levant Mine 71
   Stanhope Mine 157
   Wheal Coates 70
money 244, 249
mountains
   Brown Willy 73
   Caer Caradoc 172
   Castle Crag 34-5
   Catbells 28
   Catstye Cam 39
   Fleetwith Pike 33
   Hallin Fell 26-7
   Harrison Stickle 25
   Haystacks 32-3
   Haytor 90
   Helvellyn 36-9
   Hound Tor 90
   Ingleborough 126-9
   Kinder Low 164
   Kinder Scout 162-5
   Langdale Pikes 24-5
   Mam Tor 166-7
   Old Man of Coniston 30-1
   Pavey Ark 24-5
   Pendle Hill 130-1
   Rough Tor 72
   Scafell Pike 40-3
   Showery Tor 73
   Stanage Edge 168-9
   Striding Edge 36-9
   Swirral Edge 38-9
   Three Peaks, the 127
   Whitbarrow Scar 53
   Winshield Crags 135

Trails 000
Map Pages 000, **000**

mudlarking 229
museums & galleries
   Alexander Keiller Museum 101
   Boscastle Museum of Witchcraft & Magic 80, 81
   Brunel Museum 229
   Cutty Sark 229
   Guildhall Art Gallery 239
   London Canal Museum 225
   Mersea Museum 216
   Sill National Landscape Discovery Centre 134
   Towner Eastbourne Art Gallery 190-1
   Verulamium Museum 205
   Vindolanda 137

N

national parks & nature reserves
   Canon Hervey Nature Reserve 55
   Dartmoor National Park 62-3, 64
   Exmoor National Park 89, 104-5
   Hodbarrow Nature Reserve 47
   Lymington Beds Nature Reserve 106
   Peak District National Park 162-5, 166-7, 168-9
   Roydon Wood Nature Reserve 107
   Rye Harbour Nature Reserve 202
   Walthamstow Wetlands London Wildlife Trust 236
   Yorkshire Dales National Park 124, 126-9
New Forest, the 106-7, **106**
New River 230-1, **230**
Newcastle 124
northern England 123-57, **122**
   accommodation 125
   festivals & events 125
   internet resources 125
   transport 125
   travel seasons 124-5

O

Old Harry Rocks 121
Old Man of Coniston 30-1, **30**
Old Wives Lees 218
Once Brewed 137
opening hours 249
Other Borrowdale, the 56

P

Padley Gorge 184
palaces, *see* castles, palaces & historic buildings
Parkland Way 242
parks & gardens
   Brandlehow Park 28
   Cambridge University Botanic Gardens 196
   Camley Street Natural Park 225-6
   Castle Vale Park 146
   Finsbury Park 230
   Hampstead Heath 232
   Mile End Park 226
   Paddock Community Nature Park 235
   Prior Park 97
   Richmond Park 233
   Ridley Park 148
   Victoria Park 226
   Whiddon Deer Park 62
Pedn-mên-an-mere 76
Pendle Hill 130-1, **130**
Pennine Way 56, 135
Penzance 60
Pilgrims' Way 218
Pilley 107
planning
   clothing 16, 244
   equipment 246
   highlights 8-13
plants 53, *see also* parks & gardens, woods & forests
podcasts 17
Poldark (TV series) 69
population 249
Porlock 89
Porthcurno to Land's End 74-7, **75**
Porthgwarra 76
Pride & Prejudice (film) 169
Primrose Hill 225
Pyecombe 211

Q

Quakers 131
Quantocks, the 121
quarries, *see* mines & quarries

R

Regent's Canal 224-7, **225**
reservoirs, *see* lakes, dams & reservoirs
responsible travel 247
Richmond 242
Richmond Park 233, **233**
Ridgeway, the 108-11, **109**
Rievaulx 142, **142**
River Dart Walk 66-7, **66**
Robin Hood's Bay 140-1, **140**
rock climbing 113, 230
Rocky Valley 79
Roman London 238-41, **238**
ruins, *see* archaeological sites & ruins
Rye to Winchelsea 200-3, **201**

S

safe travel 246
Salisbury 94
Scafell Pike 40-3, **41**
seals 195
Seven Sisters, the 190-3, **191**
Sevenoaks 218
Shap & Swindale 48-51, **48**
Shipbourne 218
Silbury Hill 101
Silecroft 46, 47
Slaughterbridge 73
South Downs Way 192, 210-13
South Downs Way 219
southeast & east England 187-219, **186**
  accommodation 189
  festivals & events 189
  internet resources 189
  transport 189
  travel seasons 189
southwest England 93-121, **92**
  accommodation 95
  festivals & events 95
  internet resources 95
  transport 95
  travel seasons 95
springs 76, 98, 171
St Agnes & Chapel Porth 70-1, **70**
St Albans 189
St Albans 204-5, **204**
St Mary's 82-5
St Tudy 73
Stanage Edge 168-9, **168**
Stanhope Burn 157
stargazing 89
Start Point 91
Stonehenge 120
Stratford-upon-Avon 160
Studland 121
Swanage 115
Swindale Valley 49

T

Tarr Steps 104-5, **104**
Teign Gorge 62-3, **62**
Telford 160
Thames Path 228-9, **228**
Thames Path West 242
theatres 75-6
Three Pubs Walk 156
time zone 249
Tintagel to Boscastle 78-81, **78**
tipping 249
Totnes 60-1
Tottenham Marshes 234-7, **234**
train travel 115, 157, 245
travel insurance 246
travel seasons 14-15, *see also* individual regions
travel to/from England 244
travel within England 245
Treen 74, 77
Trevaunance Cove 71
Truro 60
Tubby's Head 70
Turner, JMW 209
TV series 16, 69
Tynemouth 150, 151

V

Viking Trail, the 206-9, **206**

W

Wainwright, Alfred 33
Wantage 111
Wasdale Head 40-1, 43
water 246
waterfalls 129, 139
Watermouth 87, 89
Weardale 157
weather 14-15, 246
websites, *see* internet resources
weights 249
Westdean 192
Whitbarrow Scar 52-5, **52**
Whitehaven 23
Whitley Bay 151
wildflowers 53
wildlife 10, 107, 235, 246, *see also* birdwatching, butterflies, deer, seals
Winchelsea 201-2
Winchester 219
windmills 211, 213
Wistman's Wood 64, **64**
witches 131
Witherslack 55
Withypool 104, 105
woods & forests
  Bathampton Wood 97
  Bathwick Woods 96
  Epping Forest 243
  Fingle Woods 62
  Hoodown Wood 66
  Lea Wood 104
  Leigh Woods 120
  Long Wood 66-7
  Moorseats Wood 169
  New Forest 106-7
  Pit Wood 104
  Westdean Forest 192
  Wistman's Wood 64
Worth Matravers 113, 115

Y

York 124
York 152-5, **152**
youth hostels 248

Z

zoos 225

THE WRITERS

Beth Pipe

Beth is a nosey hiker who writes about places off the beaten track and has published 12 books about the history, hiking, gins and beers of Cumbria. Find her on Facebook @CumbrianRambler.

Sian Lewis

Sian is an award-winning travel and outdoor writer and author who loves exploring with a tent in her backpack. Find her on Instagram @sianannalewis.

Contributing writers

Oliver Berry, Helena Smith, Neil Wilson

SEND US YOUR FEEDBACK

We love to hear from travellers – your comments keep us on our toes and help make our books better. Our well-travelled team reads every word on what you loved or loathed about this book. Although we cannot reply individually to your submissions, we always guarantee that your feedback goes straight to the appropriate writers, in time for the next edition.

Visit **lonelyplanet.com/contact** to submit your updates and suggestions or to ask for help. Our award-winning website also features inspirational travel stories and news.

Note: We may edit, reproduce and incorporate your comments in Lonely Planet products such as guidebooks, websites and digital products, so let us know if you are happy to have your name acknowledged. For a copy of our privacy policy visit **lonelyplanet.com/legal**.

BEHIND THE SCENES

This book was researched and written by Beth Pipe, Sian Lewis, Oliver Berry, Helena Smith and Neil Wilson. It was produced by the following:

Destination Editor
Amy Lynch

Production Editor
Saralinda Turner

Book Designer
Catalina Aragón

Cartographer
Vojtech Bartos

Assisting Editors
Nigel Chin, Soo Hamilton, Kellie Langdon, Jenna Myers, Charlotte Orr

Cover Researcher
Hannah Blackie

Thanks to
Ronan Abayawickrema, Darren O'Connell, Katerina Pavkova

ACKNOWLEDGEMENTS

Cover photograph
Glastonbury Tor, Somerset; Radomir Rezny/Shutterstock ©